MIND ASSOCIATION OCCASIONAL SERIES

APPEARANCE VERSUS REALITY

MIND ASSOCIATION OCCASIONAL SERIES

This series consists of occasional volumes of original papers on predefined themes. The Mind Association nominates an editor or editors for each collection, and may co-operate with other bodies in promoting conferences or other scholarly activities in connection with the preparation of particular volumes.

Publications Officer: M. A. Stewart
Secretary: C. Macdonald

Also published in the series:

Perspectives on Thomas Hobbes
Edited by G. A. J. Rogers and A. Ryan

Reality, Representation, and Projection
Edited by J. Haldane and C. Wright

Machines and Thought
The Legacy of Alan Turing, Volume I
Edited by P. J. R. Millican and A. Clark

Connectionism, Concepts, and Folk Psychology
The Legacy of Alan Turing, Volume II
Edited by A. Clark and P. J. R. Millican

Appearance versus Reality

NEW ESSAYS ON BRADLEY'S METAPHYSICS

Edited by
GUY STOCK

CLARENDON PRESS · OXFORD
1998

Oxford University Press, Great Clarendon Street, Oxford OX2 6DP

Oxford New York

Athens Auckland Bangkok Bogota Bombay
Buenos Aires Calcutta Cape Town Dar es Salaam
Delhi Florence Hong Kong Istanbul Karachi
Kuala Lumpur Madras Madrid Melbourne
Mexico City Nairobi Paris Singapore
Taipei Tokyo Toronto Warsaw

and associated companies in
Berlin Ibadan

Oxford is a trade mark of Oxford University Press

Published in the United States
by Oxford University Press Inc., New York

British Library Cataloguing in Publication Data
Data available

Library of Congress Cataloging-in-Publication Data
Appearance versus reality : new essays on Bradley's metaphysics /
edited by Guy Stock.
(Mind Association occasional series)
"This collection of papers derives from a conference held at
Merton College, Oxford, 2–5 April 1993, to mark the centenary of the
publication of Bradley's Appearance and reality"—Pref.
Includes bibliographical references.
1. Bradley, F. H. (Francis Herbert), 1846–1924. 2. Metaphysics.
I. Stock, Guy. II. Series.
B1618.B74A67 1998 192—dc21 97-36679
ISBN 0-19-823659-X

1 3 5 7 9 10 8 6 4 2

Typeset by Graphicraft Typesetters Ltd., Hong Kong
Printed in Great Britain
on acid-free paper by
Biddles Ltd., Guildford and King's Lynn

PREFACE

This collection of papers derives from a conference held at Merton College, Oxford, 2–5 April 1993, to mark the centenary of the publication of Bradley's *Appearance and Reality*. The idea of organizing such a conference was suggested by Tony Manser as a further way of developing a critical literature which made a serious attempt to locate Bradley's arguments in relation to contemporary issues within the tradition of analytical philosophy. Tony was involved with the invitation of speakers and with the selection of contributed papers. Unfortunately he was already too ill to attend the conference, and sadly died on the 19 January 1995. It was he who suggested that the title of this volume should be *Appearance versus Reality*, and it is to his memory, with much affection and respect, that it is now dedicated.

In my introductory essay I make no attempt to summarize the subsequent papers in the volume. It is an essay which represents, in a short space, a rethinking on my part of Bradley's epistemology and metaphysics. The rethinking resulted in part from reflections stimulated by a careful reading of the papers in this volume during the editorial process and in part from reading an unpublished essay on Bradley's *Appearance and Reality* by R. G. Collingwood. My attention was drawn to the existence of that essay by David Boucher, the editor of *Collingwood Studies*, and I am most grateful to him.

The secondary aim of my introduction is to place Bradley's philosophy in the context of metaphysical discussions directly or indirectly related to those currently taking place. In doing this, so far as possible, I have used Bradley's own terminology; but I have tried to do so in such a way that his thought is accessible to present-day students of philosophy from an undergraduate level upwards. Such students, I hope, even if they have no deep acquaintance with Bradley's works first hand, will be enabled to appreciate better how the particular critical discussions that form the chapters of this book relate to Bradley's logic, epistemology, and metaphysics as a whole.

Finally, my thanks are due to James Bradley for his invaluable help, and to the British Academy, the Mind Association, the Aristotelian Society, and the Fellows of Merton College for financial assistance in organizing the conference at which the papers were originally presented.

GUY STOCK

CONTENTS

LIST OF ABBREVIATIONS

References to Bradley's works will use the following abbreviations and, except where indicated, will be to the following editions:

AR   *Appearance and Reality* (Oxford: Clarendon Press, 2nd edn. 1897, corrected impression 1930)

CE   *Collected Essays* (Oxford: Clarendon Press, 1935)

ETR   *Essays on Truth and Reality* (Oxford: Clarendon Press, 1914)

PL   *The Principles of Logic*, vols. i and ii (Oxford: Oxford University Press, 2nd edn. 1922, corrected impression 1928)

NOTES ON CONTRIBUTORS

THOMAS BALDWIN is Professor of Philosophy at the University of York; previously he was a Lecturer in Philosophy at Cambridge University. He is author of *G. E. Moore* (Cambridge University Press, 1993), and edited *Selected Writings* by G. E. Moore (Routledge, 1993).

STEWART CANDLISH teaches philosophy at the University of Western Australia. He has also held visiting appointments at Clare Hall, Cambridge, the University of Sussex, the Australian National University, and Darwin College, Cambridge. Many of his publications concern the history of philosophy in the twentieth century, with special emphasis on Bradley, Russell, and Wittgenstein. He is author of the articles on Bradley and on the Private Language Argument in the forthcoming *Routledge Encyclopaedia of Philosophy*.

DAVID CROSSLEY is Professor of Philosophy at the University of Saskatchewan. His publications include several articles dealing with the ethical theory and epistemology of F. H. Bradley. The most recent of these are 'Feeling in Bradley's *Ethical Studies*', in P. MacEwen (ed.), *Ethics, Metaphysics and Religion in the Thought of F. H. Bradley* (Edwin Mellen, 1996), and 'Justification and the Foundations of Empirical Knowledge', in J. Bradley (ed.), *Philosophy after F. H. Bradley* (Thoemmes, 1996).

NICHOLAS GRIFFIN is Professor of Philosophy, McMaster University, Hamilton, Ontario, Canada. He is the author of *Russell's Idealist Apprenticeship* (Oxford: 1991), and the co-editor of two volumes of Russell's *Collected Papers*. Currently he is editing a two-volume selection of Russell's letters.

DAVID HOLDCROFT is Professor of Philosophy at the University of Leeds. His publications include: *Words and Deeds*; *Jurisprudence: Texts and Commentary* (with Howard Davies); and Saussure: *Signs, System and Arbitrariness*. He has published a number of papers on F. H. Bradley, and is currently working on his first essay *The Presuppositions of Critical History*.

JAMES LEVINE is a Lecturer in Philosophy at Trinity College, Dublin. He works largely in the area of early analytic philosophy.

TIMOTHY SPRIGGE is Professor Emeritus and Honorary Fellow of the University of Edinburgh. His books include *The Vindication of Absolute Idealism* (Edinburgh University Press, 1983), *The Rational Foundation of Ethics* (Routledge, 1987), and *James and Bradley: American Truth and British Reality* (Open Court, 1993).

GUY STOCK teaches in the philosophy department at the University of Dundee. He is joint editor (with W. J. Mander) of *Bradley Studies*, an associate editor of *Philosophical Investigations*, and Honorary Treasurer of the Mind Association. He introduced and edited (with Anthony Manser) *The Philosophy of F. H. Bradley* (Clarendon Press, 1984), introduced a new edition of Bradley's *Presuppositions of Critical History and Aphorisms* (Thoemmes, 1993), and edited (with James Allard) *F. H. Bradley: Writings on Logic and Metaphysics* (Clarendon Press, 1994).

RALPH WALKER is a Fellow and Tutor at Magdalen College, Oxford. His principal publications are *Kant* (Routledge, 1978) and *The Coherence Theory of Truth* (Routledge, 1989). He edited *Kant on Pure Reason* (Oxford Readings in Philosophy, 1982) and the *Real and the Ideal* (Garland, 1989).

I

Introduction: The Realistic Spirit in Bradley's Philosophy[1]

GUY STOCK

———•———

Within the history of philosophy, Bradley's philosophy has traditionally been classified as Hegelian and Idealist. This is not a very enlightening characterization. Neither of these terms is precise, and no doubt that is part of the reason why Bradley himself was reluctant to accept either description.[2] R. G. Collingwood, in an unpublished essay on Bradley's *Appearance and Reality*, written in 1933,[3] sketched a rather different view, which enables the contemporary reader to locate Bradley's thought more readily and to chart his philosophical motivation more accurately. Collingwood argued that Bradley was not the last significant representative of

[1] This title is borrowed from Cora Diamond's volume of her collected papers on Wittgenstein entitled *The Realistic Spirit* (Cambridge, Mass.: MIT Press, 1991). What I (with the help of Collingwood) see as fundamental for Bradley—viz. his rejection of a certain conception of mind, or thinking subject—has an obvious historical parallel in the *Philosophical Investigations*, where Wittgenstein undermines his earlier conception of (i) thought and linguistic understanding as an *inner* yet rule-governed process and (ii) the presupposed world-transcendent subject as the seat of the generative activity constitutive of thinking: conceptions which Wittgenstein had, in the *Tractatus*, taken to be requirements for the existence of determinately truth functional *a posteriori* propositional contents.

[2] *PL*, preface to 1st edn., p. x; *ETR*, supplementary note II, p. 278; and *AR*, 485, where Bradley says: 'The conclusion which we have reached, I trust, the outcome of no mere compromise, makes a claim to reconcile extremes. Whether it is to be called Realism or Idealism I do not know, and I have not cared to inquire. It neither puts ideas and thought first, nor again does it permit us to assert that anything else by itself is more real.'

[3] R. G. Collingwood, 'The Metaphysics of F. H. Bradley: An Essay on *Appearance and Reality*', MS in the Collingwood Papers, Bodleian Library, Oxford.

Hegel in Britain. He was not an apologist for an alien, already dying tradition that was finally to be discredited by Russell and Moore. On the contrary, he was within British philosophy the primary source of the realism in epistemology which, in the conventional account, Russell and Moore were credited with initiating in the course of freeing themselves from the malign influence of Bradley's idealism.

Again, the term 'realist' is not precise, but in the sense in which Russell characterized his realism in 'On the Nature of Acquaintance' Bradley certainly was a realist. Russell, when he wrote that article, and when he wrote his lectures on logical atomism which were delivered in 1918, rejected neutral monism. He then retained in his metaphysics a subject–object duality on grounds that Bradley, in his own way, also responded to, but without ascribing substantiality to finite subjects.[4] Russell argued that without presupposing an irreducible non-physical subject, there could be no 'account of that principle of selection which, to a given person at a given moment, makes one object, one subject and one time intimate and near and immediate, as no other object or subject or time can be to that subject at that time'.[5] Against the background of his non-Cartesian subject–object dualism, Russell located, by implication, his epistemological realism as follows:

I do not think that, when an object is known to me, there is in my mind something which may be called an 'idea' of the object, the possession of which constitutes my knowledge of the object. But when this is granted neutral monism by no means follows. On the contrary, it is just at this point that neutral monism finds itself in agreement with idealism in making an assumption which I believe to be wholly false. The assumption is that, *if anything is immediately present to me, that thing must be part of my mind.* The upholders of 'ideas', since they believe in the duality of the mental and the physical, infer from this assumption that only

    [4] *ETR*, 412–14; T. S. Eliot pointed out the similarity between Leibniz's monads, with their unique more or less confused viewpoints of the universe, and Bradley's non-substantial finite centres. See Eliot, 'Leibniz's Monads and Bradley's Finite Centres', *Monist*, 26 (Oct. 1916), 566–76.
    [5] Bertrand Russell, *Logic and Knowledge*, ed. R. C. Marsh (London: Allen & Unwin, 1956), hereafter *L&K*; *idem*, 'On the Nature of Acquaintance' (originally published in three parts in the *Monist*, 24 (1914), 1–16, 161–87, 435–53), 169, hereafter ONA; see also 162. But cf. Ludwig Wittgenstein, *Notebooks 1914–1916*, ed. G. H. von Wright and G. E. M. Anscombe; trans. G. E. M. Anscombe (Oxford: Blackwell, 1961), 88: 'For the consideration of willing makes it look as if one part of the world were closer to me than another (which would be intolerable).'

ideas, not physical things, can be immediately present to me. Neutral monists, perceiving (rightly, as I think) that constituents of the physical world can be immediately present to me, infer that the mental and the physical are composed of the same 'stuff', and are merely different arrangements of the same elements. But if the assumption is false, both these opposing theories may be false, as I believe they are.[6]

According to the notion of acquaintance, adopted by Russell in 1914, sensations were not construed as immediately known inner data by way of which outer things could be known, or, correspondingly, as deliverers of causal inputs to subjects. A sensation was construed as an immediate *intentional* relation, holding momentarily, between a subject and an independently existent physical particular. The subject, Russell surmised, was probably knowable not by acquaintance but merely by description as 'the x acquainted with *this*' where 'this' designated a physical particular immediately given in sensation.[7] Thus Russell's physical particulars could not be identified with three-dimensional objects of humanly perceptible sorts; nor could his percipient subjects be identified with particular human beings. Three-dimensional physical bodies and individual human subjects had the status of *logical constructions*, hence *as such* neither enjoyed independent existence.[8]

By Russell's characterization of idealism in the passage quoted, Bradley is certainly not an idealist. He, as much as Russell, can be seen as fundamentally opposed to those epistemological and metaphysical theories which portrayed the nature of the phenomena cognitively accessible to human beings in the experiences constitutive of their waking lives as a function of the nature of a postulated mind, or thinking-cum-sentient subject, construed as a locus of representative 'ideas' somehow *inner* and active within the spatio-temporally located human being. Such theories characteristically portrayed a human being's experiential knowledge of the existence of things as mediated via immediately known mind- or brain-dependent data, and in consequence as more or less illusory with respect to the nature of the postulated independently existent reality. According to the strict Kantian schema,

---

[6] ONA, 147.   [7] ONA, 164.
[8] *L&K*, 'The Philosophy of Logical Atomism', e.g. 200–2, hereafter PLA. (PLA was originally published in four parts in the *Monist*, 28 (1918), 495–527; 29 (1919), 33–63, 190–222, 345–80.)

the nature of the independently existent reality, whether delivered to a subject's inner or outer sense, was discursively utterly unknowable; according to both the Cartesian dualist tradition and the Lockean agnostic physicalist[9] tradition, the primary qualities of the consciousness-independent, independently existent reality—and thus, by inference, which qualities were the secondary merely consciousness-dependent qualities of phenomena—were in principle knowable by human beings through the fundamental theories of physics; and according to both the corrupt Kantianism of Mansel (dominant at Oxford when Bradley was a student) and the Hume–Mill phenomenalist tradition, the *merely* mind-dependent features of the objects of human beings' waking experiences were *ex hypothesi* deducible from empirical psychologists' reflections on the associative laws governing the functioning of human beings' minds: minds which, for the phenomenalist tradition, were themselves to be construed as nothing but constructions out of an ultimate reality of momentary, law-governed, independently existent sense impressions, each impression to be construed therefore as an immediate non-relational *knowing and being in one*.

Bradley rarely identified his thumb-nail epistemological-cum-metaphysical sketches with historical figures by name, and so he never found himself overburdened with a need for detailed historical accuracy. Nevertheless, his sketches are familiar to anybody with a knowledge of the history of philosophy, and they go straight to the heart of the difficulties implicit in the complex historical systems. Such sketches formed the staple diet in Book I of *Appearance and Reality* for his negative critique of attempts to give in very general terms, in the context of metaphysics, accounts of the ultimate nature of an independently existent reality.

Hence Bradley, as an essential element in his philosophy, is to be seen as rejecting the theoretical conception of an inner mind

---

[9] I use this term to indicate that Locke envisaged the possibility of self-conscious thinking subjects (his *persons*) being one in substance with physical things. This was the position embraced by J. J. C. Smart in his very influential paper 'Sensations and Brain Processes', *Philosophical Review*, 68 (1959), 141–56. There are many other examples from philosophers accepting the physicalist metaphysics entailed by Quine's conception of an epistemology naturalized. A relatively independent approach to the same end is contained in Bernard Williams's notion of an 'absolute conception' as he articulates it in *Ethics and the Limits of Philosophy* (London: Fontana, 1985, ch. 8: 'Knowledge, Science and Convergence', 138–40).

or thinking-cum-percipient subject postulated as an entity in some relation to a living human being and conceived as either (i) an independently existent reality (as in Cartesian dualism), or (ii) an entity metaphysically supervenient on a human brain (as in Locke on a physicalist construal and in contemporary scientific realism), or (iii) a transcendental ego (as with Kant and Wittgenstein in his early work), or (iv) a phenomenalist construction out of independently existent designatable sense-data (as with Hume and the Logical Positivists), or, we might now add, (v) a momentary independently existent subject having a manifold of intentional sensations in which indefinitely numerous immediately known and designatable independently existent physical particulars will be present, and which, if the subject has the requisite concepts, it will perceive as particular logical constructions of various humanly perceptible sorts (as with Russell and, possibly, with the ultimately agnostic Moore).

Bradley makes it clear both in the *Principles of Logic* and *Appearance and Reality* that the thinking sentient subjects he is concerned with are irreducibly bodily creatures, human and otherwise, living their lives in space and time. Mind, or soul, as a characteristic of a normal adult human being, Bradley describes as a 'late achievement',[10] both evolutionarily and in the history of the individual human life. He sees no Cartesian break of an absolute kind between humans and lower animal species with respect to mental capacities. As he puts it: 'It is better to treat the mind as a single phenomenon, progressing through stages, and to avoid all discussion as to whether the lines, by which we mark out this progress, fall across or between the divisions of actual classes of animals.'[11]

The break, in so far as there is one, is one of degree, and is a function of the human linguistic ability; within the history of the individual human life, he takes the development of mind proper to coincide with the gradual mastery of the use of language 'for social purposes'.[12] Like those of Collingwood, Ryle, and Strawson, his successors at Oxford, Bradley's concept of mind is Aristotelian in tenor. Correspondingly, his centrally important concept of immediate experience is not to be construed as a causal input into a mind or a centre of consciousness supervenient on a

---

[10] *ETR*, 356–7; *PL*, 28–35.   [11] *PL*, 29.   [12] *ETR*, 357.

brain.[13] For Bradley, the paradigm for a centre of immediate experience can be seen as what is enjoyed, at a waking moment, by a human infant at any early pre-linguistic stage of development or by an animal like a dog, which, in lacking command of the requisite dating-and-placing vocabulary, could not have the capacity to think systematically about particular times, past and future, or particular places in given directions at given distances from the present location of its body and current happenings in its perceptual environment.[14] On Bradley's view, reality will be given *immediately* in the activities, bodily and otherwise, of the infant and dog; but, in so far as it is present in their experiences in *ideal form*, it will be present at best inchoately and fragmentarily. So, for Bradley, the distinction between immediate and ideal experience in a *finite centre*[15] is not absolute. It will always be a distinction of degree. No matter how highly developed any aspect of a human being's intellect might be, or how systematically interrelated the communicable contents in a specific sphere of the individual's waking experience might become—we might here think of the cosmologist's current sense perceptions the contents of which he is able self-consciously to refer to particular events currently occurring on a screen in front of him and which he can, in the ideal content of his current thinking, relate in highly complex ways to a postulated physical event enormously remote in time from the present—such contents will always be present against an indefinitely complex background of merely immediate experience from which other disparate contents will, more or less inchoately, be continuously prone to emerge.[16]

So, on Bradley's view, the metaphysician's independently existent reality *ex hypothesi* will (i) be given immediately in the successive deeds and sufferings, bodily and otherwise, constitutive of the sentient individual's life, and (ii) be present in ideal form,

---

[13] Cf. Gottfried Wilhelm Leibniz: 'It must be confessed, moreover, that perception and what depends on it are *inexplicable by mechanical reasons*, that is, by figures and motions. If we pretend there is a machine whose structure enables it to think, feel, and have perception, one could think of it enlarged yet preserving its same proportions, so that one could enter it as one does a mill. If we did this, we should find nothing within but parts which push upon each other; we should never see anything which would explain a perception' ('The Monadology' (1714), sect. 17, in *G. W. Leibniz: Philosophical Papers and Letters*, ed. L. Loember (Dordrecht: Reidel, 1976), 643–53).   [14] *ETR*, 356–7, also 410–12.   [15] *ETR*, 159–60.   [16] *ETR*, 188–91; cf. *PL*, Terminal Essay V.

more or less partially and abstractly, in the disparate systems of logically interrelated ideal contents that will be present in the individual's experiences—that is, in its concurrent and temporally successive manifolds of actions and interactions with things.

Thus, in a clear sense, Bradley's epistemology is realist in intent, in that it portrays the postulated independently existent reality as both immediately known and, with more or less adequacy, discursively known in the experiences constitutive of a human life. Moreover, Bradley's epistemology is in a broad sense empiricist,[17] in that he takes a sentient animal's fundamental point of cognitive and practical contact with an independently existent reality to be provided by its present experience. Further, Bradley maintains that, as a fundamental condition[18] of acquiring any significant degree of systematic knowledge, a sentient individual must acquire the ability to exercise in its thinking what Bradley called in *propria persona* the 'ideal construction of my real world'.[19] To have this ability is equivalent to having the world picture[20] that G. E. Moore called the 'Common sense view of the world'.[21] Bradley's real world is certainly not, therefore, to be confused with the dualists' and empiricists' metaphysically postulated *external* worlds. Distinctions like those between primary and secondary qualities, self and not-self, mental and physical things, language and world, perception and thought, particular and general, life and death, and so on without limit, are distinctions that are drawn within—and are exemplifiable in given contexts by reference to paradigms existing within—the compass of our real world: they are *internal* to the ideal construction in terms of which that world is identifiable in our current thinking. The ability to think of our real world is an ability that, along with manifold others, any normal human being will gradually acquire as it progressively masters, in pursuit of the activities constitutive of early life, the dating-and-placing vocabulary in a natural language like English. To put it rather ponderously, it is the ability a normal human being will acquire to think self-consciously, at any waking moment, (i) of

---

[17] *ETR*, 209.   [18] *AR*, 336.

[19] *ETR*, 30–2, 46–9; the first mention of the notion of ideal construction appears to be *PL*, 29.

[20] Ludwig Wittgenstein, *On Certainty* (Oxford: Blackwell, 1969), hereafter *OC*; cf. paras. 93–5, 162–7.

[21] G. E. Moore, *Philosophical Papers* (London: Allen & Unwin, 1959), ch. 2, esp. 32–5, 44–5.

its body—like the body of every other historically real human being—as occupying at each moment of its life a unique position in an enduring spatial system that extends unlimited distances from its body in pointable directions, and (ii) of its experiences, bodily and otherwise, at each moment of its life—like the experiences of every other historically real human being—as occurring at successive moments in a single linear time series stretching without limit into the past and the future. We might note that the world in question is, therefore, a single spatio-temporally interrelated system of existence with global simultaneity and three spatial dimensions. Acquisition of the logically interrelated ideal contents essential to this capacity for ideal construction was seen by Bradley, as it was no doubt also by Russell[22] and Moore, as a necessary condition for a human being coming to possess, to any significant degree, cognitive access not merely to the 'worlds', present or past, culturally close or remote, of human history and geography, but also to those of the special sciences, morality, religion, magic, commerce, literature, metaphysics, or whatever.[23]

From this point of agreement Russell and Moore articulated their realism and empiricism in a divergent way from Bradley, and in a way that Bradley, for reasons falling within the philosophy of logic, had taken to be incoherent. Contemporary thinking on this has in some respects moved in Bradley's direction. Russell's empiricism in his logical atomism required all of an individual's logically complex empirical belief contents, in so far as they constituted genuine knowledge, to be ultimately founded on, and in principle analysable truth-functionally into, logically singular, unconditionally true propositions expressing incorrigible, momentarily perceived *atomic* facts. Such propositions required, as a condition of their possibility, merely *designatory* proper names capable of introducing independently existent particulars into the ideal contents of contingently true perceptual judgements.[24] Bradley rejected this requirement as incoherent.[25] He also argued that in fact human beings have no sense perceptions that are both capable of contributing ideal contents to their knowledge and are in

---

[22] ONA, 168; cf. P. F. Strawson, *Individuals* (London: Methuen, 1964), ch. 1: 'Bodies'.   [23] AR, 336–7.

[24] PLA, 200–2.

[25] PL, 59–61; cf. 66–9, 99–101, 112 n. 46, 194 n. 14; ETR, 207, 261–5.

principle incorrigible.[26] Bradley's consequent epistemological model, and his related rejection of the philosophical significance of the developments in symbolic logic, marked off his philosophy utterly from the analytical and narrowly empirical tradition which received its momentum from Russell, Moore, and, via the influence of Wittgenstein's early work, the Logical Positivists. Bradley insisted that in the early stages of a human being's life truth is utterly subservient to practice.[27] Thus the initial standing systems of ideal contents that come to operate in a sentient individual's life, as it gradually masters language, will be acquired in the practices involved in its early upbringing, and these, to a considerable extent, will be a function of it being an individual of the natural kind it is.[28] Hence Bradley's irreducible epistemological model is that of a human being confronting reality[29] as reality is immediately given in the activities constitutive of its waking experience, with a plurality of disparate, but more or less interpenetrating, acquired systems of logically interrelated ideal contents. Contents within such standing systems will, under pressure generated jointly by 'new' incoming ideal contents, perceptual or otherwise, and the intellect's own operational norms of coherence and comprehensiveness, be subject with more or less ease to reassessment with respect to their truth-values. Hence the assertion of a particular ideal content within any given acquired system of contents will be intrinsically conditional, since it will always be in principle possible to suppose inputs to the system which would entail its

---

[26] *ETR*, 206.   [27] *ETR*, 75–80.

[28] Ludwig Wittgenstein, *Philosophical Investigations*, trans. G. E. M. Anscombe (Oxford: Blackwell, 1958), p. xii.

[29] Bradley himself uses the expression 'refer to reality' and, sometimes, 'predicate of reality'. Although Bradley does not make a strict terminological distinction, it is not ideas, *qua* concepts, but ideal contents that are referred to reality in acts of judgement. These, I take it, would require for their communication verbal expressions of any amount of propositional, or syntactic, complexity. Moreover, assertion (reference to reality) is intrinsic to the thinking of an ideal content. An ideal content cannot merely *float* unreferred to reality, or be thought in a radically non-assertoric mode. However, an ideal content can be thought without involving an *explicit* or self-conscious act of judgement. Further, an ideal content need not involve reference to any specific reality existing within our real world. For example, in a negative existential judgement that is made with respect to an object in our real world, a state of affairs thought as obtaining within the negated ideal content will be explicitly excluded by the negation from existence in *this* our real world. But, as Bradley puts it, the excluded reality must 'fall somewhere'. See *ETR*, 32–42; *AR*, 350–2 (Appendix), 528–9; *PL*, 10.

rejection. The less systematically integrated a particular ideal content, the easier it would be to reject it, and the contents of what Bradley called 'analytic judgements of sense'[30] (which approach the contents that Russell and Moore putatively saw as epistemologically foundational and incorrigible) would be very low on the scale of systematic integration. Thus, on Bradley's view, a body of human knowledge is to be seen not as a superstructure deriving its firmness from the incorrigibility of empirically given, but in fact hidden, foundations from which it is in principle logically deducible. It is secure to the degree that it is systematic: that is, presents itself in the informed individual's intellect[31] as internally coherent and comprehensive.[32]

It follows that if, according to Bradley's essentially interconnected conception of human knowledge and action,[33] anything is foundational for human knowledge and practice, it is the system of logically interrelated ideal contents internal to the world picture which a normal human being will acquire in acquiring the ability to make the ideal construction of our real world. As Bradley puts it:

What is the world which I am accustomed to call 'my real world'? It is (we must reply) the universe of those things which are continuous in space with my body, and in time with the states and actions of that body. My mental changes form no exception, for, if they are to take their place in time as 'real' events, they must, I think, be dated in connexion with the history of my body. Now if I make an ideal construction of this nature in space and time, I can arrange (more or less) in one ordered scheme both myself and other animates, together with the physical world. This arrangement is practical since I can act on it, and since I must act on it if I am to continue what I call my 'real' life. Again this arrangement is true theoretically, so far as it serves to bring facts before my mind harmoniously.[34]

Now Bradley maintains, not unreasonably, that any system of ideal contents to which a human being could have cognitive access, and through which it could come to have discursive knowledge of any sort of object whatsoever, must be realized in the thoughts, perceptions, inferences, desires, dreams, spoken and

[30] *PL*, 48–51.   [31] *ETR*, 219–23; *PL*, 99–101.
[32] *ETR*, 210; cf. *OC*, paras. 105, 140–2, 225, 279.
[33] *PL*, Terminal Essay XII, 713–28.   [34] *ETR*, 460–1.

written utterances, and so on occurring at moments in the lives of human beings living in the time series of our real world. Such ideal contents must in that sense appear in our real world. However, it does not follow from this that the specific systems of objects that are known through such ideal contents must exist in the time series of our real world, let alone be locatable in the space of our real world. Among the objects Bradley alludes to in this context are objects of mathematical, logical, scientific, moral, and theological thinking; the objects of negations true with respect to objects in our real world; objects of illusions, dreams, and fictional descriptions in literature, and so on. The latter objects may well be spatio-temporally ordered objects of humanly perceptible sorts, but *as such* will not exist in our historically real world.

In this regard Bradley argued forcefully in the *Principles of Logic*, and with great significance for the whole of his philosophy, that the idea of a spatio-temporal system of existence is simply an ideal content, and thus, like any such content, is intrinsically general. Therefore, no matter how much further discursive content we might write into the descriptions of our real world, it could not conceivably guarantee the *uniqueness* of its own application.[35] Hence he concluded that we cannot take the uniqueness of our real world to derive from its general *character* as a spatio-temporally extended system. We must take it to rest on the uniqueness of the immediate experience in the ideal contents of which reality is given as a time-ordered life in a three-dimensional spatially extended environment in which *here* and *now* we are thinking, perceiving, feeling, and acting. We can think of, and have knowledge of, spatio-temporal systems not spatio-temporally related to our real series, but we cannot *here* and *now* act in them. With respect to thinkable systems of objects which are excluded from existence in our real world (e.g. objects merely dreamt of by somebody), whether or not of spatio-temporally locatable sorts, Bradley refused to countenance as an acceptable option within metaphysics a psychologistic reduction of their reality—a reduction of a kind that would be open to both the Cartesian dualist and the Lockean physicalist—to the datable

---

[35] *PL*, 62–6, 77–8; see also *PL*, Terminal Essay IV, and Hidé Ishiguro, 'Inscrutability of Reference, Monism, and Individuals', in J. Hopkins and A. Savile (eds.), *Psychoanalysis, Mind and Art* (Oxford: Blackwell, 1992), esp. 216–18.

psychological acts occurring in our real time series and through which individual human beings have cognitive access to them.[36] Bradley sums up his position as follows:

[A] building up of the sense-world from the ground of actual presentation is a condition of all our knowledge. It is not true that everything, even temporal, has a place in *our* one 'real' order of space or time. But, indirectly or directly, every known element must be connected with its sequence of events, and, at least in some sense must show itself even there. The test of truth after all, we may say, lies in presented fact.[37]

Bradley, of course, is not saying here that the test of truth lies in the presentation of facts accessible through the contents of momentary sense perceptions of the chimerical kind postulated in the Russell–Moore empiricism as lying at the limit of analysis of the propositional systems of our empirical knowledge. On Bradley's view, reality will be present in the waking life of a normal adult human being more or less adequately through an indefinite multiplicity of more or less disparate acquired systems of logically interrelated ideal contents which will inform *phenomenologically* the character of that life. These systems will inevitably, as Bradley puts it, 'on the one side penetrate and on the other side transcend the common visible facts'.[38] Moreover, they will do so in a way that leaves no room for an application of a dichotomous distinction *true or false* to the various systems of contents that currently inform the character of an individual's experience.[39] Only particular contents that are internal to acquired and currently standing systems will present themselves in the individual's experience as determinately *bivalent*. Correspondingly, there will be no room for an application of the dichotomous distinction *real or unreal* to specific systems of objects known through such systems of ideal contents, in the way that there will be to particular objects of sorts known as *possible* within particular systems of existents.

The test of truth, or reality, for a system, on Bradley's view, can never be other than satisfaction of a human being's intellect,[40]

---

[36] *ETR*, 34–5; also *AR*, 186–7, 528–9; but see *AR*, 337, where Bradley says: 'The dollar, merely thought of, or imagined, is comparatively abstract and void of properties. But the dollar, verified in space, has got its place in, and is determined by, an enormous construction of things.'   [37] *AR*, 336–7.
[38] *ETR*, 31.   [39] *ETR*, 261–2.   [40] *ETR*, 219–20.

and such an intellect can only operate in a particular historical, and continuously changing, situation within our real world. A human being's intellect constrained, *qua* intellect, by a constant quest for truth and by the operational norms of coherence and comprehensiveness, can operate only on specific realities (historical, geographical, scientific, mathematical, moral, theological, logical, or whatever) that present themselves from out of the background of the individual's immediate experience in terms of the ideal contents internal to particular systems of logically interrelated contents that the individual has in fact acquired through life. Non-bivalent concepts of truth and reality that allow for increasing *degrees* of truth and reality will apply to such systems of ideal contents and the systems of objects identifiable by means of them. This is because of the intrinsic proneness of systems of content to supplant one another through time as a result of the constant drive of intellectually active individuals for increasing systematicity (i.e. coherence and comprehensiveness) in the specific systems of their knowledge. Any system more comprehensive than a competitor that brings to coherence, and thus to internality, data that were left merely external by the previously standing system of contents will be the truer. Correspondingly, the specific system of existence identifiable in terms of ideal contents internal to the more comprehensive system of contents will be more real. Bradley saw no necessity for human knowledge either generally, or in any specific sphere of human interest, to increase with the passage of time; but, no doubt, the kinds of advances that have in fact occurred in the Western world within specific natural sciences dealing with particular aspects of reality would provide a paradigm for the kind of movement to increasing comprehensiveness that he had in mind.[41] For Bradley, only experts in the given field of a special science could conceivably apply the joint criteria of coherence and comprehensiveness within the contents of a particular theoretical context; but in general, he claims, the application of the notion of comprehensiveness must make reference to the spatial and temporal series of our real world.[42]

---

[41] *AR*, 5, 251–5; see also F. H. Bradley, *Aphorisms and Presuppositions of Critical History* (Bristol: Thoemmes, 1993), aphorism 7, p. 6: '*The Unity of Science.* Whatever you know it is all one.' [42] *AR*, 327–8.

Here it can be seen that the system of ideal contents constitutive of the ideal construction of our real world, embedded in the practices and nature of human beings' daily lives as those contents are, must be construed to have an entirely different epistemological and logical status from that of specific systems of ideal contents that are, as, say, in the natural sciences, developed by individuals in pursuit of knowledge of particular aspects of reality. Certainly, as we well know, the contents internal to the system in which we identify our real world will be continuously prone at given points to a degree of penetration and modification as a result of advances in particular sciences; but the relation of the system as a whole to the contents of specific scientific systems can never be analogous to that between competing systems within a given science. The contents that are systematically integrated into the ideal construction of our real world do not have the status of *hypotheses*.[43] We cannot intelligibly regard them as being in principle falsifiable either in our own lives or in the lives of future human beings.

So far in the above account, no positive commitment to what Bradley would call a 'metaphysics' has been mentioned. It has been indicated that particular accounts of the nature of the postulated independently existent reality taken from the history of philosophy were rejected as unsatisfactory by Bradley. And it has been asserted that in Bradley's account the independently existent reality is *ex hypothesi* both immediately given and discursively present in the waking experiences of human beings and sentient creatures generally. Finally, it has been indicated that while Bradley insists that acquisition of the system of ideal contents in terms of which we are able at waking moments to think of our historically and geographically real world is of utterly fundamental importance both practically and cognitively in an individual's life, he nevertheless holds that the world in question cannot in the context of metaphysics be regarded as uniquely or, therefore, *as such* as maximally real.

What of Bradley's positive attempt to characterize in general terms the ultimate nature of the postulated independently existent reality? Before considering Bradley's account, we should note a constraint that he takes the metaphysician to be bound by. At

---

[43] Cf. OC, para. 167.

the beginning of the chapter in *Appearance and Reality* entitled 'Solipsism', Bradley says in speaking of metaphysics: 'Any view which will not explain, and also justify, an attitude essential to human nature, must surely be condemned.'[44]

The attitudes essential to human nature that Bradley has in mind here are no doubt those that a human being will have in taking itself to have been born at a determinate place and time, to be facing a death inevitably to come, to have a known past and an unknown future, to be capable of acting, for better or worse, successfully and unsuccessfully, to be capable of knowledge and error, happiness and misery, and so on. However, the kind of explanation and justification which Bradley can demand from his metaphysics will have to be significantly different from the detailed kinds of explanation and justification—whether everyday or scientific—that can be given for the existence and occurrence of specific things knowable from within the compass of our real world. So long as his outline account of the ultimate nature of the independently existent reality can be shown to be compatible[45] with the main attitudes essential to human nature, and so long as it presents itself to the intellect as not further corrigible[46] in the kinds of way that competitors have shown themselves to be, he will be satisfied.

As is well known, in Book I of *Appearance and Reality*, Bradley argues that the key ideas (e.g. the concepts of space, time, movement, causation, activity, self, and not-self) that are internal to the ideal contents in terms of which, in our thinking, we identify our real world can, on reflection, be seen to involve contradictions. Consequently, metaphysical theories which proceed by taking some one or more sorts of thing known to exist within our real world and presenting things of that sort or sorts as independently existent must fail. Further, the fundamental source of these contradictions Bradley locates in the intrinsically abstract nature of our linguistically communicable predicative thought. He is not, of course, claiming that contradictions are always, as he puts it, visible[47] in the specific systems of ideal contents with which we confront reality in our lives. Moreover, when a contradiction does become visible, and because of some 'new' input of content to

---

[44] *AR*, 218; *ETR*, 14.   [45] *AR*, 163–4.   [46] *AR*, 482–5.
[47] *ETR*, 223–4.

a system, a logical conflict appears between particular contents internal to a currently standing system of ideal contents, the possibility will always remain, on Bradley's view, for the intellect to resolve the conflict by bringing the ideas involved together, modified in presently unforeseeable ways, within the context of a more comprehensive system of ideal contents.[48] For paradigms of the complex and subtle kinds of identity and change in meanings, and thus in logical interconnections between ideal contents, that can occur in hitherto conflicting ideas internal to specific systems of contents when those ideas reappear harmoniously in the context of more comprehensive systems, we can, no doubt, look again to the history of the natural sciences. However, given that there are contradictions latent in any system of communicable ideal contents, and given the intrinsically partial character of the theories in any special science, no matter how comprehensive and fundamental such theories might become with respect to their specific sphere of reality—like those of mathematical physics have in fact become—it follows that no science, natural or social, could conceivably help the metaphysician in his quest.

Nevertheless, Bradley saw philosophical logic as giving a glimmer of light at the end of the metaphysical tunnel. In his account of negative judgement in the *Principles of Logic* he argued against the intelligibility of *bare* negation. By this, in effect, he meant the function of the operator in the standard truth table. Bradley maintained that if a negative judgement is true with respect to any specific reality, that reality must have some positive feature incompatible with the feature denied and in virtue of which the negation is true. He therefore concluded that an independently existent reality must have a feature in virtue of which it is the case that any internally inconsistent system of ideal contents, as it stands, can be denied of it.[49] He designated that feature *harmoniousness*. Moreover, given that contradictions are latent not only in the ideal construction of our real world, but also in any possible specific system of ideal contents through which a finite individual could have cognitive access to any particular sphere of reality, Bradley argued that, within the lives of finite sentient creatures, only the *knowing and being in one* constitutive of their immediate

---

[48] e.g. *AR*, 332–3.
[49] *AR*, 120–4; *PL*, i. ch. 3; cf. Guy Stock, 'Negation: Bradley and Wittgenstein', *Philosophy*, 60 (1985), 465–76.

experiences in which the ideal contents which are the vehicles of their discursive and self-consciously possessed knowledge must be realized could be allowed in metaphysics to possess independent existence.

Thus Bradley concluded that the independently existent reality must be one in substance with such finite centres of immediate experience, and hence in its ultimate nature must be conceived as an all-encompassing utterly harmonious immediate experience. This reality will be (i) given both immediately and, with varying degrees of adequacy, in ideal form in any finite centre of immediate experience, (ii) the ultimate source of the existence both of any finite centre of immediate experience and of any of the worlds, or specific realities, to which such individuals have cognitive access through their systems of ideal contents, and (iii) that in which all the aspects and strivings of any finite existent, which in a finite life must be more or less unfulfilled, will be completely realized.

However, Bradley warns that we cannot think of the Absolute as one in the sense in which, in our real world, we can think of some general sort of thing as being countably one, or unique: it is not one of a general sort within a world in which there could be more than one.[50] Nor can we think of the Absolute as an experience in the sense which that term has within our real world when we distinguish sentient animals, as subjects of consciousness and inner experiences, from inanimate things like trees which lack such experiences, or from merely physical things—whether the merely physical things be things of humanly perceptible sorts, or things of the kinds that are identifiable only in terms of ideal contents internal to the fundamental theories of physics. Nor, *a fortiori*, is Bradley's concept of experience that of the Lockean physicalist: an impotent centre of self-conscious, self-deluded epiphenomena realized in the temporally successive physico-chemical happenings in a human being's brain that is contingently not a brain-in-a-vat. Bradley emphasizes that almost the whole point of his philosophy is to avoid the trap in metaphysics of attributing independent existence to one or more of the ontological categories of thing of which we have discursive knowledge from within the compass of our real world, and of reducing the rest of reality to

[50] *AR*, 460–1.

the status of a mere appearance supervenient on, or somehow constructed out of, things of the favoured category or categories.[51]

It follows that Bradley's idea of experience as that is allowed to qualify the independently existent reality must like that of the neutral monists have, with respect to the ontological categories we are familiar with in our real world, a *neutrality* about it. Nevertheless, it is clear that Bradley intends to sustain a metaphysics which (i) leaves standing an individual human life, in all its diverse aspects, with all its achievements and failures, theoretical, emotional, and practical, scientific, artistic, moral, political, religious, or whatever, as a fundamental and ineliminable reality, and (ii) portrays such a life as the locus of the material sufficient for us in metaphysics, by some profound extension of meaning to the point of ineffability, to get an inkling of the character of an all-encompassing utterly harmonious experience within which all the intentional distinctions that language has made available to us and that have enabled us in the deeds and sufferings of our individual lives, for better or worse, to transcend and transform phenomenologically— and so give value to—the merely sentient, minimally active immediacy of our temporal beginnings, are themselves, each to its own measure, transcended and transformed in an altogether higher kind of immediacy.[52]

[51] *AR*, 128–9; *PL*, 590–1, 595 n. 25; but see also *AR*, 298–300.
[52] *PL*, Terminal Essay VIII, 689–90.

2

The What and the That: Theories of Singular Thought in Bradley, Russell, and the Early Wittgenstein

JAMES LEVINE

———◆———

As has become widely recognized in recent years, one of the fundamental differences between Frege and Russell concerns their views of the constituents of singular sentential 'contents'. Frege and Russell agree that at least one purpose of a proper name is to stand for an object, and both agree that sentences containing proper names, as well as the contents such sentences express, are *about* the objects designated by the names in those sentences (if those names succeed in designating at all). But they do not agree as to what the relation is between the content expressed by a singular sentence and the object(s) which that sentence is about.

In particular, once he makes his distinction between sense and *Bedeutung*,[1] Frege holds that what a name contributes to a content is not the object which it designates (the *Bedeutung* of the name) but rather its sense. Russell, on the other hand, rejects Frege's distinction between sense and *Bedeutung*, and holds that proper names serve only to designate objects. Thus, as opposed to Frege, Russell holds that the content expressed by a singular sentence includes among its constituents the actual object designated by that name.

Both Frege and Russell, then, adhere to:

---

[1] In order to avoid issues surrounding the translation of Frege's *Bedeutung*, I have left it untranslated throughout.

ST   At least some contents (call them singular thoughts[2]) are, or
     at least purport to be, about objects.[3]

But since Russell makes the object which a singular thought is
about an actual constituent of that singular thought, his singular
thoughts differ in certain respects from Frege's. First, there is a
metaphysical difference in that Russell, but not Frege, accepts:

ST$_M$ What singular thoughts there are depends on what objects
         there are.

For by placing the object which a singular thought is about in the
thought itself, Russell's singular thoughts become, in contemporary terminology, 'object-dependent':[4] the being of a singular thought
depends upon the being of the object it is about. A singular
thought lacking an object would be no thought at all, for it would
be lacking a component—the object itself—needed to make it into
a complete and genuine thought. Frege, on the other hand, holds
that the being of a singular thought depends on the being of
the senses composing that thought; and since he holds that a
name may have sense even when it fails to designate an object,
he thereby holds that the being of a singular thought does not

---

[2] Here and in what follows, I am not using 'thought' in the specifically Fregean
way, as a sentential content whose components are senses; rather, I am using it
as I use the phrase 'sentential content'—i.e. as neutral between Frege's and
Russell's views of the constituents of sentential contents.

[3] A list of the labelled principles used throughout this chapter is given in an
appendix.

[4] See e.g. John McDowell, 'Singular Thought and the Extent of Inner Space',
in P. Pettit and J. McDowell (eds.), *Subject, Thought and Context* (Oxford:
Clarendon Press, 1986), 142. Both McDowell and Gareth Evans, *Varieties of
Reference* (Oxford: Clarendon Press, 1982), 27–30, attempt to find this view
of 'object-dependent' thoughts in Frege's post-1890 writings; and, in order to
do so, they must deny or dismiss passages in which Frege clearly indicates that
names may express sense without having any *Bedeutung*. Like David Bell, 'How
"Russellian" was Frege?', *Mind*, 99 (1990), 267–77, I believe that Evans and
McDowell have little, if any, textual support for claiming that Frege himself (post-
1890) has any general difficulty in holding that a singular sentence may have a
sense, or express a thought, without succeeding in being about an object. And,
to this extent, I believe that Evans and McDowell have little, if any, textual support for attributing an 'object-dependent' view of singular thought to Frege.
(I recognize, however, that by focusing on the few passages where Frege discusses
demonstratives, Evans and McDowell suggest a way to develop a broadly 'Fregean'
account of 'object-dependent' singular thoughts, even if such a position does not
accurately reflect Frege's overall view of singular thoughts.)

depend on there being an object which that thought succeeds in being about.[5]

Second, Russell, but not Frege, accepts the epistemological doctrine:

ST_E Apprehending a singular thought requires knowing (or being acquainted with) the object which that thought is about.

Russell and Frege both hold that apprehending a content (or thought) requires being in direct cognitive contact with each of its constituents, something which, at a minimum, enables one to know the existence (or being) of each constituent.[6] In the terminology of Russell and Frege, apprehending a content will require knowing, or being acquainted with (*kennen*), or 'grasping', each of its constituents.[7] Since Russell makes the object which a singular thought is about a constituent of that thought, he thereby holds, in accordance with ST_E, that apprehending a singular thought requires knowing (or being acquainted with) the object which

---

[5] See e.g. Gottlob Frege, 'Logic in Mathematics', in his *Posthumous Writings*, ed. H. Hermes, F. Kambartel and F. Kaulbach, trans. P. Long and R. White (Oxford: Blackwell, 1979), 225: '. . . when we say "Scylla has six heads", what are we making a statement about? In this case, nothing whatsoever; for the word "Scylla" designates nothing. Nevertheless we can find a thought expressed by the sentence, and concede a sense to the word "Scylla".' Here, then, Frege indicates that the singular sentence 'Scylla has six heads' expresses a genuine content (or thought) even though it is not about anything. Passages such as this are in opposition to the reading of Evans and McDowell (see n. 4).

[6] Because of this, accepting ST_E requires accepting ST_M. For if, as ST_E requires, apprehending a singular thought requires coming in contact with the object which that content is about, then, as ST_M requires, the being of that singular thought depends upon the being of the object which that thought is about and with which we must come into cognitive contact to apprehend that thought. Accepting ST_M, on the other hand, need not require accepting ST_E; and, as I mention in n. 18 below, some contemporary direct theorists of reference seem to take this course of accepting ST_M but not ST_E. Throughout this essay, my main focus is on how Bradley, Russell, and the early Wittgenstein come to apply the stronger principle ST_E.

[7] Thus Russell's principle of acquaintance: 'Every proposition which we can understand must be composed wholly of constituents with which we are acquainted' ('Knowledge by Acquaintance and Knowledge by Description', in *Mysticism and Logic* (London: Longmans, Green and Co., 1919), 219). Likewise, in discussing the sentence 'Sea water is salty', Frege writes that 'knowledge [*Die Kenntnis*] of the sense of the word "salt" is required for an understanding of the sentence, since it makes an essential contribution to the thought' ('My Basic Logical Insights', in *Posthumous Writings*, 251). Thus for Frege, as for Russell, apprehending a sentential content requires knowledge (*Kenntnis*) of each component part of that content.

that thought is about.[8] On the other hand, since Frege denies that the object which a singular thought is about is a constituent of that thought, and holds instead that only senses are constituents of thoughts, he thereby rejects ST_E. While he holds that apprehending a singular thought will require knowing (or grasping) the senses composing that thought, he denies that it will require knowing (or grasping or being acquainted with) the object which that thought is about. For, according to Frege, in grasping the sense of a name, we are not thereby acquainted with the object designated by that name, and do not even know whether it succeeds in designating any object at all.[9]

When these sorts of differences between Frege and Russell were recognized in recent years, it was the Russellian, not the Fregean, position that seemed more strange. For although the Russellian view is simpler (in that names serve only one symbolic function), and although Frege himself seems to have accepted the Russellian view prior to 1890, from the 1930s to the 1960s, the Fregean view was the more widely accepted, so much so that it had become philosophical common sense. Hence, when philosophers increasingly recognized in the 1970s and 1980s that Russell allowed actual objects to be constituents of propositions, it was presented as a somewhat remarkable point, worthy of emphasis. Commentators felt the 'need to stress' that, 'counter-intuitive' though it may seem, Russell held that in propositions such as 'Socrates is human' or 'Brown is taller than Smith', Socrates, Brown, and Smith themselves, the very people, actually occur as constituents.[10]

Furthermore, when philosophers such as David Kaplan and others advocating 'new' or 'direct' theories of reference not only point out these differences between Russell and Frege, but further

[8] Hence in defending his principle of acquaintance, Russell writes: 'we cannot make a judgement or a supposition without knowing what it is that we are making our judgement or supposition about' ('Knowledge by Acquaintance', 221).

[9] Thus Frege writes: 'In grasping a sense, one is not certainly assured of meaning [*bedeuten*] anything' ('On Sense and Meaning' trans. M. Black, in *Collected Papers*, ed. B. McGuinness (Oxford: Blackwell, 1984), 159). Again, this passage is obviously opposed to the Evans–McDowell reading of Frege.

[10] See e.g. Richard Cartwright, 'A Neglected Theory of Truth', in his *Philosophical Essays* (Cambridge, Mass.: MIT Press, 1987), 83; Peter Hylton, 'Russell's Substitutional Theory', *Synthese*, 45 (1980), 7, 28 n. 3; David Kaplan, 'Dthat', in P. Yourgrau (ed.), *Demonstratives* (Oxford: Oxford University Press, 1990), 13. These examples come from Russell's pre-1905 writings, when he still held that expressions like 'Socrates', 'Brown', 'Smith' may be genuine proper names.

side with Russell against Frege, they readily acknowledge that by so doing they are challenging ingrained philosophical doctrine. Thus Kaplan describes himself as having 'been raised on Fregean semantics'[11] and writes of the 'Golden Age of Pure Semantics' during the 1930s, 1940s, and 1950s, when 'meanings and entities of the world' were 'each properly segregated and related to one another in rather smooth and comfortable ways'.[12] Hence, in maintaining ('despite Frege's incredulity'[13]) that Russellian singular propositions have a role to play in semantics, Kaplan recognizes that he is not only rebelling 'against [his] own Fregean upbringing[14] but is, more generally, 'reviv[ing] a view of language alternate to that of the Golden Age'.[15] Kaplan sees himself, that is, as 'contribut[ing] to the redevelopment of an old and common-sensical theory of language which—at least in the philosophical literature—has rather been in decline during the ascendency' of the 'Golden Age of Pure Semantics'.[16] As some have described them, 'new' or 'direct' theories of reference are an attempt to return to a state of 'pre-Fregean semantic innocence'.[17]

My purpose here is to show that this Russellian view of singular thoughts, which was so out of favour during the 'Golden Age of Pure Semantics', but which has become increasingly popular in recent years, is at the heart not only of Russell's philosophy, but also of the views of his immediate predecessor, F. H. Bradley, as well as of his immediate successor, the early Wittgenstein. I will argue that all three philosophers accept ST

---

[11] David Kaplan, 'Demonstratives', in J. Almog, J. Perry, and H. K. Wettstein (eds.), *Themes from Kaplan* (Oxford: Oxford University Press, 1989), 486.

[12] Kaplan, 'Dthat', 13–14.

[13] David Kaplan, 'Opacity', in L. E. Hahn and P. A. Schilpp (eds.), *The Philosophy of W. V. Quine* (La Salle, Ill.: Open Court, 1986), 240.

[14] David Kaplan, 'Afterthoughts [to "Demonstratives"]', in Almog *et al.* (eds.), *Themes from Kaplan*, 568.   [15] Kaplan, 'Dthat', 19.

[16] Ibid. 13.

[17] The phrase comes from Donald Davidson, 'On Saying That', repr. in his *Inquiries into Truth and Interpretation* (Oxford: Clarendon Press, 1984), 108, and others have used it to characterize the position of 'new' theorists of reference generally. See e.g. Jon Barwise and John Perry, 'Semantic Innocence and Uncompromising Situations', in P. A. French, T. E. Uehling, and H. K. Wettstein (eds.), *Midwest Studies in Philosophy VI* (Minneapolis: University of Minnesota Press, 1982), 387–403, and Herman Parret, 'Perspectival Understanding', in H. Parret and J. Bouveresse (eds.), *Meaning and Understanding* (Berlin: de Gruyter, 1981), 249: 'causal theories of proper names and of meaning—Putnam's say, or Kripke's—together with their related philosophies of language, are trying to recover a pre-Fregean semantic innocence'.

along with ST_M and ST_E, and will attempt to make clear that understanding some of the central doctrines of these philosophers amounts to understanding the different ways they apply these shared principles.

Once one accepts ST_M and ST_E, one may not avoid relating one's views of sentential contents to one's views of objects. During the 'Golden Age of Pure Semantics', when meanings (or Fregean senses) were sharply segregated from the entities of the world, one's views of objects were independent of one's views of sentential contents. But, by ST_M and ST_E, if one begins with certain views of the nature of objects, then one will be forced to accept corresponding views of the nature of singular thoughts; conversely, by those same principles, antecedent views of the nature of singular contents will translate into views of the nature of objects. What I will argue, then, is that Russell, Wittgenstein, and Bradley arrive at their widely divergent philosophical positions by bringing different concerns to bear upon their shared principles, ST_M and ST_E. In particular, I will argue that Russell conjoins these principles with views as to what we are acquainted with in experience; that Wittgenstein conjoins them with views regarding the apprehension of sentential contents; and that Bradley conjoins them with views as to what is involved in knowing an object. By doing so, I hope to clarify not only the views of Bradley, Russell, and the early Wittgenstein, but also some of the issues that become pressing and some of the positions that become available, once one accepts the 'semantically innocent' notion of Russellian singular thoughts.[18]

I

During the period with which I am here concerned (roughly 1905 to 1919), Russell comes to hold that the only particulars with

[18] I recognize that not all contemporary 'direct' theorists of reference would accept ST_E along with ST_M. For some 'direct' theorists sharply distinguish the task of 'semantics' from that of analysing the 'cognitive significance' of a sentence— i.e. from the task of analysing what we need to know to understand a sentence. Thus they might hold that while Russellian singular thoughts have a role to play in 'semantics', they are not all that is needed for a proper account of what is involved in understanding a sentence. In the concluding section, however, I mention briefly the views of certain contemporary philosophers who seem to accept ST_E along with ST_M.

which we are acquainted (indeed, the only particulars there *are*) are sense-data.[19] Thus, for Russell, the only singular thoughts (or singular propositions, in his terminology) we can apprehend (indeed, the only singular propositions there *are*) are about sense-data. Hence, by ST_M and ST_E, Russell's views of sense-data transmit themselves into his views of singular propositions.

Thus, for example, Russell accepts:

S-D$_1$ Sense-data exist only fleetingly or momentarily; they are apprehended *a posteriori*; they are private to the person apprehending them.[20]

Hence, by accepting ST_M and ST_E, Russell is forced to accept:

R$_1$ Singular thoughts exist only fleetingly; they are apprehended *a posteriori*; and they are private to the person apprehending them.

For if, by ST_M, the existence of a singular thought depends upon the existence of the object it is about, and if the only objects

---

[19] Before 1905, Russell seems to have had no difficulty in holding that we may be acquainted with physical objects, such as Mr Arthur Balfour. (See the pre-'On Denoting' MSS quoted by Richard Cartwright in his chapter 'On the Origins of Russell's Theory of Descriptions', in his *Philosophical Essays*, 112.) In 1911, Russell held that while sense-data (taken widely to include the particulars apprehended by inner as well as outer sense and also by memory—see his 'Knowledge by Acquaintance', 212) are the only particulars with which we are acquainted, there are other particulars (including physical objects and other minds—see ibid. 214) with which we may never be acquainted. From 1913 to 1919, Russell pursued the view that the only particulars there are (or at least the only particulars he is going to countenance) are those sense-data with which we may be acquainted. On this view, physical objects as well as minds are logically 'constructed' out of (ontologically neutral) sense-data. Here, the only particulars which Russell recognizes as being part of 'the ultimate constituents of the world' are sense-data; all other apparent particulars or 'things', such as physical objects, will be 'logical fictions'. See e.g. 'The Philosophy of Logical Atomism', in *Logic and Knowledge*, ed. R. C. Marsh (London: George Allen & Unwin, 1956), lecture VIII.

[20] Thus, in 'Philosophy of Logical Atomism', Russell states: 'A particular [i.e. a sense-datum], as a rule, is apt to last for a very short time indeed' (203–4). In his 1913 *Theory of Knowledge*, ed. E. R. Eames (London: George Allen & Unwin, 1984), 66, he writes: 'The object of a sensation we will call a *sense-datum*', thereby indicating that we are acquainted with sense-data through sensory experience. (Here, as elsewhere, the emphasis in the quotation is original unless noted otherwise.) And in 'Philosophy of Logical Atomism', 201, Russell writes: 'when you use "this" quite strictly, to stand for an actual object of sense . . . [it] does not mean the same thing to the speaker and to the hearer'. For Russell, that is, since sense-data are private, the word 'this', when taken to refer to a sense-datum, cannot stand for something which both speaker and hearer may apprehend.

which singular thoughts are about exist fleetingly, then singular thoughts themselves will have only a fleeting or momentary existence. Likewise, if, by ST_E, apprehending a singular thought requires acquaintance with the object it is about, and if our acquaintance with that object is *a posteriori* and essentially private, then apprehending that singular thought will also be *a posteriori* and essentially private.[21]

Furthermore—what will be central in distinguishing his position from both Wittgenstein's and Bradley's—Russell has quite specific views as to what is involved in knowing, or being acquainted with, a sense-datum, views which, by ST_E, will also affect his view of the apprehension of singular propositions. In particular, Russell accepts:

S-D$_2$ In being acquainted with a sense-datum, we immediately know it fully and completely; in being acquainted with it, we know both *that* it is (or exists) and also *what* it is; in knowing *what* it is, we thereby know some truths about it.

In the remainder of this section, my main purpose is to show how Russell accepts the three parts of S-D$_2$ and to consider some consequences which S-D$_2$ has for Russell's view as to what is involved in apprehending singular propositions.

First of all, for Russell, since sense-data are objects of acquaintance, each sense-datum is given to us in its entirety, and no error is possible with regard to any sense-datum. For, on Russell's view, an object of acquaintance is an object which is wholly present to us; and, on Russell's view, no error is possible with regard to any object of acquaintance. Thus, for Russell, in being acquainted with a sense-datum, we can neither be ignorant nor mistaken regarding that sense-datum. And thus Russell accepts the first part

---

[21] Thus in 'Philosophy of Logical Atomism', 201, Russell claims: 'if you try to apprehend the proposition I am expressing when I say "This is white", you cannot do it'; and writes more generally (p. 198): 'A logically perfect language . . . would be very largely private to one speaker. That is to say, all the names that it would use would be private to that speaker and could not enter into the language of another speaker.' Note also in this context that G. E. Moore, *Lectures on Philosophy*, ed. C. Lewy (London: George Allen & Unwin, 1966), 130–1, indicates that singular propositions 'subsist contingently'. For Moore, since particulars (sense-data) exist contingently and are constituents of singular propositions, then singular propositions themselves have contingent being.

of S-D$_2$, according to which our immediate acquaintance with a sense-datum gives us a complete knowledge of that sense-datum. As Russell writes in *The Problems of Philosophy*:

I know the [sense-datum] perfectly and completely when I see it, and no further knowledge of it itself is even theoretically possible. Thus the sense-data which make up the appearance of the table are things with which I have acquaintance, things immediately known to me just as they are.[22]

More specifically, Russell holds, in accordance with the second part of S-D$_2$, that acquaintance with a sense-datum gives us knowledge *that* that sense-datum is (or exists), as well as a full knowledge as to *what* that sense-datum is. First, according to Russell, we cannot be acquainted with an object unless that object exists; and, for Russell, in being acquainted with that existing object, we thereby know that that object exists. As he writes in *The Problems of Philosophy*: 'If I am acquainted with a thing which exists, my acquaintance gives me the knowledge that it exists.'[23] Second, by holding that acquaintance gives us a complete knowledge of a sense-datum, Russell thereby holds that acquaintance gives us a full knowledge of *what* that sense-datum is. As he states in his 1918 lectures on logical atomism: 'When you have acquaintance with a particular, you understand that particular itself quite fully . . . [Y]ou . . . know *what* the particular itself is.'[24] For Russell, that is, to 'understand' a particular (a sense-datum) 'quite fully', or to know it 'perfectly and completely', just is to 'know *what* that particular itself is'.

Finally, in accord with the third part of S-D$_2$, Russell holds that knowing *what* a sense-datum is will enable one to know at least some truths about that sense-datum. The point does not follow for Russell as a matter of logic. For Russell sharply distinguishes 'knowledge of things' from 'knowledge of truths'. According to Russell, knowing a 'thing', or being acquainted with a particular, 'is a two-term relation [between a subject and a particular] in which the object [i.e. the particular, the object of acquaintance] can be *named* but not *asserted*, and is inherently incapable of

---

[22] Bertrand Russell, *The Problems of Philosophy* (London: Oxford University Press, 1959), 47.

[23] Ibid. 45. See also 'The Relation of Sense-Data to Physics', in *Mysticism and Logic*, 148: 'Concerning sense-data, we know that they are there while they are data.'   [24] 'Philosophy of Logical Atomism', 204; emphasis added.

truth or falsehood'.[25] On the other hand, in knowing a truth, what the mind entertains is propositional in nature, for only what is propositional in nature is capable of being asserted or of being either true or false. Hence, for Russell, acquaintance with a sense-datum is not the same as knowledge of truth; for, as Russell writes: 'The actual sense-data are neither true nor false. A particular patch of colour which I see, for example, simply exists: it is not the sort of thing that is true or false.'[26]

Nevertheless, even though he holds that the logical structure of acquaintance with a particular is different from that of knowledge of a truth, and even though he writes that 'We may have knowledge of a thing by acquaintance even if we know very few propositions about it—theoretically we need not know any propositions about it',[27] he also holds that 'it would be rash to assume that human beings ever, in fact, have acquaintance with things without at the same time knowing some truth about them'.[28] For, according to Russell, given the actual particulars with which we humans have acquaintance—namely, sense-data—mere acquaintance with a particular will enable us to know some truths about that particular.

Specifically, Russell writes of 'self-evident truths of perception' which are 'immediately derived from sensation'.[29] Even though he sharply distinguishes these 'self-evident truths' from the particulars given in sensation from which they are 'immediately derived',[30] he still holds that mere acquaintance with particular

---

[25] 'Relation of Sense-Data to Physics', 147.

[26] *The Problems of Philosophy*, 113.

[27] Ibid. 144. See also p. 46, where Russell writes that 'knowledge by *acquaintance* is essentially simpler than any knowledge of truths, and logically independent of knowledge of truths'. Again, in *Our Knowledge of the External World* (Chicago: Open Court, 1915), 144, Russell writes: 'Acquaintance, which is what we derive from sense, does not, theoretically at least, imply even the smallest "knowledge about," *i.e.* it does not imply knowledge of any proposition concerning the object with which we are acquainted.' See also a similar passage in *Theory of Knowledge*, 95. In all these passages, Russell indicates that it is only 'theoretically' or 'logically' that acquaintance with an object does not imply knowledge of any truth about that object. I argue that Russell holds that while *theoretically*, acquaintance with a particular does not imply any knowledge of truth, *in fact* our human acquaintance with sense-data always enables us to know (immediately) truths about those sense-data.　　　　　　[28] *The Problems of Philosophy*, 46.

[29] Ibid. 113–14.

[30] Since, again, the particulars are not themselves capable of being true or false (ibid. 114).

sense-data will enable us to know some truths about those sense-data. Thus he writes that one kind of 'self-evident truth' which is 'immediately derived from sensation' 'arises when the object of sense is complex, and we subject it to some degree of analysis. If, for instance, we see a *round* patch of red, we may judge "that patch of red is round".'[31] For Russell, that is, if we are acquainted with a red sense-datum which is also round, we thereby immediately know the truth that that red sense-datum is round. And, more generally, if a sense-datum is red and round, the sense-datum itself (a particular) is different from the properties of being red or being round, and is different also from the facts (or truths) that it is red or that it is round. But, for Russell, in merely being acquainted with the sense-datum, we thereby know immediately both that it is red and that it is round. For according to him, in knowing *what* sense-datum we are acquainted with, we thereby know what sensible qualities it has (as e.g. its colour and shape), and thereby know as well some truths about that sense-datum (viz. that it has those sensory qualities).

Just as accepting S-D₁ affects Russell's view of what is involved in apprehending a singular proposition, so too does accepting S-D₂. First of all, Russell's views of acquaintance enable him to accept:

R₂ We can fully apprehend a singular proposition (or thought) immediately; in immediately apprehending that proposition, we know *that* it is about something and know fully *what* it is about.

According to Russell, apprehending a proposition requires acquaintance with each of its constituents. But for him, whatever we are acquainted with, we fully apprehend immediately. For Russell, that is, there are no degrees of knowing an entity by acquaintance: either we are acquainted with that entity and thereby know

[31] Ibid. In his discussion here, Russell distinguishes 'two kinds of self-evident truths of perception'. The first kind 'simply asserts the *existence* of the sense-datum, without in any way analysing it'—i.e. in accordance with passages cited in n. 23, Russell holds that acquaintance with a sense-datum enables us to 'immediately derive' the 'self-evident truth' *that* that sense-datum is (or exists). Russell's second kind of 'self-evident truth of perception'—the kind with which I am concerned here—consists, in effect, of truths regarding *what* that sense-datum is, truths regarding what sensible qualities that sense-datum has.

it fully, or we are not acquainted with it.[32] Hence, since Russell holds that all the constituents of a singular proposition are entities with which we may be acquainted, he is thereby able to hold as well, in accordance with R_2, that we can fully apprehend singular propositions immediately. For Russell, just as there are no degrees of knowing a sense-datum, there are also no degrees of apprehending a singular proposition: we apprehend it fully and immediately or not at all.

Furthermore, by accepting S-D$_2$ along with ST$_E$, Russell is forced to accept the second part of R_2. By ST$_E$, apprehending a singular proposition requires acquaintance with the object it is about; and by S-D$_2$, acquaintance with a sense-datum (for Russell, the only kind of object which a singular proposition may be about) enables us to know immediately both *that* that sense-datum is and *what* that sense-datum is. Hence Russell is forced to hold, in accordance with R_2, that in immediately apprehending a singular proposition, we know *that* it is about something and also know fully *what* it is about. And since Russell holds that in knowing *what* a sense-datum is, we thereby know 'self-evident truths of perception' about that sense-datum, he thus holds that in immediately apprehending a singular proposition, we thereby know some truths about the object (or particular) which that proposition is about.[33]

More specifically, by adhering to S-D$_2$ along with ST$_E$, Russell is forced to accept:

[32] See e.g. *Our Knowledge of the External World*, 144–5: 'It is a mistake to speak as if acquaintance had degrees: there is merely acquaintance and non-acquaintance. . . . [A]cquaintance . . . is either complete or non-existent.'

[33] In 'Philosophy of Logical Atomism', Russell writes: 'The whole question of what particulars you actually find in the real world is a purely empirical question which does not interest the logician as such. The logician as such never gives instances, because it is one of the tests of a logical proposition that you need not know anything whatsoever about the real world in order to understand it' (199). What I have attempted to make clear, in effect, is how Russell comes to hold that understanding singular propositions (as opposed to logical propositions, all of which for Russell are general) requires knowing something 'about the real world'. Russell holds that understanding singular propositions requires empirical acquaintance with the particulars (the sense-data) those propositions are about; and he holds further that in being acquainted with sense-data, we thereby know truths about those sense-data. We not only know that they exist; we also know truths regarding what sensible qualities they have. And since, for Russell, sense-data are among 'the ultimate constituents of the world', he thereby holds that merely understanding a singular proposition requires knowing something 'about the real world'.

R₃ Fully apprehending some singular propositions (or thoughts) enables us to know their truth-values.

For, by ST_E, apprehending a singular proposition requires acquaintance with the object which that proposition is about; but, by $S\text{-}D_2$, acquaintance with a sense-datum enables us to know some truths about that sense-datum. Thus, for Russell, merely apprehending a singular proposition—such as one expressed by the sentence 'This is red'—which predicates a sensible quality of a sense-datum will suffice for knowing the truth-value of that proposition. For apprehending that proposition will require acquaintance with the sense-datum which it is about, and, by $S\text{-}D_2$, that will suffice for knowing whether or not that sense-datum has the sensible quality being predicated of it. For Russell, that is, in understanding the sentence 'This is red'—or in apprehending the proposition expressed by that sentence—we will have to be acquainted with the sense-datum designated by the word 'this'; and in being acquainted with that sense-datum, we will thereby know fully *what* that sense-datum is; and that in turn will involve knowing whether or not that sense-datum is red, which will thus suffice for knowing the truth-value of the sentence 'This is red'.[34]

---

[34] In the 1930s, Moritz Schlick came to hold views of 'observation statements'—statements such as 'Here now blue', which he also calls 'affirmations'—similar to Russell's views of singular sentences such as 'This is red'. In particular, Schlick explicitly accepts the view to which I have argued Russell is committed: viz. that to understand such a sentence is thereby to know its truth-value. As Schlick writes in 'On the Foundations of Knowledge', trans. P. Heath, in Schlick, *Philosophical Papers*, ii, ed. H. Mulder and B. F. B. van de Velde-Schlick (Dordrecht: Reidel, 1979), 385: 'the process of understanding [affirmations] is at the same time the process of verification. Along with their meaning I simultaneously grasp their truth.' (See also *idem*, *The Problems of Philosophy in their Interconnection*, ed. H. Mulder *et al.*, trans. P. Heath (Dordrecht: Reidel, 1987), 123–4.) Furthermore, Schlick recognizes that this view of 'affirmations' is at odds with his characterization of the analytic/synthetic distinction. For, in general, Schlick holds that whereas understanding an analytic sentence suffices for knowing what is true, understanding a (true) synthetic sentence does not. By this characterization of the analytic/synthetic distinction, then, each (true) 'affirmation' should be regarded as analytic. Schlick recognizes this, but nevertheless regards 'affirmations' as synthetic, because he holds that they are not 'empty of content' and 'relate to reality'. Hence, for Schlick, 'affirmations' are the 'one exception' ('On the Foundations of Knowledge', 385) to his characterization of the analytic/synthetic distinction. As I mention below (n. 45), Russell does not characterize the analytic/synthetic distinction in terms of what we do or do not know in merely understanding a sentence and so does not face this problem of reconciling his views of 'judgements of perception' with the analytic/synthetic distinction.

In what follows, I turn to consider how the early Wittgenstein and Bradley view what is involved in apprehending singular contents and in knowing objects. By accepting ST_E with Russell, both philosophers hold that issues regarding what is involved in apprehending singular contents are intimately connected with issues regarding what is involved in knowing an object. However, whereas Russell generates his position by conjoining ST_E with the view that the only particulars with which we are acquainted are sense-data, and thus conjoins ST_E with such views as S-D_1 and S-D_2, Wittgenstein and Bradley generate their positions, I argue, by bringing other considerations to bear on ST_E. And what result from bringing these other considerations to bear on ST_E are radically different views of the nature of experience, of objects, and of singular thought.

In particular, I will argue that Wittgenstein and Bradley are led to diametrically opposite positions, each of which incorporates different features of Russell's view. Wittgenstein, I will argue, is led to accept R_2 but reject R_3; Bradley, on the other hand, is led to accept R_3 but reject R_2. In doing so, Wittgenstein, like Russell, holds that in knowing merely *that* an object is, we thereby know fully *what* that object is; but, unlike Russell, he denies that in knowing fully *what* an object is, we thereby know any *truths about* that object. By contrast, Bradley agrees with Russell that knowing fully *what* an object is requires knowing *truths about* that object; but, unlike Russell, he denies that knowing *what* an object is comes immediately with knowing *that* that object is. Hence, from their opposed positions, both Wittgenstein and Bradley reject Russell's view that we may know, immediately and simultaneously, *that* an object is, *what* that object is, and *truths about* that object.

II

Following Russell, Wittgenstein accepts ST, ST_M, and ST_E. Thus, for example, in *Tractatus*, 4.1211, Wittgenstein writes: 'a sentence "fa" shows that the object a occurs in its sense, two sentences "fa" and "ga" show that they are about the same object'.[35] Here,

---

[35] Ludwig Wittgenstein, *Tractatus Logico-Philosophicus*, trans. C. K. Ogden (London: Routledge and Kegan Paul, 1922). Here I have used the Ogden translation of the second main clause rather than that of D. F. Pears and B. F. McGuinness (London: Routledge and Kegan Paul, 1961), because the translation (using the word 'about') was actually suggested by Wittgenstein. See his *Letters*

then, by writing that 'fa' and 'ga' (sentences with predicates 'f' and 'g' and the proper name 'a') are both about the same object, Wittgenstein is indicating that, like both Russell and Frege, he accepts ST, according to which there are at least some sentential contents about objects—that is, that there are singular thoughts.[36]

Furthermore, by writing here that the object a *occurs* in the sense of the sentence 'fa', Wittgenstein is siding with Russell, not Frege, on the issue as to what a proper name contributes to the content expressed by a sentence containing that name. For, like Russell and unlike Frege, Wittgenstein is thereby placing the object itself designated by a name, and not something else, like the Fregean sense of that name, in the content (or sense) expressed by a sentence containing that name. And in so doing, Wittgenstein is thereby indicating with Russell, and in accord with ST_M, that the object which a singular thought is about is integral to the being of that thought. He is indicating, that is, that what objects there are determines what singular contents may be expressed.[37]

Besides following Russell, but not Frege, in accepting ST_M, Wittgenstein also follows Russell, but not Frege, in accepting ST_E. Thus, for example, in 3.263, Wittgenstein writes: '[S]entences that contain the primitive signs . . . can only be understood if the meanings [*Bedeutungen*] of those signs are already known [*bekannt*].' Similarly, shortly after writing in 4.024 that '[A sentence] is understood by anyone who understands its constituents',

to C. K. Ogden, ed. G. H. von Wright (Oxford: Blackwell, 1973), 28. Unless noted otherwise, I will use the Pears and McGuinness translation in what follows and cite the remark number in the text. (Throughout, however, I have rendered Wittgenstein's *Satz* as 'sentence', rather than 'proposition', to avoid confusion with Russell's use of 'proposition'.)

[36] More specifically, he is indicating, with both Russell and Frege, that sentences containing proper names (and hence the contents expressed by such sentences) are about the objects designated by those names (even if he need not agree with either Frege or Russell as to which expressions turn out to be genuine proper names).

[37] See also in this context 5.4733, where Wittgenstein indicates that a sentence will lack sense if some constituent of that sentence lacks *Bedeutung*. Since Wittgenstein holds that the *Bedeutung* of a name is the object it stands for (3.203), he is thereby indicating, with Russell and in accord with ST_M, but as against Frege, that sentences containing empty names express no contents. He is indicating, that is, that what singular contents (or sense) may be expressed depends on what objects there are to be referred to. Further, in 5.5561, Wittgenstein indicates that the 'totality of objects' there are manifests itself in the 'totality of elementary sentences' there are, again connecting what singular senses may be expressed with what objects there are.

Wittgenstein adds in 4.026: 'The meanings [*Die Bedeutungen*] of simple signs (words) must be explained to us if we are to understand them.' In these remarks, then, Wittgenstein is indicating that understanding a sentence requires knowing (*kennen*) the meanings (*Bedeutungen*) of the primitive signs in that sentence. Hence, since he holds that a proper name, a primitive sign, has as its meaning (*Bedeutung*) the object it stands for (see 3.203), he thereby holds with Russell, but not Frege, that understanding a singular sentence—or apprehending a singular content—requires knowing (*kennen*) the objects designated by the names in that sentence.[38]

However, although Wittgenstein follows Russell, but not Frege, in accepting ST_M and ST_E, he does not apply these principles in the same way that Russell does. Whereas Russell conjoins those principles regarding singular thoughts with his views regarding the objects (viz. sense-data) he believes such thoughts are about, Wittgenstein conjoins those same principles regarding singular thoughts with certain other (Fregean) views regarding the nature of thoughts generally. By so doing, Wittgenstein arrives at positions fundamentally at odds with Russell's. In the remainder of this section, I turn first to introduce these other Fregean views of thought, and then discuss the consequences, for Wittgenstein, of conjoining these Fregean views with the Russellian view ST_E.

As I mentioned at the outset, for Frege, and during what Kaplan calls the 'Golden Age of Pure Semantics', meanings (or senses) are sharply separated from 'entities of the world'. In this regard, then, Wittgenstein, like anyone who adheres to the Russellian principles ST_M and ST_E, does not follow Frege. For, like Russell, Wittgenstein holds that the thoughts expressed by singular sentences include among their constituents the 'entities of the world' which those sentences are about—entities (objects) which Wittgenstein holds 'make up the substance of the world' (2.021). However, even if Wittgenstein connects singular thoughts to 'entities of the

---

[38] Wittgenstein's remarks on identity (see e.g. 4.243 and 6.2322) also indicate that, like Russell, but unlike Frege, he accepts ST_E. For, like Russell, but unlike Frege, Wittgenstein denies that there can be any genuinely informative identity statements. In particular, in accord with ST_E, Wittgenstein holds that understanding a sentence containing a name will require knowing the *Bedeutung* of that name—i.e. the object it stands for; thus, he holds, with Russell but not Frege, that merely understanding a sentence containing two (genuine) names will already suffice for knowing whether or not those names refer to the same object.

world' in a wholly un-Fregean manner, he still sharply separates thoughts from the world in ways that are in accord with Frege before him and the 'Golden Age of Pure Semantics' that followed.

According to Frege, thoughts are 'timeless, eternal, and unvarying'[39] entities which occupy a 'third realm' wholly independent of what occurs either in the 'inner world' of one's own mind or in the external world of physical objects.[40] We apprehend these thoughts not by sense perception, but rather *a priori*, through a non-sensible or intellectual 'grasping'.[41] Frege, then, sharply separates apprehending thoughts from knowing truths about the world:[42] we apprehend thoughts *a priori*; we gain knowledge of the world *a posteriori*. That is to say, Frege accepts the following two principles regarding the apprehension of thoughts:

A-T₁ We apprehend thoughts *a priori*.

and

A-T₂ In apprehending a thought, we do not thereby have any knowledge about the world.

Although Wittgenstein does not accept Frege's distinction between sense and *Bedeutung*, and although he does not accept Frege's metaphysics of a 'third realm' of thought, he does follow Frege in accepting A-T₁ and A-T₂. Thus, for example, in 3.05 Wittgenstein writes: '*A priori* knowledge that a thought was true would be possible only if its truth were recognizable from the thought itself (without anything to compare it with)', thereby indicating that *a priori* knowledge would be knowledge that we have merely by apprehending a thought. And in indicating this, Wittgenstein thereby holds, in accordance with A-T₁, that we apprehend thoughts *a priori*.

[39] Frege, 'Thoughts', in *Collected Papers*, 370. Here, Frege is indicating specifically that 'the thought we express by the Pythagorean theorem is surely timeless, eternal, unvarying'. He then goes on to argue that these same features apply to all thoughts. [40] Ibid. 363.
[41] See ibid. 369–70, where Frege characterizes thoughts as belonging to 'the realm of what is non-sensibly perceptible'.
[42] As I use it, the phrase 'truths about the world' does not require (nor does it preclude) that the world itself is an object about which there are truths. For Wittgenstein, it will turn out that the world is not an object (but rather an arrangement of objects); for Bradley, it will turn out that the world is an object (or individual).

Furthermore, in *Tractatus*, 4.024, Wittgenstein writes that 'one can understand [a sentence] without knowing whether it is true'; and beyond this, in the *Notebooks*, he remarks: 'What do I really know when I understand the sense of "ϕa" but do not know whether it is true or false? In that case I surely know no more than ϕa v ~ ϕa; and that means I *know* nothing.'[43] Hence, Wittgenstein holds, in accordance with A-T$_2$, that in merely understanding the singular sentence 'ϕa'—or in merely apprehending the singular content it expresses—we do not thereby know any truth about the world. Not only do we not know whether what that sentence itself says about the world is true; we do not thereby know any truth about the world whatsoever. For, according to Wittgenstein, all we thereby know is that ϕa v ~ ϕa, a tautology which makes no claim on reality, and thus we thereby know nothing about the world.

These views, A-T$_1$ and A-T$_2$, are incorporated in the analytic/synthetic distinction as it came to be articulated during the 'Golden Age of Pure Semantics'. For central to that distinction as formulated during that period are more general distinctions between 'meaning' (or sense) and 'fact' (or truth about the world) and between what is involved in understanding a sentence and what is involved in determining the 'facts'. During the 'Golden Age', an analytic sentence was said to be one whose truth may be determined merely by apprehending its meaning, or merely by understanding it; a synthetic sentence, on the other hand, is one whose truth may be determined only by going beyond the apprehension of meaning to a determination of 'fact'.[44] This very characterization of the analytic/synthetic distinction, then, assumes a sharp

---

[43] Ludwig Wittgenstein, *Notebooks 1914–1916*, ed. G. H. von Wright and G. E. M. Anscombe, trans. G. E. M. Anscombe, 2nd edn. (Chicago: University of Chicago Press, 1979), 31.

[44] See e.g. Rudolf Carnap, *Introduction to Symbolic Logic and its Applications*, trans. W. H. Meyer and J. Wilkinson (New York: Dover Publications, 1958), 16–18. There Carnap indicates that we may distinguish two steps involved in 'investigat[ing] a given sentence with a view towards establishing its truth-value'. The first is to understand the sentence, i.e. determine its meaning (sense). The second is to use observation to compare the sentence with the relevant facts: 'If the facts are as the sentence says, then the sentence is true; otherwise false.' Carnap goes on to indicate that a sentence is logical or analytic if its truth is 'grounded only in the analysis of sense (the first step [above]) and does not require any observations of fact (the second step above)'. On the other hand, a sentence is synthetic if determining its truth-value 'requires the second step'—i.e. requires going beyond merely understanding the sentence to making observations of fact.

distinction between 'meaning' and 'fact'; in particular, it assumes A-T_2, that to apprehend meaning is not thereby to have any knowledge of 'fact'.[45] Moreover, during the 'Golden Age', the analytic/synthetic distinction coincided with the *a priori/a posteriori* distinction. And by doing so, it thereby incorporated A-T_1, the Fregean view that we apprehend meanings (or senses or contents) *a priori*. For if the analytic is arrived at merely by knowledge of meaning, and if the analytic coincides with the *a priori*, then knowledge of meaning must thereby be *a priori*.[46]

Indeed, consistent with his accepting A-T_1 and A-T_2, the early Wittgenstein was influential in formulating the analytic/synthetic distinction in the way that was to become standard during the 'Golden Age of Pure Semantics'. For Wittgenstein identifies the analytic sentences with tautologies,[47] and according to him, what

[45] Hence this characterization of the analytic/synthetic distinction cannot apply to Russell's position. For, as I have discussed in Sect. I, Russell holds that merely understanding the sentence 'This is red' will suffice for knowing its truth-value. But, for Russell, if that sentence is true, it will be so because there is a 'fact' corresponding to it. By the criteria of the 'Golden Age', then, that sentence is both analytic and synthetic: 'analytic' in that (if true) understanding the sentence— knowing its meaning—suffices for knowing that it is true; 'synthetic' in that it is true in virtue of 'fact'. The analytic/synthetic dichotomy of the 'Golden Age' does not apply here, because Russell does not accept the Fregean view that knowledge of meaning (or content) is wholly independent of knowledge of fact. In n. 34, I indicated, in effect, that Moritz Schlick wishes to accept the analytic/synthetic dichotomy of the 'Golden Age' while also accepting a 'Russellian' view of observation sentences. In doing so, Schlick was then led to regard observation sentences as the 'one exception' to that characterization of the analytic/synthetic distinction. Russell, on the other hand, has no difficulty squaring his account of singular propositions with the analytic/synthetic distinction, for his account of that distinction involves no general distinction between 'meaning' and 'fact'. Rather, for Russell, a sentence is analytic if and only if it is of the form 'An SP is P', where 'S' and 'P' are to be replaced by general terms. (See *Problems of Philosophy*, 82–3.) For Russell, that is, a sentence is analytic or synthetic simply in virtue of its form, not in virtue of considerations involving 'meaning' or 'fact'. And since no singular sentence is of the form 'An SP is P', Russell has no difficulty in holding that all singular sentences are synthetic. (See *Theory of Knowledge*, 94–5.)

[46] Again, Russell is in no position to accept this view. For according to him, merely understanding 'This is red' suffices for knowing its truth-value; but understanding this sentence also requires appeal to sense experience (acquaintance with a sense-datum). Given his account of singular thought, that is, Russell cannot hold that what we know in merely understanding a sentence is what we know prior to experience. Furthermore, Russell's early view that mathematics and logic are synthetic and *a priori* (see *Problems of Philosophy*, ch. 8) is also opposed to the view of the 'Golden Age' that everything we know prior to experience is analytic.

[47] See *Tractatus*, 6.1–6.11: 'The sentences of logic are tautologies. . . . They are the analytic sentences.'

is characteristic of these sentences is that they make no claim on reality,[48] and that understanding them is sufficient for knowing that they are true.[49] Moreover, Wittgenstein also identifies the analytic sentences with those which are knowable *a priori*.[50] Thus, like later philosophers during the 'Golden Age', he holds that the analytic and *a priori* is what we know merely by understanding language, without having any knowledge of fact. And in doing so, he holds, in accordance with A-T$_1$ and A-T$_2$, that we apprehend thoughts (or sentential contents) *a priori* and without any knowledge of fact.

Combining these Fregean principles A-T$_1$ and A-T$_2$ with the Russellian principle ST$_E$ forces Wittgenstein to accept certain views as to what is involved in knowing or being acquainted with (*kennen*) objects. First, by conjoining

ST$_E$ Apprehending a singular thought requires knowing (being acquainted with) the object which that thought is about

with

A-T$_1$ We apprehend thoughts *a priori*,

Wittgenstein is thereby forced to accept

W$_1$ We know (*kennen*) objects *a priori*.

For if, as A-T$_1$ requires, we are to apprehend all thoughts, including singular ones, *a priori*, and if, by ST$_E$, apprehending singular thoughts will require knowing (*kennen*) the objects those thoughts are about, then we will have to know those objects *a priori* as well.

Further, by conjoining ST$_E$ with

A-T$_2$ In apprehending a thought, we do not thereby have any knowledge about the world,

---

[48] See e.g. ibid. 4.461–4.462, where Wittgenstein indicates that tautologies 'say nothing', are not 'pictures of reality', and 'do not represent any possible situations'.

[49] See ibid. 6.113: 'It is the peculiar mark of logical sentences that one can recognize that they are true from the symbol alone.' For Wittgenstein, recognizing a symbol (as opposed to a mere sign) requires understanding it: i.e. knowing how it is used with sense (see 3.326).

[50] See e.g. ibid. 6.3211: 'as always, what is certain *a priori* proves to be something purely logical'.

Wittgenstein is forced to accept

W$_2$ In knowing (*kennen*) an object, we do not thereby know any truth about that object.

For if, as ST$_E$ requires, apprehending a singular thought requires knowing (*kennen*) the object which it is about, but, by A-T$_2$, does not require knowing any fact or truth about the world, then knowing (*kennen*) an object cannot require knowing any facts or truths about the world. By A-T$_2$ together with ST$_E$, that is, in knowing an object, we do not thereby know any truth about *any* object (any constituent of 'the substance of the world'); and thus as one consequence of this general conclusion, in knowing an object, we do not thereby know any truth about *that* object. As Wittgenstein writes to Ogden in discussing the translation of *Tractatus*, 2.0123, which concerns what is involved in *kennen* an object: 'to know here just means: I know *it* but needn't know anything *about* it'.[51]

The way Wittgenstein sustains these views is by making a sharp distinction between objects (the only entities he countenances) and facts (or states of affairs or situations). Thus at the outset of the *Tractatus*, Wittgenstein writes: 'The world is the totality of facts, not of things' (1.1), and adds shortly thereafter: 'A state of affairs is a combination of objects (entities, things)' (2.01).[52] For Wittgenstein, that is, a fact (or state of affairs or situation) is not itself an object or entity; rather, it is a combination or arrangement of objects (or entities). And for Wittgenstein, having knowledge of the world requires knowing not what objects there are, but rather how those objects are arranged.

In particular, the way that Wittgenstein sustains W$_1$, the view that we know objects *a priori*, is by holding (as opposed to Russell) that sensory experience is not the same as acquaintance with an object, but is rather apprehension of how objects are arranged. Thus in 5.552, Wittgenstein remarks:

[51] Wittgenstein, *Letters to C. K. Ogden*, 59. In this letter, Wittgenstein indicates that he does not wish to translate *kennen* as 'acquaintance' because 'acquaintance' 'seems to me to imply somehow that one knows a lot about an object'. Russell, as I have discussed, holds that (human) acquaintance with an object (a sense-datum) *does* enable one to know truths about that object; so perhaps Wittgenstein is here intending to distinguish his view from Russell's.

[52] Here I have incorporated part of the more literal Ogden translation.

The 'experience' which we need to understand logic is not that such and
such is the case, but that something *is*; but that is *no* experience.
Logic *precedes* every experience—that something is *so*.
It is before the How, not before the What.[53]

Here, then, Wittgenstein indicates that what we experience is
always an arrangement of objects (that something is *so* or that
something is the case), not a single object (that something *is*).[54]
For Wittgenstein, that is, it is '*no* experience' to apprehend 'that
something *is*'; rather, 'every experience' is 'that something is
so'. And, further, Wittgenstein indicates here that apprehending
'that something *is*' '*precedes* every experience'. That is to say, he
is indicating, in accordance with W_1, that we know *a priori*, or
prior to experience, what objects there are; and he is indicating
that we know *a posteriori* how objects are arranged. Hence,
he indicates here that 'the What', but not 'the How', is prior to
experience: prior to experience we know *what* objects there are,
but not *how* those objects are arranged.[55]

Furthermore, by making his sharp distinction between objects
and arrangements of objects (or facts), Wittgenstein is able to sustain W_2, the view that in knowing (*kennen*) an object, we do not
thereby know any truth about that object. For, according to
Wittgenstein, knowing a truth about an object requires knowing
how that object is arranged with other objects, and in his view,
we may know this only by experience. But, for Wittgenstein, we
know an object fully—we know fully *what* it is—prior to experience. So, for Wittgenstein, unlike Russell, in knowing *what* an
object is, we do not thereby know any truth about that object,
we do not thereby know *how* that object is.

More specifically, for Wittgenstein, in knowing *what* an object
is, we know its possible arrangements with other objects, but not
how it is actually arranged with them. Thus he writes:

[53] I have here used the more literal Ogden translation.

[54] See also here *Tractatus*, 5.5423, where Wittgenstein indicates that what we
perceive are complexes—i.e. arrangements of objects.

[55] I recognize that in 5.552, one of Wittgenstein's main points is that *logic* precedes experience; and in my discussion of this passage I have not considered
Wittgenstein's view of logic. What is important for my purposes here, however,
is that Wittgenstein indicates that the reason logic 'precedes experience' is that
while logic requires knowing *that* something is and requires knowing *what* there
is, it does not require knowing *how* objects are arranged. And to hold this,
Wittgenstein must thereby hold, in accordance with W_1, that we know objects—
we know *that* they are and *what* they are, if not *how* they are—prior to experience.

If I know [*kennen*] an object I also know all its possible
occurrences in states of affairs.
(Every one of these possibilities must be part
of the nature of the object.)
A new possibility cannot be discovered later.
If I am to know [*kennen*] an object, though I need not know its
external properties, I must know all its internal properties.

(2.0123–2.01231)

For Wittgenstein, then, the internal properties of an object—those
that constitute its 'nature' or 'essence'—are simply the possible
ways it is related to other objects, the possible states of affairs
(or facts or arrangements of objects) it may occur in. The external properties of an object—those that are not part of its
'nature'—are the ways it actually is arranged with other objects.
Thus, for Wittgenstein, in accordance with W_2, in knowing an
object—in knowing *what* that object is, in knowing the 'essence'
or 'nature' of that object—we do not thereby know any facts
or truths about that object. Further, as Wittgenstein indicates in
these remarks, if we know an object at all, we know its 'nature'
in its entirety. For Wittgenstein, that is, if we know *any* of the
possible states of affairs an object may occur in, we thereby know
all its possible occurrences in states of affairs. As he writes: 'A
new possibility cannot be discovered later.' Whereas Russell holds
that we know objects (or particulars) *a posteriori*, and that in
doing so, we know some truths about those objects, Wittgenstein
holds that we know objects fully *a priori*, and that in doing so,
we do not thereby know any truths about them.

More generally, Russell conjoins ST_E with the view that the
objects which our singular thoughts are about are sense-data; and
from his views of sense-data, such as $S-D_1$ and $S-D_2$, he is then
forced to reach conclusions, such as R_1-R_3, regarding the apprehension of singular thoughts. Wittgenstein, on the other hand,
conjoins ST_E not with antecedent views regarding the objects which
our singular thoughts are about, but rather with views, including
$A-T_1$ and $A-T_2$, regarding what is involved in apprehending thoughts
generally; and, from this combination of views, he is forced to
reach conclusions, including W_1 and W_2, regarding our knowledge of objects. And since accepting ST_E precludes accepting
Russell's initial views regarding the objects which our singular
thoughts are about together with Wittgenstein's initial views

regarding the apprehension of thoughts, Russell and Wittgenstein are forced to reject features of each other's positions.

Thus, by ST_E, one cannot hold both that we apprehend singular thoughts *a priori* and that we know the objects which those thoughts are about *a posteriori*. Here Russell assumes, by $S-D_1$, that we know those objects *a posteriori*, and then is forced to conclude, in accordance with R_1, that we apprehend singular thoughts *a posteriori* as well. Wittgenstein, on the other hand, assumes, by $A-T_1$, that we apprehend singular thoughts *a priori*, and is then forced to accept W_1, that we know the objects which those thoughts are about *a priori* as well.

Likewise, accepting ST_E precludes holding both that we can apprehend any singular thought without thereby knowing its truth-value and that knowing the object which a singular thought is about enables us to know some truths about that object. For, by ST_E, apprehending a singular thought requires knowing the object which that thought is about; hence, if knowing that object enables us to know some truth about that object, then merely apprehending the singular thought which expresses that truth will suffice for knowing the truth of that thought. Here Russell assumes, by $S-D_2$, that knowing objects (sense-data) enables us to know some truths about those objects, and is then forced to accept R_3, according to which there are some singular thoughts (such as that expressed by 'That is red') which are such that apprehending them suffices for knowing their truth-value. Wittgenstein, on the other hand, assumes, by $A-T_2$, that apprehending a singular thought never suffices for knowing its truth-value; for, by $A-T_2$, apprehending a singular thought never suffices for knowing any facts or truths about the world, including the fact or truth which would have to obtain for that thought to be true. And thus, as opposed to Russell, Wittgenstein is then forced to accept W_2, according to which knowing an object never suffices for knowing any truth about that object.

However, while Wittgenstein rejects R_1 and R_3, he at least agrees with Russell in accepting R_2. He agrees, that is, that we fully apprehend singular thoughts immediately, and that in doing so, we thereby know *that* it is about something and know fully *what* it is about. For, by $A-T_1$, Wittgenstein holds that prior to any experience we can apprehend a singular thought fully. Thus he holds that we may fully apprehend singular thoughts immediately or without needing any explanation.[56] And since he holds, by ST_E, that apprehending a singular thought requires knowing the object which it is about, he thereby holds, with Russell, that in immediately apprehending a singular thought, we thereby fully know the object it is about. We know immediately both *that* the object is and (fully) *what* the object is. Unlike Russell, Wittgenstein holds that the immediacy with which we apprehend singular thoughts involves the immediacy of *a priori* apprehensions, not of sensory experience. And, unlike Russell, Wittgenstein holds that in knowing immediately *what* an object is, we do not thereby know any truths about that object. But, for all their differences as to how we know objects (*a priori* or *a posteriori*) and as to what we know in knowing objects (whether or not we thereby know any truths about those objects), Russell and Wittgenstein are able to agree that full or complete apprehension of a singular thought comes immediately, and with it comes the knowledge *that* it is about something, as well as the full knowledge as to *what* it is about.

What I turn to show now is how it is that Bradley's relation to Russell's position is the opposite of Wittgenstein's. I show, that is, that where Wittgenstein agrees with Russell (i.e. in accepting R_2), Bradley disagrees, and that where Wittgenstein disagrees with Russell (i.e. regarding R_1 and R_3), Bradley agrees. And in so doing, I show how Bradley applies the same principles of singular thoughts which are common to both Wittgenstein and Russell in a wholly different way.

III

I begin by showing that, like Russell and Wittgenstein, Bradley accepts ST, ST_M, and ST_E. First of all, like Russell and Wittgenstein (as well as Frege), Bradley holds that there are contents or thoughts about objects (or individuals)—that is, that there are singular thoughts in the sense of ST. Indeed, one of the main claims Bradley wishes to establish in Book I of *The Principles of Logic* is that *all* thought or judgement is singular.

Thus Bradley writes:

---

[56] See *Tractatus*, 4.02–4.021: 'I understand the sentence without having had its sense explained to me.'

A judgement, we assume naturally, says something about some fact or reality. If we asserted or denied about anything else, our judgement would seem to be a frivolous pretence. We not only must say something, but it must also be about something actual that we say it.[57]

Here, then, Bradley indicates generally that each judgement is about 'something actual', or is about 'some fact or reality'. But shortly thereafter, he goes on to emphasize that the 'something actual' or 'fact' or 'reality' which a judgement is about is always individual, not universal. For he writes that 'the simplest account [of the real] . . . is given in the words, The real is self-existent. And we may put this otherwise by saying, The real is what is individual,'[58] and in contrasting 'fact' and 'ideas', he writes: 'A fact is individual, an idea is universal; a fact is substantial, an idea is adjectival; a fact is self-existent, an idea is symbolical.'[59] For Bradley, then, since every judgement is about 'some fact or reality', and since a 'fact' or 'reality' is always individual, then every judgement is about an individual.[60] (Below, it will become clear how it is that, in sharp contrast to the early Wittgenstein, Bradley is able to equate what is 'individual' with what is 'fact' or 'reality'.)

Moreover, Bradley not only agrees with Frege, Russell, and the early Wittgenstein in accepting ST; he also holds, with Russell and the early Wittgenstein and in accord with ST_M but as against Frege, that the existence of the individual which a singular judgement is about is required for that judgement. Thus, in *The Principles of Logic* Bradley argues at some length against the view that a judgement is composed wholly of ideas. By an 'idea', Bradley does not mean a mental image or a psychic state, but rather the 'content' or 'universal meaning' of the mental image.[61] As such, as 'idea' is not a mental particular, or any sort of particular, physical or mental. In *The Principles of Logic*, after discussing his notion of idea, Bradley introduces his view of judgement by writing:

Judgement proper is the act which refers an ideal content (recognized as such) to a reality beyond the act. . . . The ideal content is the logical idea, the meaning as just defined. It is recognised as such, when we know that,

---

[57] *PL*, 41.   [58] *PL*, 45.   [59] *PL*, 43–4.

[60] Unlike Russell, Frege, and the early Wittgenstein, Bradley does not hold that the object which a singular thought is about is designated by a genuine proper name. Thus, unlike Russell and Wittgenstein, Bradley does not connect his search for the object which a singular thought is about with a search for the 'genuine' proper name designating that object.   [61] See *PL*, 5–10.

by itself, it is not a fact but a wandering adjective. In the act of assertion we transfer this adjective to, and unite it with, a real substantive,[62]

and adds shortly thereafter:

in every judgement there is a subject of which the ideal content is
asserted. But this subject of course can not belong to the content or fall
within it, for, in that case, it would be the idea attributed to itself. We
shall see that the subject is, in the end, no idea but always reality.[63]

Again, in *Appearance and Reality*, Bradley writes:

Now a thought only 'in my head', or a bare idea separated from all relation to the real world, is a false abstraction. For we have seen that to
hold a thought is, more or less vaguely, to refer it to Reality. And hence
an idea, wholly un-referred, would be a self-contradiction.[64]

For Bradley, then, thought or judgement always consists of two
elements: the 'logical idea' (or 'ideal content' or 'meaning'), which
is adjectival and universal, and the reality, which is substantive
and individual, about which the judgement is made. And hence
Bradley holds, in accordance with ST_M, that singular thoughts (i.e.
for Bradley, all thoughts) depend for their being on the objects
(or individuals) they are about.

Furthermore, Bradley also agrees with Russell and Wittgenstein
in accepting ST_E, according to which apprehending a singular
thought or making a singular judgement requires knowing or
being acquainted with the individual which that judgement is
about. Thus, in *The Principles of Logic*, Bradley writes: 'all judgements predicate their ideal content as an attribute of the real
which appears in presentation',[65] thereby indicating that 'the real',
or individual, about which we are judging 'appears in presentation'. In Russellian terms, Bradley is indicating that we must be
'acquainted with' that which a singular judgement is about. Indeed,
by writing here that 'the real', the subject of a judgement, 'appears
in presentation', Bradley is not only indicating that he adheres
to the general Russellian principle (which the early Wittgenstein
also accepts) that we must be acquainted with what our judgement is about; he seems to be suggesting further with Russell (but
not the early Wittgenstein), that the way we are acquainted with
the subject of a judgement is through sensory experience. Again,
in *The Principles of Logic*, Bradley writes: 'How am I to judge

[62] *PL*, 10.   [63] *PL*, 13.   [64] *AR*, 350.   [65] *PL*, 50.

unless I go to presentation? Let the past and future be as real as you please, but by what device shall I come in contact with them, and refer to them my ideas, unless I advance directly to the given . . .'[66] Here again, Bradley is indicating not only that we must 'come in contact with' whatever we are making judgements about, but also that the only way that we can come in contact with it is through 'presentation' or the apprehension of 'the given'. At this point, I am not yet concerned with how Bradley relates his view of judgement to his view of experience; I am concerned only to show that however he comes to apply it and relate it to experience, Bradley accepts ST_E, the general principle common to both Russell and the early Wittgenstein, that whenever we make a singular judgement, we must 'come in contact', or be acquainted, with the object or individual which that judgement is about.

That Bradley accepts this principle but does not actually apply it in the way Russell does is suggested at the outset of his paper 'What is the Real Julius Caesar?' For Bradley begins that paper by writing:

Mr. Russell in a recent essay ['Knowledge by Acquaintance and Knowledge by Description'] ventures on the following assertion: 'Returning now to Julius Caesar, I assume that it will be admitted that he himself is not a constituent of any judgement which I can make.' To my mind the opposite of this admission appears to be evident. It seems to me certain, if such an admission is right, that about Julius Caesar I can have literally no knowledge at all, and that for me to attempt to speak about him is senseless. If on the other hand I am to know anything whatever about Caesar, then the real Caesar beyond doubt must himself enter into my judgements and be a constituent of my knowledge.[67]

For Russell, Caesar may not be a constituent of any judgement we make, because we are not acquainted with Caesar himself (but only with our present sense-data). Thus accepting ST_E, Russell willingly accepts the conclusion that none of our judgements are, strictly speaking, about Caesar.[68] Bradley, on the other hand,

---

[66] *PL*, 62.

[67] F. H. Bradley, 'What is the Real Julius Caesar?', in *ETR*, 409.

[68] Thus, in 'Knowledge by Acquaintance', 222–3, Russell writes: 'we must substitute for "Julius Caesar" some description of Julius Caesar, in order to discover the meaning of a judgement nominally about him'. For Russell, that is, because we are not acquainted with Julius Caesar, judgements which seem to be about him are only *nominally*, not really, about him.

holds that it is obvious that we can make judgements and have knowledge about Caesar. Then, applying the same principle, he concludes that Caesar himself must 'enter into' our judgements and be a 'constituent' of them; he concludes, that is, in effect that we must somehow 'come in contact' with Caesar himself, that he must somehow be 'present' to us.

In the remainder of this section, my purpose is to clarify how Bradley comes to apply ST_E—to show, in effect, how Bradley can agree with Russell that the only way we can 'come in contact' with the object which a singular thought is about is by 'advanc[ing] directly to the given' while also holding, as opposed to Russell, that 'the real Julius Caesar . . . must himself enter into my judgements and be a constituent of my knowledge'. I will argue that Bradley conjoins ST_E not with antecedent views as to the objects which our singular thoughts are about (as Russell does), or with general views as to what is involved in apprehending thoughts (as Wittgenstein does), but rather with two general views as to what is involved in knowing *what* object a singular thought or judgement is about. The first concerns how our knowledge of that object is related to sensory, or 'immediate', experience; the second concerns what would be required to know *fully what* object a singular thought is about. Together with ST_E, these views commit Bradley to many of his characteristic positions regarding the nature of judgement and reality.[69]

First of all, as I have just mentioned, Bradley may seem inclined to go in the direction of Russell and to hold that the acquaintance with particulars (or individuals) needed for apprehending singular thoughts is achieved through sensory experience. For, by

---

[69] I am thus presenting Bradley as accepting ST_E, with Russell and the early Wittgenstein, as an antecedently obvious view, and then as bringing other considerations to bear on ST_E which distinguish his position from both Russell's and Wittgenstein's. Accordingly, in the passages I have cited so far from *PL*, Bradley is not already presuming his ultimate metaphysics, but is rather indicating what 'we assume naturally' (41). Rather than considering 'very ultimate principles' or 'enter[ing] at once on a journey into metaphysics, the end of which might not soon be attained', Bradley is seeking in these passages only to present 'the account which represents the ordinary view, and in which perhaps we may most of us agree' (44). Thus, when Bradley initially introduces such principles as ST_M and ST_E in *PL*, he presents them as commonsensical and initially obvious, as Russell also would (see the passage cited in n. 8). What differentiates Bradley's position from Russell's and the early Wittgenstein's is how he comes to apply these shared principles.

writing that 'all judgements predicate their ideal content as an attribute of the real which appears in presentation', Bradley may seem to be indicating that acquaintance with the individual which a singular judgement is about simply *is*, or consists in, apprehending what 'appears in presentation'. And if this were Bradley's position, then it would be no different from Russell's, according to which the knowledge of the object which a singular judgement is about is achieved immediately and fully when we are acquainted with the relevant sense-datum 'given in experience'. However, while Bradley agrees that in all judging we must 'go to presentation' if we wish to 'come in contact' with the individual which our judgement is about, he does not agree that mere sensory experience alone gives us, as Russell claims, a 'perfect and complete' knowledge of that individual.

Thus, in *The Principles of Logic*, Bradley writes:

Are we to hold that the real, which is the ultimate subject, and which, as we said, appears in perception, is identical with the merely momentary appearance? We shall see that this cannot be.... The subject ... to which we attribute our ideas as predicates, must itself be real. And, if real, it must not be purely adjectival. On the contrary it must be self-existent and individual. But the particular phenomenon, the momentary appearance, is not individual, and so is not the subject which we use in judgement.[70]

And, then, to reconcile the view that the subject 'appears in presentation' but is not itself 'identical with the merely momentary appearance', Bradley writes:

the real, which appears in perception, is not identical with the real just *as* it appears there. If the real must be 'this', must encounter us directly, we cannot conclude that the 'this' we take is all the real, or that nothing is real beyond the 'this'. It is impossible perhaps to get directly at reality, except in the content of one presentation: we may never see it, so to speak, but through a hole. But what we see of it may make us certain that, beyond this hole, it exists indefinitely,[71]

and adds on the following page: 'The real can not be identical with the content that appears in presentation. It for ever transcends it, and gives us a title to make search elsewhere.'[72] According to Bradley, that is, in 'the endeavour to find the completeness

[70] *PL*, 51.   [71] *PL*, 70.   [72] *PL*, 71.

of the real, which we feel can not exist except as an individual',[73] we must go beyond immediate experience. As he writes: 'The real then itself transcends the presentation, and invites us to follow it beyond that which is given.'[74]

For Bradley, then, the real—the individual about which a judgement is made—appears in, but is not identical with, what is 'given in experience'. Experience gives us access to that individual, but does not give us a complete knowledge of it; to have knowledge of that individual, we must begin with experience, but cannot remain there. To complete that knowledge, we must follow the real 'beyond that which is given'; we must 'transcend experience' and 'make search elsewhere'. Whereas Wittgenstein holds that we have a full knowledge of the object which a singular thought is about *prior* to experience, and whereas Russell holds that we have a full knowledge of such an object *immediately in* 'given experience', Bradley holds that we can have a full knowledge of the object which a singular judgement is about neither before experience nor in immediate experience, but only *after* immediate experience. Like Russell (and unlike Wittgenstein), Bradley holds that we must appeal to experience to know what object a singular thought is about; but, unlike Russell, he holds that, by itself, immediate experience does not suffice for a full knowledge of that individual.

Central to Bradley's view here is his account of 'immediate experience', one which is opposed to many features of sense-datum theory. Sense-datum theorists hold that what are 'given in experience' are, metaphysically speaking, particulars (or individuals or things); Bradley holds that if we confine ourselves to what is merely 'given' as such, we are not presented with whole individuals.[75] Sense-datum theorists assume, prior to their analysis of experience, a dualism between what is 'inside' and what is 'outside' the mind, and they hold that since sense-data are 'objects' of 'mental acts', sense-data exist, strictly speaking, 'outside' the mind.[76] Bradley,

---

[73] Ibid.   [74] *PL*, 72.

[75] Thus he writes, in the passage cited in n. 70: 'the particular phenomenon, the momentary appearance, is not individual, and so is not the subject which we use in judgement'.

[76] See e.g. Russell, 'Relation of Sense-Data to Physics', 150–2, where Russell indicates that sense-data are 'external objects' and hence not 'in the mind': 'The sense-datum . . . stands over against the subject as that external object of which in sensation the subject is aware' (152).

on the other hand, holds that 'immediate experience' is prior to any distinction between 'self and not-self', or 'subject and object', and thus denies that, in itself, 'the given' may be said to exist either 'in the mind' or 'outside' it.[77] Again, sense-datum theorists hold that in mere acquaintance with 'the given' we thereby know some 'self-evident' facts which may then be formulated in indubitable judgements (such as Russell's 'This is red'). While Bradley agrees that 'immediate experience' provides us with 'the material of our knowledge', he denies that 'immediate experience' may be 'carried over intact' into indubitable judgements or knowledge of any 'facts of perception'.[78]

Bradley, then, has a more minimal, less metaphysically laden, view of 'immediate experience' than do sense-datum theorists.[79] Nor is he alone in holding that, taken in itself, 'immediate experience' is 'below the level' of fact, or judgement, or the distinction of subject and object, or knowledge of an individual. Bradley himself credits the view to Hegel.[80] And, outside the tradition of Absolute Idealism, William James finds similarities between his own view of 'pure experience' (as a 'blooming buzzing confusion' which is prior to all 'conceptual interpretation'[81]) and the views of both Bradley and Henri Bergson.[82] Furthermore, later logical empiricists, including Rudolf Carnap, A. J. Ayer, and C. I. Lewis, similarly hold that in itself 'the given' is neither subject nor object; and Lewis, in particular, stresses that, by itself, mere apprehension of 'the given' does not give us any knowledge of fact or enable

[77] Thus, e.g., in 'On Appearance, Error and Contradiction', in *ETR*, 247, Bradley writes: 'in truth neither the world nor the self is an ultimately given fact. On the contrary each alike is a construction and a more or less one-sided abstraction. There is even experience in feeling where self and not-self are not yet present and opposed.' Similarly, in *AR*, 128, Bradley writes that in immediate experience, 'what we certainly do *not* find is a subject or an object, or indeed any other thing whatever, standing separate and on its own bottom'.

[78] See e.g. Bradley, 'On Truth and Coherence', in *ETR*, 203–4, 206–7.

[79] For a more detailed discussion of this sort of view of 'immediate experience' and its relevance to contemporary philosophical disputes, see my paper 'Putnam, Davidson and the Seventeenth-Century Picture of Mind and World', *International Journal of Philosophical Studies*, 1/2 (1993), 193–230.

[80] See *ETR*, 207 n.; also *ETR*, 152–3.

[81] William James, *Some Problems of Philosophy* (New York: Longmans, Green and Co., 1911), 50.

[82] William James, 'Bradley or Bergson?', repr. in his *Collected Essays and Reviews* (New York: Russell and Russell, 1920), 491–9.

us to make any indubitable judgements.[83] Whatever else they may hold, these philosophers agree that when we reach the level of 'immediate experience', we are not thereby 'given' whole objects (or individuals or things); as opposed to sense-datum theorists, these philosophers all hold that full knowledge of an object (or individual or particular) requires transcending 'immediate experience'.

My concern here is not with how these philosophers accept this view of 'immediate experience'. Rather, what is of concern is that by accepting this view of 'immediate experience', Bradley accepts the following principle regarding our knowledge of the individual which a singular judgement is about:

K-I$_1$ We know the individual (or object) which a singular thought or judgement is about by degrees, over time.

For by holding that we need to appeal to 'immediate experience' to know the individual which a singular judgement is about, while also holding that, by itself, 'immediate experience' does not suffice for a full knowledge of that individual, Bradley is forced to hold that while knowledge of that individual begins with 'immediate experience', it does not end there, but must be completed (if ever) over time.

In accepting K-I$_1$, Bradley rejects views that are common to Russell and Wittgenstein. First of all, Russell and Wittgenstein both hold, as opposed to K-I$_1$, that we immediately have full and complete knowledge of the individual which a singular judgement is about; both hold, that is, that such knowledge does not come by degrees, but rather all at once. For Wittgenstein, such knowledge comes *a priori*; for Russell, it comes in 'immediate experience'. But for both philosophers, and by contrast with Bradley, in knowing an object at all, we know that object fully.

Put another way, by accepting K-I$_1$, Bradley holds, as opposed to both Russell and Wittgenstein, that there is a gap between

---

[83] See Rudolf Carnap, *The Logical Structure of the World*, trans. R. George (Berkeley: University of California Press, 1967), 101, 103 ff., e.g.; A. J. Ayer, *Language, Truth and Logic* (New York: Dover Publications, 1952), 123 f.; C. I. Lewis, *Mind and the World-Order* (New York: Dover Publications, 1929), chs. 2 and 5. For a more detailed discussion of Lewis's view of the 'given'—and how it is used by him to reject the kind of metaphysics common to Bradley, Russell, and the early Wittgenstein, the kind which seeks to characterize the 'ultimate furniture of the universe'—see my 'Putnam, Davidson'.

knowing *that* an object is (or that it exists) and knowing *what* that object is. Russell and Wittgenstein both hold that any cognitive contact with an object which enables us to know *that* that object is also enables us to know that object fully: it enables us to have a full knowledge of *what* that object is (even if, as I have discussed above, Russell and Wittgenstein disagree as to what that knowledge consists in or how it is arrived at). By accepting K-I$_1$, however, Bradley holds that while 'immediate experience' may give us knowledge *that* an individual is, it by no means gives us knowledge (let alone full knowledge) of *what* that individual is. For, according to Bradley, only by 'transcending' immediate experience and by 'making our search elsewhere' may we hope to gain a more complete knowledge of *what* individual a singular judgement is about.

Furthermore, by conjoining K-I$_1$ with ST$_E$, Bradley is forced to reject R$_2$, the view common to Russell and Wittgenstein, according to which we may fully apprehend singular thoughts immediately. For, by ST$_E$, apprehending a singular thought requires knowing the object which that thought is about; and, by K-I$_1$, we know that object only by degrees, over time. Hence Bradley is forced to accept:

B$_1$ We apprehend a singular thought (or the content of a singular judgement) by degrees, over time.

By ST$_E$, one cannot hold both that we immediately apprehend singular thoughts fully and that we know the objects those thoughts are about by degrees, over time. That is to say, in accepting ST$_E$, one cannot accept both R$_2$ and K-I$_1$. Russell and Wittgenstein accept ST$_E$ along with R$_2$, and hence must hold, as opposed to K-I$_1$, that we immediately know fully the object a singular thought is about. Bradley accepts ST$_E$ along with K-I$_1$, and hence must hold, as opposed to R$_2$, that we apprehend a singular thought by degrees, over time.

By holding that there are degrees of knowing the individual which a singular thought is about—by holding that full knowledge of that individual may be completed (if ever) by degrees over time—Bradley is faced with the question as to what *full* or *complete* knowledge of that individual would consist in. To consider how Bradley answers this question—and to elicit a second principle regarding knowledge of individuals that Bradley combines with ST$_E$—I turn to consider passages in which Bradley argues that our judgements are 'defective' or 'faulty' and are incapable of 'absolute truth'. For in these passages Bradley argues that the 'defect' in our judgements, and the reason why they cannot be absolutely true, is that, in making a judgement, we do not know fully *what* that judgement is about. And by indicating what would be needed to overcome the 'defect' in our judgements, Bradley thereby indicates as well what would be needed to have *full* knowledge of *what* individual a judgement is about.

Consider, for example, the following passage from Bradley's paper 'On Appearance, Error and Contradiction':

> ... our truth fails to reach beyond generality, and hence the opposite of our truth becomes also tenable. 'Caesar crossed the Rubicon,' we say 'or not'; but this 'either-or' is only true if you are confined to a single world of events. If there are various worlds, it may be also true that Caesar never saw the Rubicon nor indeed existed at all. And, with this, obviously our truth has ceased to be absolute.[84]

In this passage, Bradley is explaining why a judgement such as 'Caesar crossed the Rubicon' cannot be 'absolutely true'; he is explaining, that is, why the truth of that judgement as well as its 'opposite' both 'become tenable'.[85] And he indicates that the reason why such judgements fail to attain 'absolute truth' is that they 'fail to reach beyond generality'.

More specifically, Bradley holds that when we make such a judgement, the reason we 'fail to reach beyond generality' is that we have failed to specify fully *what* individual that judgement is about. According to Bradley, that is, because we do not have a full knowledge of *who* Caesar is, we do not pick out a unique individual when we say 'Caesar crossed the Rubicon'. Instead, we merely pick out certain properties which may be satisfied by different individuals in different possible worlds (or perhaps, in a certain world, by no individual at all). And since there is nothing in our judgement to specify one of these individuals uniquely, our judgement is, in effect, ambiguous or general, capable of applying to more than one individual. Hence, for Bradley, the

---

[84] *ETR*, 261–2.
[85] According to Bradley, 'truth is not found except in judgements' (*PL*, 43). So in arguing that 'our truth fails to reach beyond generality' or fails to be 'absolute', he is arguing that our judgements fail 'to reach beyond generality', and cease to be absolutely true.

judgement is not 'absolutely true', since it may be true of some of the individuals it applies to and false of others. As Bradley adds on the following page: 'If truth as to matter of fact falls short of uniqueness, that truth, we have seen, is defective. Without contradicting yourself you can affirm and deny that Caesar crossed the Rubicon.'[86] For Bradley, that is, because we fail to pick out a unique individual when we say 'Caesar crossed the Rubicon', the judgement may be either affirmed or denied, depending on which of the many possible individuals we think of it as applying to.

Similarly, Bradley indicates that whenever we 'omit' something from the subject or 'take it too narrowly or abstractly'—that is, whenever we fail to make our subject apply to only one possible individual—then our judgement will become 'defective' because 'ambiguous', capable of being both affirmed and denied. Thus he writes:

If the predicate is true of the subject only by virtue of something omitted and unknown, such a truth is defective. The condition left out is an *x* which may be filled in diversely. And, according to the way in which the unspecified condition is actually filled in, either the judgement or its denial is true. The judgement therefore, as it stands, is ambiguous, and it is at once true and false, since in a word it is conditional.[87]

And again:

The fault of every judgement may be said to consist in the taking its subject too narrowly or abstractly. The whole of the conditions are not stated. And hence, according to the way in which you choose to fill in the conditions (and no special way belongs to the judgement), the assertion and its opposite are either of them true.[88]

For Bradley, the 'conditions' which are 'left out' in our specification of the subject are those which would secure unique reference. And so long as any condition is left out—so long as we have not fully specified a unique individual, and hence so long as we do not know fully *what* individual our judgement is about—then the judgement 'fails to reach beyond generality'. It could be taken to apply to different individuals (depending on how the conditions are filled in), and so could be either affirmed or denied, depending

---

[86] ETR, 263.   [87] ETR, 252.   [88] ETR, 257.

on which individual we take it to be about (or how we fill those conditions in).

For Bradley, then, the only way we could avoid the 'defect' in judgement—the only way we could secure unique reference—would be if the properties we have used to pick out the individual which the judgement is about could not apply to any other possible individual. As Bradley writes in describing what is needed in order to obtain 'uniqueness': 'The possibility of another fact [i.e. for Bradley another individual] in another series must be excluded, so that in your fact and truth . . . you have nevertheless no general sort but a determinate thing.'[89] On this view, knowing fully *what* individual we are thinking of would require knowing, with regard to any property that may be predicated of that object, whether or not it applies to that individual. For if we fail to know, with regard to even one property, whether or not that property applies to that object, we will have failed to reach 'beyond generality'. In such a case, what we are judging about could be either of two different individuals: one which has the property in question and one which lacks it.

Hence, besides accepting K-I_1, Bradley accepts the further view:

K-I_2 Knowing fully *what* individual (or object) a singular thought or judgement is about would require knowing, with regard to any property, whether or not it applies to that individual.

And by adhering to K-I_2 along with ST_E, Bradley is forced to accept:

B_2 Were we to fully apprehend a singular thought (were we to fully apprehend the content of a singular judgement), we would thereby know its truth-value.

For, by K-I_2, knowing fully *what* object that thought is about will require knowing the truth-value of any predication, or any judgement, that can be made about that object. Hence, to accept ST_E, according to which fully apprehending a singular thought requires knowing fully *what* object that thought is about, along with K-I_2 guarantees that fully apprehending a singular thought suffices for knowing whether the predication made of the object in that thought is true or false; it suffices, that is, for knowing the truth-value of that thought.

[89] *ETR*, 264.

In fact, for Bradley, knowing fully *any* object requires knowing *every* object fully, and thus requires knowing every truth about the world. For, by K-I$_2$, knowing a given object fully requires knowing every truth about that object; hence, if there is more than one object, knowing every truth about a given object includes knowing every truth regarding that object's relations to each other object. And, for Bradley, we could truly (or 'non-defectively') know how two objects are related to each other only if we knew fully *what* each of those objects is. Thus, for Bradley, knowing one object fully requires knowing its relations to every other object, which in turn requires knowing every other object fully, which finally requires knowing every truth about every object— that is, every truth about the world.

Hence, for Bradley, there is ultimately no distinction between knowing different objects, since knowing any object will amount to knowing the same—namely, every truth about the world. And since knowing any object will amount to the same, for Bradley, there are not, ultimately, any different objects to know. For Bradley, that is, there is ultimately only one individual, and *what* that individual is determines every truth about the world; hence, for him, ultimately every judgement is about the same individual, and in making any judgement, we are attempting to know more fully *what* that individual is.[90]

Bradley's position, then, is diametrically opposed to Wittgenstein's. Whereas Wittgenstein holds that the world consists of a plurality of objects in contingent arrangements with each other, Bradley holds that the world consists of only one individual and that every truth about the world follows necessarily from the nature or essence of that individual. Whereas Wittgenstein holds that in knowing fully *what* objects the world consists of, we do not thereby know any truths about the world, Bradley holds that to know fully *what* individual the world consists of is thereby to know every truth about the world.

Russell claims that Bradley's position 'seems to rest upon some law of sufficient reason, some desire to show that every truth

---

[90] Thus the reason why Bradley can hold that 'the real Julius Caesar' can 'enter into' our judgements and be a 'constituent of' our knowledge is because he holds that the reality of Julius Caesar extends beyond 'the mere period in which he lived' (*ETR*, 423), and ultimately merges with the all-encompassing Absolute.

is "necessary" '.[91] And throughout his writings, Bradley does, indeed, display an aversion to the view that there are mere contingent facts—mere 'brute' or 'bare conjunctions' of objects— whose obtaining does not depend on any reason deeper than the brute contingency that that is the way things happen to be. Thus Bradley criticizes any view in which 'you are left in short with brute conjunctions where you seek for connexions, and where this need for connexions seems part of your nature',[92] and writes that 'a mere "together", a bare conjunction in space and time, is for thought unsatisfying and in the end impossible'.[93] However, in response to Russell, Bradley denies that he is 'arguing downwards from some assumption or axiom'.[94] And what I have argued, in effect, is that Bradley's position does not rest upon a demand or a vague longing for sufficient reasons, but rather upon certain views as to what is involved in knowing the individual which a (singular) judgement is about.[95]

More generally, I have attempted to make clear that the reason why Bradley and Wittgenstein take such diametrically opposed positions is that they bring opposite concerns to bear on the view ST_E, which they both accept. Both agree, that is, that apprehending a singular thought requires knowing what object that thought is about. But whereas Wittgenstein conjoins ST_E with general views as to what is involved in apprehending thoughts to arrive at conclusions as to what is involved in knowing the object a singular thought is about, Bradley conjoins ST_E with general views as to what is involved in knowing the object a singular thought is about to arrive at conclusions as to what is involved in apprehending thoughts. And since Bradley's assumptions, $K\text{-}I_1$ and $K\text{-}I_2$, regarding what is involved in knowing objects are the opposite of Wittgenstein's conclusions, W_1 and W_2, Bradley's conclusions, B_1 and B_2, regarding what is involved in apprehending thoughts

---

[91] Bertrand Russell, 'Some Explanations in Reply to Mr. Bradley', *Mind*, 19 (1910), 374.   [92] *ETR*, 115.

[93] *AR*, 505.   [94] See *ETR*, 289 ff. See also *ETR*, 311 ff.

[95] As Bradley writes in his reply to Russell (*ETR*, 290), 'the ground of objection to externality and to mere fact' is: 'You want . . . to say something about something and not about something else, particularly when the something else is unknown.' For Bradley, that is, the source of his objection to contingent or 'mere' or 'brute fact' is a concern with securing unique reference, a concern with identifying one thing and not another as the subject of a judgement.

are likewise the opposite of Wittgenstein's assumptions A-T$_1$ and A-T$_2$.

Thus, whereas Wittgenstein assumes that we fully apprehend all thoughts *a priori* (A-T$_1$) and is then forced, by ST$_E$, to conclude that we fully know objects *a priori* (W$_1$), Bradley assumes that we know objects by degrees through experience (K-I$_1$) and is then forced, by ST$_E$, to conclude that we apprehend thoughts by degrees through experience (B$_1$). And whereas Wittgenstein assumes that we apprehend thoughts independently of any knowledge of fact (A-T$_2$) and is then forced, by ST$_E$, to conclude that we know objects independently of any knowledge of fact (W$_2$), Bradley assumes that full knowledge of any object would require all knowledge of fact (K-I$_2$) and is then forced, by ST$_E$, to conclude that full apprehension of a singular thought would also require knowledge of fact (B$_2$).

Wittgenstein conjoins ST$_E$, in effect, with a view of the perfection of our apprehension of thought (that it is *a priori* and independent of knowledge of fact), and is then led to a metaphysics of mere contingent facts and 'brute connection', a metaphysics which Bradley would find far from perfect and wholly unsatisfying. Bradley, on the other hand, conjoins ST$_E$ with a view as to what is involved in securing uniqueness of reference, a view which leads both to his 'perfect' view of reality as an all-encompassing whole in which all parts are necessarily related to all others and to a view of thought or judgement which Wittgenstein would find wholly unacceptable, and which would upset Wittgenstein's view of logic. For on Wittgenstein's view, logical truth is ascertained merely by apprehending thoughts, prior to all experience and all knowledge of fact. But on Bradley's view, there is no apprehension of thought prior to experience, and the more our apprehension of thought is divorced from knowledge of fact, the less perfect and the more defective and ambiguous that thought is. The same principle, ST$_E$, which forces Wittgenstein to accept a view of reality which is wholly unacceptable to Bradley, forces Bradley to accept a view of thought which is wholly unacceptable to Wittgenstein. This principle guarantees that if one begins with Wittgenstein's 'perfect' view of thought, one is forced to accept what is for Bradley a wholly imperfect view of reality; and it guarantees as well that if one begins with Bradley's 'perfect' view of what is involved in knowing an object, one is forced to accept what is for Wittgenstein a wholly imperfect view of thought.[96]

Unlike Wittgenstein and Bradley, Russell conjoins ST_E not with general principles regarding what is involved in apprehending thoughts or what is involved in knowing objects, but rather with the view that the only objects (or particulars or individuals) which our singular thoughts are about are sense-data. Neither Wittgenstein nor Bradley begin their reasoning, that is, with actual examples in mind of objects which our singular thoughts are about; rather, they are forced to reach conclusions as to what those objects must be like, given the general principles they conjoin with ST_E. Russell, on the other hand, combines ST_E with specific views as to what the objects are which our singular thoughts are about—namely, that those objects are sense-data. Hence, what determine Russell's views of what is involved in apprehending singular thoughts and in knowing what object a singular thought is about are not general abstract principles, but rather his specific views of sense-data and what is involved in knowing them. Because of this, Russell's position falls in between the extremes of Bradley's and Wittgenstein's.

For Russell's sense-data have certain features in common with Wittgenstein's objects and certain features in common with Bradley's all-encompassing individual. Like Wittgenstein's objects, sense-data are such that to know them at all is to know them fully: to know *that* they are is to know fully *what* they are. Like Bradley's individual, a sense-datum is such that to know it fully, we must know at least some truths about it and must appeal to experience. Thus, while Russell agrees with Wittgenstein that we may immediately know objects fully, he cannot agree with Wittgenstein that we know objects *a priori*, or that in knowing objects fully we do not thereby know any truths about them. And while Russell agrees with Bradley that we know an object by appeal to experience, and that in knowing it fully we thereby have some knowledge of fact, he cannot agree with Bradley that we come to know an object progressively, by degrees, and that with full knowledge of *what* an object is, we would thereby

---

[96] It was through reading Josiah Royce, *The World and the Individual*, 1st ser. (New York: Dover Publications, 1959), Lecture VII, that I first came to suppose that central features of Wittgenstein's early views and Absolute Idealism may amount to opposite applications of the same shared principle ST_E.

achieve a complete knowledge of all of reality.[97] Thus Russell's view of reality is neither that of Wittgenstein's objects in merely contingent arrangement with each other nor Bradley's single individual from which all truths flow by necessity.[98]

Likewise, Russell's view of singular thought falls in between Wittgenstein's and Bradley's. Like Wittgenstein, Russell holds (by R_2) that we may immediately apprehend a singular thought fully; like Bradley, he holds (by R_1) that we need to appeal to experience to apprehend a singular thought and (by R_3) that fully apprehending a singular thought will give us knowledge of fact. Thus Russell's singular thoughts, unlike Wittgenstein's, are not apprehended *a priori* and wholly independently of knowledge of fact; and, unlike Bradley's singular thoughts, Russell's may be apprehended fully immediately. Just as Russell's view of reality falls in between Bradley's 'perfect' individual and Wittgenstein's objects in mere 'brute conjunction' with each other, so too Russell's view of singular thought falls in between Wittgenstein's 'perfect' *a priori* apprehensions independent of all knowledge of fact and Bradley's *a posteriori* 'endeavour' to achieve an ever fuller knowledge of *what* our thoughts are about.

However, by sharing views with Wittgenstein as well as Bradley, Russell is led to at least one view which neither Wittgenstein nor Bradley could accept. With Wittgenstein, Russell holds that

---

[97] See e.g. *Problems of Philosophy*, 144–5; 'Philosophy of Logical Atomism', 204.

[98] Russell, I recognize, did not wish to acknowledge any fundamental metaphysical distinction between necessity and contingency. Thus, e.g., in a letter to Bradley he writes: 'my view is that, possibility and necessity are not fundamental notions.' (*The Collected Papers of Bertrand Russell*, vi, ed. J. Slater (London: Routledge, 1992), 351.) Nevertheless, Russell clearly wishes to hold, as opposed to Bradley, that we can know *what* an object is without thereby knowing all truths about that object (see passages cited in n. 97), and in this sense he wishes to hold that at least some truths about an object do not follow from the 'nature' or 'essence' of that object, that some such truths are contingent. Furthermore, in holding that knowing what a sense-datum is requires knowing some truths about that sense-datum, Russell seems committed to holding that those truths, at least, follow necessarily from the 'intrinsic nature' of *what* that sense-datum is. This is a conclusion that G. E. Moore willingly accepts in 'The Concept of Intrinsic Value', in his *Philosophical Studies* (London: Routledge and Kegan Paul, 1922), 268 ff., where he indicates that being yellow is an intrinsic property of a yellow sense-datum, a property which that sense-datum *must* have. Similarly, in his 1912 manuscript 'On Matter', Russell suggests that through acquaintance we can know of the 'intrinsic nature' of an entity. For he argues that if we cannot be acquainted with matter, then we can know nothing of its 'intrinsic nature'. (See *Collected Papers*, vi. 93, 95.)

we can immediately apprehend any singular thought fully; and, with Bradley, he holds that fully apprehending some singular thoughts enables us to know their truth-values. Hence, for Russell, immediately apprehending some singular thoughts enables us to know their truth-values. Thus, for example, he holds that we immediately apprehend fully the thought expressed by 'This is red'; and in fully apprehending this thought, we thereby know its truth-value. So, for Russell, what we know in immediately apprehending this thought suffices for knowing its truth-value.

Neither Wittgenstein nor Bradley could accept this conclusion. While Wittgenstein agrees with Russell that we may immediately apprehend any singular thought fully, he denies that apprehension of a singular thought ever suffices for knowledge of fact (and hence for knowledge of the truth-value of that thought). While Bradley agrees with Russell that fully apprehending a singular thought may suffice for knowledge of its truth-value, he denies that we may ever fully apprehend a singular thought immediately.

More generally, Wittgenstein and Bradley agree that for a judgement or a thought to be genuine, we may not determine its truth-value in immediately apprehending it. Thus Bradley indicates that if it were immediately clear, upon apprehending an apparent thought, that the predicate inhered in the subject, 'then there would be no judgement at all, and but a pretence of thinking without thought'.[99] And, for Wittgenstein, a genuine thought, being a 'picture of reality', is such that its truth-value may not be determined immediately upon apprehending it, but may only be determined by comparing it to reality.[100] Indeed, both Wittgenstein and Bradley agree that something whose truth-value may be determined immediately upon apprehending it is a mere 'tautology', which 'says nothing', and which, therefore, is not a genuine thought or judgement.[101] On Russell's view, however, 'This is red' expresses

[99] *AR*, 148. As Bradley writes: 'if the subject is the same as the predicate, why trouble oneself to judge?'

[100] Hence *Tractatus*, 2.224: 'It is impossible to tell from the picture alone whether it is true or false.'

[101] See *PL*, 141, where Bradley indicates that a 'tautology' is 'no judgement at all' and 'really says nothing'. For Bradley, 'we can not have the reality of judgement, unless some difference actually enters into the content of what we assert'. For Wittgenstein on tautology, see passages cited in nn. 47–9. In *Problems of Philosophy*, 82–3, Russell writes, apparently similarly, that 'a purely analytic judgement' is 'trivial' and 'would never be enunciated in real life except by an

a genuine thought or judgement, but it is also such that we know its truth-value immediately upon apprehending it. But for both Wittgenstein and Bradley, this is to embrace the unacceptable conclusion that some genuine thoughts or judgements are tautologous.

Wittgenstein and Bradley, however, avoid Russell's view in opposite ways. Both agree that there must be a gap between immediately apprehending a thought and knowing the truth-value of that thought, if there is to be genuine thought; but they characterize that gap in different ways. For Wittgenstein, the gap is between knowing *that* that thought is about some object and knowing *what* object that thought is about, on the one side, and knowing what is true of that object or, in Wittgenstein's terminology, *how* that object is, on the other. For Wittgenstein, that is, in immediately apprehending a thought, we know *that* it is about something and know fully *what* object it is about, but do not thereby know *how* that object is arranged with other objects, and thus do not know the truth-value of that thought.

Bradley characterizes the gap between immediately apprehending a thought and knowing its truth-value as a gap between knowing *that* that thought is about something, on the one side, and knowing *what* that thought is about, on the other. For Bradley, that is, if we knew fully *what* object a thought is about, we would know fully *how* that object is, and would thus know the truth-value of that (as well as every other) thought; hence, for Bradley, the reason we do not know the truth-value of that thought in immediately apprehending it is because, in immediately apprehending that thought, we do not know fully *what* it is about. In immediately apprehending that thought, we know *that* it is about something, but do not know fully *what* object it is about, and thus do not know *how* that object is or, hence, the truth-value of that thought. In Bradley's terminology, in genuine judgement, the subject of the judgement remains 'a "that" beyond a mere "what" '[102]—that is, it remains an object, a 'that', not fully individuated by any 'what' we are able to specify.

---

orator preparing the way for a piece of sophistry'. But Russell has defined 'purely analytic judgements' so that they will always be general, never singular (see n. 45); and he does not consider whether his account of a singular judgement such as 'This is red' would be 'trivial' in the sense that anyone immediately apprehending it would thereby know its truth-value.

[102] *AR*, 149.

Wittgenstein, then, explains the gap between what we know in immediately apprehending a thought and what we know in knowing its truth-value as a gap between knowing *what* an object is and knowing *how* that object is (knowing truths about that object); Bradley explains the same gap between immediately apprehending a thought and knowing its truth-value as a gap between knowing *that* an object is and knowing *what* that object is. Wittgenstein's way of maintaining the gap between immediately apprehending a thought and knowing its truth-value enables him to preserve a 'perfect' view of thought (since we can know immediately, and *a priori*, *what* that thought is about), but forces him to accept an 'imperfect' view of reality (in which any truth about *how* objects are is contingent); Bradley's way of maintaining that gap enables him to preserve a 'perfect' view of reality (in which *how* an object is—or each truth about an object— becomes intrinsic to *what* that object is), but forces him to accept an 'imperfect' view of thought (in which in having a thought, we never know fully *what* our thought is about).

For Russell, however, in immediately apprehending the thought expressed by 'This is red', we know all at once not only *that* that thought is about something, but also *what* object that thought is about, as well as *how* that object is. Hence, by failing to separate either the *what* from the *how*, as Wittgenstein does, or the *that* from the *what*, as Bradley does, Russell cannot distinguish, in this case, immediately apprehending that thought from knowing its truth-value. And for both Wittgenstein and Bradley, this amounts not to an 'imperfect' account of thought, but to its total collapse into mere tautology.[103] Indeed, it is to prevent this sort of collapse of thought into tautology that Bradley is led to

---

[103] Unlike Russell, Schlick comes close to acknowledging that his 'observation statements' or 'affirmations' amount to the collapse of judgement and thought. For, like the early Wittgenstein, Schlick regards the analytic/synthetic distinction as the 'absolutely sharp' difference between 'tautology' and 'real assertion' (*Problems of Philosophy in their Interconnection*, 121). Furthermore, he holds that what distinguishes 'tautologies' from 'real assertions' is that 'in the one case [tautologies] mere understanding already includes insight into their truth', while in the case of 'real assertions' it does not (ibid. 122–3). Hence Schlick's admission (see n. 34) that in 'affirmations', as in tautologies, 'the process of understanding is at the same time the process of verification' is tantamount to an admission that 'affirmations' cannot be 'real assertions'. While Schlick thus recognizes a problem in regarding his 'affirmations' as 'real assertions', Russell does not question whether his 'This is red' can be a genuine judgement.

hold that the 'consummation' of thought is at the same time its 'happy suicide', wherein it ceases to be genuine thought.[104] For, on Bradley's view, thought would reach its 'consummation' if we attained a full knowledge of *what* our thought or judgement is about. At that moment, there would no longer be any gap between the 'that', on the one side, and the 'what' and the 'how', on the other; and at that moment, our judgement would become something else, something like a tautology, in which our immediate apprehension of it would suffice for knowing its truth-value. For Bradley, with this collapse of judgement, we would have attained a 'mode of apprehension' different from thought or judgement: we would have attained union with the Absolute.[105]

Whereas the Bradleyan collapse of judgement is the 'end' toward which our thought and judgement aims,[106] the Russellian collapse of judgement occurs in his lowest level, 'judgements of perception'. For on Russell's view, it is here—in judgements about sense-data—that the 'that', the 'what', and the 'how' come together to yield cases where there can be no gap between immediately apprehending a judgement and knowing its truth-value. For both Wittgenstein and Bradley, this is unacceptable. For Wittgenstein, once we fully apprehend a thought (*a priori*), there always remains a gap between the 'that' and the 'what', on the one side (which we know *a priori* in apprehending the thought), and the 'how', on the other (which we do not). Hence, for Wittgenstein, the sort of collapse of thought and judgement to which Russell is committed can never occur. Bradley, on the other hand, seeks such a collapse of judgement, but not in our encounter with 'immediate experience', where Russell is forced to find it. Instead, Bradley holds, as against Russell, that what is 'given' in 'immediate experience' cannot itself be identical with the object about which we judge; and, for Bradley, it is only when we go beyond 'given experience' to seek an individuating knowledge of *what* object our thought is about that we embark on the path whose 'end' is the 'suicide' of thought in our union with the Absolute.

IV

I mentioned at the outset that when contemporary philosophers of language endorse the view that actual objects (or particulars

---

[104] *AR*, 148–52.   [105] *AR*, 151–2.   [106] *AR*, 153.

or individuals) may be constituents of sentential contents, they typically cite Russell as the historical source for their position. There is, however, something of an irony in their using Russell in this way.

For while Russell does, indeed, accept the view that singular thoughts are 'object-dependent', he does not hold that *all* thoughts are. In addition to singular thoughts or propositions, Russell recognizes general propositions. For Russell distinguishes particulars—entities designated by genuine proper names—from universals—entities designated by general terms and relation expressions; and, according to Russell, whereas singular propositions have particulars (along with universals) among their constituents, general propositions are composed only of universals. And since Russell holds that universals are apprehended *a priori* and independently of any knowledge of the actual world, he is able to hold, for example, that, unlike singular propositions, general propositions are apprehended *a priori* and independently of any knowledge of the actual world.[107]

Moreover, from Russell's perspective, what is innovative in his position is not the view that some propositions—the singular propositions—are object-dependent; rather, it is the view that some propositions—the general propositions—are wholly object-*independent*. Emerging as they do against the background of the 'Golden Age of Pure Semantics', during which all propositions (or sentential contents) are taken to be object-independent, recent 'direct' theorists of reference find it striking that Russell held that singular propositions are object-dependent. But Russell himself developed his position against the background of Bradleyan idealism, according to which all propositions (or judgements) are object-dependent. Hence, in historical context, what is original in Russell's position is not the view that some propositions are object-dependent, but rather that some are not.

In fact, one central component of Russell's and, before him, G. E. Moore's original break with idealism is their attack on Bradley's view that each judgement (and hence, for Bradley, each truth[108]) makes reference to an existing individual. Thus, in his

---

[107] Hence, in *Our Knowledge of the External World*, 41, Russell claims that confusing the difference between singular and general propositions 'obscured not only the whole study of the forms of judgement and inference, but also the relations of things to their qualities, of concrete existence to abstract concepts, and of the world of sense to the world of Platonic ideas'.   [108] See n. 85.

1899 paper 'The Nature of Judgement', Moore argues that 'it is
. . . impossible that truth should depend on a relation to existents
or to an existent'.[109] And following Moore, Russell argues in *A
Critical Exposition of the Philosophy of Leibniz* (1900) and *The
Principles of Mathematics* (1903) against 'the existential theory
of judgement—the theory, that is, that every proposition is concerned with something that exists',[110] the theory that 'all truth
consists in propositions about what exists'.[111] In making these
arguments, both Moore and Russell are specifically attacking
Bradley's view that all propositions are object-dependent, and
they are replacing it with the view that some propositions, at
least, are 'non-existential'[112]—that is, that some propositions are
not about any existing individual, that some propositions are
wholly object-independent.

Moreover, even if singular, object-dependent propositions come
to play an important role for Moore and Russell in our knowledge of the external world (when these propositions come to be
about sense-data), the general, object-independent propositions
are fundamental to Russell's account of mathematics and logic
and to Moore's account of what is 'good in itself'. In the years
immediately following their break with idealism, Moore and
Russell were primarily concerned with these issues and, more
generally, with issues regarding the nature of the *a priori*. What
they argue is that none of these issues can be properly addressed
unless one rejects Bradley's view that each proposition is about
an existing individual and holds instead that some propositions,
at least, are wholly object-independent.[113] Again, viewed in context,

---

[109] G. E. Moore, 'The Nature of Judgement', repr. in *Moore's Early Essays*,
ed. T. Regan (Philadelphia: Temple University Press, 1986), 65.

[110] Bertrand Russell, *The Principles of Mathematics* (London: George Allen &
Unwin, 1903), 449–50. Of course, on Bradley's 'existential theory of judgement',
judgements are not 'existential' in the sense of contemporary logic. For the existential propositions of contemporary logic are quantified (and hence, for Russell,
are generally object-independent), rather than singular (and hence, for Russell,
object-dependent).

[111] Bertrand Russell, *A Critical Exposition of the Philosophy of Leibniz*
(London: George Allen & Unwin, 1900), 177.

[112] Russell, *Principles of Mathematics*, p. xviii.

[113] See e.g. G. E. Moore, *Principia Ethica* (Cambridge: Cambridge University
Press, 1903), 125 ff., where he argues that to accept Bradley's view that '*all* propositions . . . assert either that something exists or that something which exists
has a certain attribute' is at 'the root of the naturalistic fallacy' and precludes
a proper analysis of statements of intrinsic value. Likewise, chapters 7–10 of

Moore and Russell contribute more to the decline of object-dependent views of thought than to their development.[114]

Furthermore, contemporary philosophers of language who endorse object-dependent views of singular thought typically emphasize that while they follow Russell in holding that objects themselves 'figure in', or are 'constituents of', singular thoughts, they do not wish to restrict the objects which singular thoughts may be about to sense-data. Rather, they defend the view that object-dependent singular thoughts may be about ordinary, external physical objects. Hence this 'externalist' version of singular thought theory is

Russell's *Problems of Philosophy* are a sustained argument to the effect that a proper account of *a priori* knowledge requires recognizing general (object-independent) propositions. In later writings, Bradley noted and criticized Russell's attack on 'the existential theory of judgement'. See 'On Appearance, Error and Contradiction', 253 n. 1, and 'What is the Real Julius Caesar?', 425–6 n. 1.

[114] While Moore and Russell depart from Bradley's view that all thought is object-dependent, and come to hold that only some thought is object-dependent, the early Wittgenstein returns to a position which (in this respect at least) is Bradleyan. For Wittgenstein holds that all thought requires acquaintance with objects. Hence, like Bradley, he holds that there can be no thought without there being objects (or individuals) for that thought to be about; and, again like Bradley, he holds that in all thought we are acquainted, or 'come in contact', with the objects which that thought is about. (Whereas Russell sharply distinguishes general propositions from their singular instances, the early Wittgenstein regards general propositions as the logical sums or products of their singular instances, and so makes the general propositions object-dependent, along with the singular propositions.) In this regard, both Bradley and the early Wittgenstein accept a kind of 'ontological argument' according to which the mere being of thought (or judgement) guarantees the existence of an individual for that thought to be about. (Of course, this kind of ontological argument does not establish that the existing individual has the characteristics traditionally associated with God.) As Nicholas Griffin explains in *Russell's Idealist Apprenticeship* (Oxford: Clarendon Press, 1991), 70–8, Russell accepted Absolute Idealism (in 1894) because he accepted this kind of 'ontological argument'. (Griffin bases his discussion there on Carl Spadoni, ' "Great God in Boots!—The Ontological Argument is Sound" ', *Journal of the Bertrand Russell Archive*, 23–4 (1976), 37–41.) Further (as Griffin also points out), in his 1900 book on Leibniz, Russell explicitly relates this version of the ontological argument to Bradley's 'existential theory of judgement' (see *Critical Exposition of the Philosophy of Leibniz*, 177 ff.). By this time, however, Russell no longer accepts such an argument; for, following Moore, he now holds that some propositions, at least—those which were to become the general propositions —can have being even in the absence of all existing particulars. Russell comes to hold, that is, that there can be thought (general thought) and there can be truth (general truth) without there being any existing objects for that thought or truth to be about. (See also in this context Russell's *Introduction to Mathematical Philosophy* (London: Allen & Unwin, 1919), 203–4.) But even though Russell, following Moore, had come to reject this type of 'ontological argument', Russell's student Wittgenstein reinstates it in the *Tractatus*.

closely associated with Hilary Putnam's slogan that ' "meanings" just ain't in the head';[115] for on this view, the 'meaning' or 'content' of a singular sentence depends upon, or is composed in part of, an external physical object.

Because of this, contemporary 'externalist' singular thought theorists are faced with rejecting R_2, the view common to Russell and the early Wittgenstein, that we may immediately apprehend singular thoughts fully.[116] For if fully apprehending a singular thought requires knowing the (external) object which that thought is about, and if we do not immediately know that external object fully, then we cannot immediately apprehend that singular thought fully either. Thus, for example, John McDowell argues that his externalist account of singular thoughts is 'radically anti-Cartesian' in that it rejects the view that 'the inner life takes place in an autonomous realm, transparent to the introspective awareness of the subject'.[117] According to McDowell, that is, we do not have immediate or 'transparent' access to our singular thoughts, since we do not have immediate or transparent access to the objects which those thoughts are about. Thus for McDowell, this externalist account of singular thought 'open[s] the possibility that a subject may be in error about the contents of his own mind';[118] for in so far as we may be in error about the external objects which our thoughts are about, we will likewise be mistaken about the singular 'contents' we are apprehending.

Furthermore, closely associated with 'externalist' views of singular thought is the view that some entities have 'essences' which are discoverable only *a posteriori*, and hence that some necessary truths are not knowable *a priori*. To hold, then, that an entity has an 'essence' which is discoverable only *a posteriori*, while also holding that fully apprehending a thought about that entity requires knowing *what* that entity is, is thereby to hold that we can fully apprehend such a thought only after we have discovered *a posteriori* the 'real essence' of that entity, and only after we have thus discovered *a posteriori* truths about that entity. Thus Ruth

---

[115] See Hilary Putnam, 'The Meaning of "Meaning"', in *Mind, Language and Reality* (Cambridge: Cambridge University Press, 1975), esp. 223–7.

[116] Those contemporary 'externalists' inclined to reject R_2 are those inclined to accept ST_E. As I mentioned above (see n. 18), not all contemporary 'direct' theorists of reference would seem to do so.

[117] McDowell, 'Singular Thought and the Extent of Inner Space', 146.

[118] Ibid. 145.

Barcan Marcus holds that no one can genuinely believe that Hesperus is not Phosphorus.[119] For, on Marcus's view, believing that would require fully apprehending the content expressed by 'Hesperus is different from Phosphorus'; and, for Marcus, fully apprehending that content would require knowing *what* object each name in that sentence stands for. But we could not know fully *what* objects are designated by those names without knowing (*a posteriori*) that those names designate the same object. Thus, for Marcus, anyone who fully apprehended that content would thereby know that it is false.

Similarly, and more directly related to the issue of 'essences', Marcus would seem to be committed to the view that anyone who fully apprehended the content expressed by 'Water is H_2O' would thereby know that it is true. For, like Kripke, she holds that water has a 'real essence' which it is the task of science to discover, and on account of this, she holds that (if true) a claim like 'Water is H_2O' will be necessarily true.[120] But now, for Marcus, if fully apprehending the content expressed by 'Water is H_2O' requires knowing fully *what* that content is about, then apprehending that content will require knowing (*a posteriori*) the 'real essence' of water, which will in turn require knowing the truth of that content.

In all these respects, then, contemporary 'externalist' singular thought theorists have more in common with Bradley than with either Russell or Wittgenstein. Bradley holds that 'a thought only "in my head", or a bare idea separated from all relation to the real world, is a false abstraction',[121] and that 'the real Caesar' may be a constituent of our singular thoughts. Likewise, contemporary externalists hold that 'meanings ain't in the head', and that ordinary physical objects, and not merely Russell's sense-data, let

---

[119] Ruth Barcan Marcus, 'Rationality and Believing the Impossible', *Journal of Philosophy*, 80 (1983), esp. 329 ff.

[120] See e.g. Ruth Barcan Marcus, 'A Backward Look at Quine's Animadversions on Modalities', in R. Barrett and R. Gibson (eds.), *Perspectives on Quine* (Oxford: Blackwell, 1990), 239, where she endorses the view that 'a particular instance of a species such as tiger, or of a physical kind such as gold would seem to have non-purely logical necessary properties as was argued by Aristotle as well as contemporary philosophers [here she cites Kripke and Putnam]'. Marcus holds that we cannot believe what is impossible (see her 'Rationality and Believing the Impossible'); thus, in so far as she believes that it is necessary that water is H_2O, she holds that we cannot genuinely believe that it is not.   [121] *AR*, 350.

alone Wittgenstein's objects, may 'figure in', or be constituents of, our singular thoughts. Like Bradley and Russell, but unlike Wittgenstein, they hold that we know the objects which our thoughts are about by means of experience, and that knowing those objects fully requires knowing some truths about them. Thus, like Bradley and Russell, but unlike Wittgenstein, they hold, in accordance with R_1 and R_3, that we apprehend singular thoughts by means of experience, and that fully apprehending some singular thoughts requires knowing their truth-values. But, like Bradley, and unlike either Russell or Wittgenstein, contemporary externalists hold that we do not have immediate access to the objects which our singular thoughts are about, but know those objects only by degrees over time. Hence, like Bradley, but unlike either Russell or Wittgenstein, contemporary externalists hold, in opposition to R_2, that we do not fully apprehend singular thoughts immediately, but apprehend them only by degrees, over time.

Like Bradley, that is, contemporary 'externalists' do not combine the notion of an object-dependent singular thought with Russell's view that the only objects which our singular thoughts may be about are given to us fully in 'immediate experience'. Nor do they combine it with Wittgenstein's view—characteristic of the 'Golden Age of Pure Semantics', against which many contemporary 'externalists' are reacting—that we fully apprehend thoughts *a priori* and independently of any knowledge of fact. Instead, like Bradley, contemporary 'externalists' tend to combine the notion of object-dependent singular thoughts with the view that we know the objects which those thoughts are about by degrees, over time.[122] Hence, not only does Bradley contribute more than Russell to the actual development of object-dependent views of thought; he also has more in common with the ways in which certain contemporary analytic philosophers tend to pursue the notion of object-dependent thoughts than do either Russell or the early Wittgenstein.[123]

---

[122] I have not, however, addressed the issue as to whether contemporary 'externalists' also hold, or are committed to, Bradley's principle K-I_2. Nor, obviously, have I attempted to characterize the positions of all contemporary externalists, or to indicate that all of them are inclined to a Bradleyan view of singular thought. I am only pointing to some tendencies among some contemporary externalists.

[123] An earlier version of this essay was presented at the Bradley Colloquium, April 1993. I thank the participants in the colloquium, especially Guy Stock and Ralph Walker, for their helpful comments. I also thank Paul Loeb for his comments on another version of this material.

INDEX OF VIEWS CITED

Introduction

ST At least some contents (call them singular thoughts) are, or at least purport to be, about objects.

ST_M What singular thoughts there are depends on what objects there are.

ST_E Apprehending a singular thought requires knowing (or being acquainted with) the object which that thought is about.

Russell

$S\text{-}D_1$ Sense-data exist only fleetingly or momentarily; they are apprehended *a posteriori*; they are private to the person apprehending them.

$S\text{-}D_2$ In being acquainted with a sense-datum, we immediately know it fully and completely; in being acquainted with it, we know both *that* it is (or exists) and also *what* it is; in knowing *what* it is, we thereby know some truths about it.

R_1 Singular thoughts exist only fleetingly; they are apprehended *a posteriori*; and they are private to the person apprehending them.

R_2 We can fully apprehend a singular proposition (or thought) immediately; in immediately apprehending that proposition, we know *that* it is about something and know fully *what* it is about.

R_3 Fully apprehending some singular propositions (or thoughts) enables us to know their truth-values.

Wittgenstein

$A\text{-}T_1$ We apprehend thoughts *a priori*.

$A\text{-}T_2$ In apprehending a thought, we do not thereby have any knowledge about the world.

W_1 We know (*kennen*) objects *a priori*.

W_2 In knowing (*kennen*) an object, we do not thereby know any truth about that object.

Bradley

$K\text{-}I_1$ We know the individual (or object) which a singular thought or judgement is about by degrees, over time.

$K\text{-}I_2$ Knowing fully *what* individual (or object) a singular thought or judgement is about would require knowing, with regard to any property, whether or not it applies to that individual.

B$_1$ We apprehend a singular thought (or the content of a singular judgement) by degrees, over time.

B$_2$ Were we to fully apprehend a singular thought (were we to fully apprehend the content of a singular judgement), we would thereby know its truth-value.

3

Thought's Happy Suicide

THOMAS BALDWIN

———•———

I

In the appendix to *Appearance and Reality* Bradley says that the main thesis of the work is contained in chapter 15 on 'Thought and Reality'. The central theme of that chapter is that reality lies beyond any system of thoughts, however harmonious and comprehensive: the pursuit of truth, which is an essential characteristic of thought, carries thought beyond itself—to the Absolute. For the condition under which thought attains *absolute* truth is that it commit suicide, albeit, as Bradley puts it, a 'happy suicide',[1] as it attains its consummation in the burning flames of the Absolute. Now it is a central presupposition of this thesis that no judgements are absolutely, or unconditionally, true—a claim explicitly made by Bradley on several occasion;[2] and it is primarily this claim that I want to discuss here.

Despite the presence here of the qualifying adverbs 'absolutely', 'unconditionally' (which will require some attention), Bradley's claim is *prima facie* paradoxical, for it implies that it itself is not absolutely true; it embodies a form of scepticism that threatens itself. Bradley can of course respond that his claim is nearly true— as nearly true as any judgement ever gets. But there is a dilemma here for Bradley: either his theory prescribes suicide for itself, as a system of thought incapable of absolute truth (which does not appear to be a happy suicide); or, if this incapacity is not, after all, a serious incapacity for Bradley's own theory, then why is the

---

[1] *AR*, 173.   [2] *AR*, 544; *ETR*, 232, 252–3.

same incapacity nevertheless of fundamental importance for metaphysics? Bradley's philosophy, in this respect, is comparable to Wittgenstein's *Tractatus*: Bradley may say that, having climbed up the ladder of thought, one is free to throw it away; but that very statement seems to get discarded in the process.

To deal adequately with these matters, one needs a deeper understanding of Bradley's position, and it is useful to start by comparing it with some contemporary sceptical theses which, at first sight, it resembles—if only to appreciate the difference between Bradley's problematic and that of much contemporary philosophy. Bradley holds that there is something inherently problematic in the conception of judgement: he writes of 'the fundamental inconsistency of judgement which remains in the end unremoved'.[3] Now there are many contemporary philosophers who, like Bradley, think that judgement, or, as it would now be said, 'intentionality' (or 'meaning', or 'content'), is inherently problematic. Here, very briefly, are three examples. According to Quine, intentionality as we normally conceive it is an illusion, because the physical facts of behaviour, including speech, radically underdetermine ascriptions of meaning to utterances, and yet there are no other facts.[4] For Kripke, intentionality is problematic because, he argues, its essential normative dimension cannot be adequately comprehended in an account which appeals only to physical or, more broadly, natural facts about speakers.[5] According to Stich, finally, ascriptions of intentional content involve too many assumptions about the external context of the subject for such ascriptions to enter into a proper causal theory about the subject, which should draw only on intrinsic 'narrow', non-intentional descriptions of the subject's psychology.[6]

These contemporary arguments start from presumptions of a broadly realist kind concerning the physical world; the anxiety they manifest is that intentionality does not readily fit into the conception of the world thus attained. As with Bradley, the resulting sceptical thesis concerning intentionality threatens paradox;

---

[3] *ETR*, 231.

[4] W. V. O. Quine, *Word and Object* (Cambridge, Mass.: MIT Press, 1960), esp. ch. 2.

[5] Saul Kripke, *Wittgenstein on Rules and Private Language* (Oxford: Blackwell, 1982), esp. ch. 2.

[6] Stephen Stich, *From Folk Psychology to Cognitive Science* (Cambridge, Mass.: MIT Press, 1983).

for, given that knowledge and truth involve intentional content, the initial affirmation of physical realism and the subsequent statement of the sceptical thesis are themselves called into question by this very thesis.[7] But does Bradley share this starting-point? Surely not. His philosophy does not rest upon any specific assumptions concerning reality, least of all a physicalist assumption. On the contrary, as the whole structure of *Appearance and Reality* manifests, he argues that one can attain a grasp of reality only by working through problems which are internal to experience and thought itself—including, in particular, this very problem about the truth of judgement itself. So, despite the similarity between his scepticism concerning judgement and contemporary scepticisms concerning intentionality, the source of Bradley's problem concerning judgement must be sought elsewhere.

At its simplest, I think Bradley's problem arises from the combination of two claims concerning the relationship between thought and reality: first, that in judgement an ideal content is attributed to reality:[8] secondly, that 'the real is inaccessible by way of ideas'.[9] For it seems clear that if the real is inaccessible by way of ideas, then the attribution of ideas to reality must fail. It is an easy step from this to the conclusion that no judgements are true; for, according to Bradley, a judgement is true just where its ideal content is real—'By the truth of a judgement', he says, 'we mean that its suggestion is more than an idea, that it is fact'.[10] Hence if no ideal content can be real, no judgement can be true.

It is clear that the burden of this argument rests on the second claim, that 'the real is inaccessible by way of ideas'. But what reason does Bradley offer for this claim? Consider the following passage:

How is it possible for truth to embrace the whole sensible past and future? Truth might understand them (do you say?) and so include them *ideally*. Well but, if truth could do as much as this, which I myself think not possible, truth after all would not include these facts *bodily*.[11]

---

[7] For a detailed discussion of this point with respect to Quine, cf. Jane Heal, *Fact and Meaning* (Oxford: Blackwell, 1989), esp. ch. 6. More generally, cf. Paul A. Boghossian, 'The Status of Content', *Philosophical Review*, 99 (1990), 157–84.

[8] *PL*, 10.   [9] *PL*, 63.

[10] *PL*, 10. Stewart Candlish and I have argued that this identification of the truth of a judgement with the reality of its ideal content is central to Bradley's theory of truth. See Stewart Candlish, 'The Truth about F. H. Bradley', *Mind*, 98 (1989), 331–48; Thomas Baldwin, 'The Identity Theory of Truth', *Mind*, 100 (1991), 35–52.   [11] *ETR*, 115.

This might tempt one to interpret Bradley as, after all, relying on an assumption of 'bodily' realism concerning physical facts, which, in comparison with the merely 'ideal' contents of judgement, immediately yields the conclusion that the contents of true judgement cannot comprise reality. The physical fact that snow is white, with all its causal roles in relation to electromagnetic radiation and sensory systems, cannot, we naturally feel, be identified with a bare mental content that does not seem to have anything like the same causal profile. But this temptation, however attractive to a common-sense point of view, must be resisted; for the prior assumption of physical realism conflicts with Bradley's internalist approach to the conception of reality. Hence, although Bradley agrees with the physical realist that judgement cannot 'include these facts *bodily*', his route to this conclusion has to be of a different kind.

What, then, is Bradley's route? At one point, where he is trying to envisage how his account of the relationship between thought and reality might be criticized, Bradley writes as follows: 'The general position here taken must, so far as I see, be attacked either by falling back on designation or by the acceptance of mere external relations.'[12]

The implication of this remark is that Bradley sees his position as depending upon a thesis, essentially critical, concerning both the possibility of 'designation' and his rejection of 'mere external relations'. Although this remark also suggests that he conceives of these points as different parts of a single line of argument, I think it is helpful to think of them as providing the basis for two different routes to his conclusion, one arising from the rejection of external relations, the other from the critique of 'designation'; and I propose to treat them in this way.

II

Of the two points, Bradley's rejection of external relations will be most familiar. Yet it is not at first clear why this should lead us to the conclusion that no judgements at all are true, as opposed to the conclusion that all judgements which involve external

---

[12] *ETR*, 230.

relations are false. After all, Bradley acknowledges that we can frame judgements involving internal relations; but he is equally dismissive of them.[13] So the conclusion involves a double generalization: if *all* judgements involve relations, and *all* relations are unreal, then, given Bradley's conception of the relationship between reality and truth, it will follow that no judgements are true. But why should we accept the premisses of this argument? And how do they relate to the rejection of external relations?

The roots of Bradley's position on these matters lie in his conception of immediate experience. Immediate experience is that rich preconceptual manifold which, according to Bradley, persists as an essential background to conceptual thought.[14] The fact that it thus persists, that it is not exhaustively taken up and transformed through conceptualization, already shows, according to Bradley, that judgement has its limitations—'the moment's felt immediacy remains for ever outstanding'.[15] Thus judgement cannot provide an exhaustive account of reality. But it does not follow from this that it does not provide a partial account unless it is further added that such a partial account cannot be satisfactory as such, on the grounds that by missing something out it fails to deal properly with the material that it purports to cover. This addition returns us to the rejection of external relations and, more broadly, to Bradley's holism. But we cannot leave the matter there, for Bradley's critical treatment of external relations is itself bound up with his conception of immediate experience and its role in relation to conceptual thought.

Bradley makes three claims on this matter. The first is that immediate experience offers us an experience of identity amidst diversity which is not intrinsically problematic; the second is that the conceptualization of those aspects of experience which involve identity and diversity, as subjects and predicates, or terms and relations, is intrinsically problematic; and the third is that conceptual thought manages to persist despite this problem only by means of a surreptitious dependence upon immediate experience. These are difficult claims. The easiest to understand is the second one: Bradley's claim is, in effect, that the 'problem of universals' is insoluble within its own terms, in that the conception of substances as self-standing objects and of universals as their properties

[13] *ETR*, 228.   [14] *ETR*, 177.   [15] *ETR*, 115.

does not yield us any way of understanding how a fact, in which a property qualifies an object or a relation combines some terms, has any unity of its own. Bradley usually expresses this point as a point about relations, concerning the difficulty of combining a relation with its terms.[16] But there is nothing in his point that restricts it to relations as opposed to universals; indeed, Bradley criticizes the account of universals which Russell advances in *The Problems of Philosophy*[17] in a way which exactly parallels his usual critique of relations, by objecting both to the very idea of a 'bare universal' and to the possibility of such a thing entering into a relation of instantiation, or whatever, with anything else.[18] Bradley's fundamental point concerns the combination of identity and difference that is characteristic of all predication, monadic or dyadic:

> If the predicate is different from the subject, what is the sense and justification of their unity? And, if the predicate is not different, is there any sense left at all? If we take the 'is' as *mere* identity, the assertion disappears. It once more vanishes if the 'is' is understood as mere difference. And the question is whether we have any other way of taking the 'is' which in the end satisfies us and is tenable. We do not, in my opinion, possess any other way.[19]

We may well disagree with Bradley's last claim here; but at least the general import of his position is reasonably clear.

It is not so easy for me to make a similar claim concerning his other two points. These both concern immediate experience, and I have to confess that I find Bradley's treatment of immediate experience one of the chief obstacles to genuine sympathy on my part for his metaphysics. This is not because I am unsympathetic to the very idea of immediate, non-conceptual experience.[20] What I object to in Bradley is the *beatification* of immediate experience, whereby it is held to possess extraordinary virtues by comparison with which conceptual thought is but a pale and inadequate substitute. James Bradley has well shown how (F. H.) Bradley's conception of immediate experience involves a delicate fusion of

---

[16] *ETR*, 238.

[17] Bertrand Russell, *The Problems of Philosophy* (London: Williams & Norgate, 1912), ch. 9.   [18] *ETR*, 296.

[19] *ETR*, 255.

[20] Cf. my paper 'The Projective Theory of Sensory Content', in T. Crane (ed.), *The Contents of Experience* (Cambridge: Cambridge University Press, 1992), 177–95.

German idealism and British empiricism.[21] But there is a further aspect of Bradley's conception which he fails to bring out: its involvement in a late romantic Neoplatonism. It is this, I suggest, which stands behind his account of the relative merits of immediate experience and conceptual thought on this issue of predication and the unity of judgement.

Bradley's account of immediate experience is comparable to the account which Wordsworth gives of the experience of a child in his 'Intimations of Immortality from Recollections of Early Childhood' (I):

> There was a time when meadow, grove, and stream,
> The earth, and every common sight,
> To me did seem
> Apparelled in celestial light,
> The glory and the freshness of a dream.

Furthermore, just as, according to Bradley, in conceptual thought we lose that primordial unity of immediate experience, Wordsworth's dream faded with manhood:

> It is not now as it hath been of yore;—
> Turn whereso'er I may
> By night or day,
> The things which I have seen I now can see no more.

Finally, we can note that Bradley's response to the inadequacy of conceptual thought is straightforwardly Platonist: by an exercise of dialectic we are to make explicit within ourselves the ever present but half-forgotten background of immediate experience, and by combining this experience with the abstract rationality of conceptual thought we are to recapture at a self-conscious level the primordial unity from which, in bare conceptual thought, we were estranged.

It is this late romantic Neoplatonism in Bradley which leaves me cold. This is not because I am unmoved by Wordsworth, or, indeed, by the whole Platonist myth; it is just that I do not believe that such myths have a proper place in the discursive dialectic of philosophy—and certainly not when such matters as the problem

---

[21] James Bradley, 'F. H. Bradley's Metaphysics of Feeling and its Place in the History of Philosophy', in A. Manser and G. Stock (eds.), *The Philosophy of F. H. Bradley* (Oxford: Clarendon Press, 1984), 227–42.

of universals are at issue. None the less, I think I can set out Bradley's position in outline. His first claim is that immediate experience has a holistic structure whereby each aspect is conditioned by, and acts upon, every other aspect—'in immediate experience the whole qualifies every part while the parts qualify all and each both one another and the whole'.[22] This is supposed to provide us with a paradigm of unity in diversity, and it is as such that it provides the basis for Bradley's other claim, that conceptual thought, lacking the resources for a self-sufficient predicational structure, has to depend tacitly upon the kind of non-conceptual unity which immediate experience furnishes. Here is a typical statement of this second claim:

But when you ask for the unity, which in relational experience has come in and taken the place of the unity so superseded—you find that there is no answer. There is no unity left, except by a tacit and illegitimate appeal to that which the relational view has discarded. You can have the terms, without which you cannot have the relation, only so far as (in order to have the relation) you abstract from the former mode of unity, on which (to keep your relation, which requires some unity) you are forced vitally to depend.[23]

I want for the moment to bracket critical discussion of this whole line of thought, and to consider just its supposed implications: in particular, the support it provides for the fundamental claim I am examining, that no judgements are absolutely true. Bradley's line of thought is, I think, as follows: on the one hand, if a judgement is absolutely true, then its content is real and can be detached to stand alone as a fact. On the other hand, the conceptual content of judgement lacks the resources to 'unify' subject and predicate, or relation and terms, in a self-standing fact; so no such content can stand alone as a fact. Hence no judgements can be absolutely true. So far as I can see, if one is prepared to accept the premisses of this argument, it does deliver its conclusion. So at least this whole line of argument, this route to Bradley's paradoxical conclusion, does actually get us there— as long as we are prepared, for the sake of the argument, to entertain some contentious assumptions *en route*.

A question which arises here, however, is what all this has to do with 'external relations'—whose rejection by Bradley gave us

²² 'Relations', in *CE*, 631.   ²³ *CE*, 637.

the initial impetus for this line of thought. The answer to this is that the unity characteristic of immediate experience is of an entirely holistic variety, and since this is, for Bradley, the only genuine type of unity, it follows that reality excludes external relations—relations which do not have the requisite holistic structure. By contraposition, therefore, to accept 'mere external relations' as ultimately real would be to reject Bradley's account of unity, and thus, as he observes, to undermine this argument for the claim that no judgements are true.[24]

There might seem to be some tension here with Bradley's commendation of the intellectual virtues of coherence and comprehensiveness; for these are manifestly holistic, and yet, as we have seen, Bradley takes the view that judgement necessarily lacks the unity characteristic of immediate experience, which is the only genuine unity there is. The solution to this problem is that, for Bradley, possession of these virtues brings us nearer to truth precisely because, as he puts it, 'the aspects of coherence and comprehensiveness are each a way in which this one principle [sc. the holistic principle of unity] appears and in which we seek further to realise it'.[25] But, Bradley also holds, we can never attain absolutely perfect coherence and comprehensiveness: we always confront 'brute conjunctions where we seek for connexions'.[26] If, *per impossibile*, one were to attain perfect coherence, one would thereby pass beyond judgement, for 'Absolute truth is corrected only by passing outside the intellect. It is modified only by taking in the remaining aspects of experience. But in this passage the proper nature of truth is, of course, transformed and perishes.'[27]

I want now to return to the issue I bracketed before: that of what we are to think of Bradley's discussion of the unity of immediate experience and its relationship to the problem of universals. Bradley presents the matter as if, to use William James's phrase, 'the jungle' of immediate experience 'in which hallucinations, dreams, superstitions, conceptions, and sensible objects all flourish

---

[24] In my discussion of Bradley's treatment of unity in *G. E. Moore* (London: Routledge, 1990) I misrepresented him by ascribing to him a Kantian thesis to the effect that it is through the activity of the subject that judgement is unified (cf. 31). The present discussion is intended to correct that mistake, which was pointed out to me by Stewart Candlish.   [25] *ETR*, 231.
[26] *ETR*, 115.   [27] *AR*, 545.

alongside of each other, unregulated'[28] has a type of unity in diversity which is what is needed to elucidate the identity in difference of predication (the fact that different things can have the same property). I take this to be a pretty uninviting thought: even if we grant Bradley his holistic account of immediate experience, it seems just a massive *non sequitur* to suppose that this kind of structure is the only one available for an account of the structure of facts. The Neoplatonic theme in Bradley's philosophy provides some motivation for this supposition, but no defensible reason for it.

Is there any way to reconstruct Bradley's argument? I do not see much prospect of doing so on the basis of reflections about relations or universals. I myself favour a Fregean conception of universals as intrinsically 'unsaturated', so that the question as to how they combine with objects in fact does not require any further combinatorial relation; for this enables one to avoid the vicious regress to which, Bradley alleges, all conceptions of relations are vulnerable.[29] This still leaves open the issue of just how the identity in difference of universals is to be understood, and here I myself tentatively favour the view which assigns priority to 'tropes', particular property instances, as constituents of facts, with universal properties themselves as types of such tropes.[30] This, of course, is disputable; but I do not see such disputes as leading back to anything remotely like Bradley's position. The problem of universals and the non-conceptual structure of immediate experience belong to altogether different philosophical agenda.

But perhaps one should explore a different strategy. One point that Bradley seeks to establish is that conceptual thought is dependent upon immediate experience, and this is a thesis that we can get to by less contentious empiricist lines of argument. Take, for example, the familiar thesis that the conceptual content of the judgement that snow is white is dependent upon the non-conceptual content of visual experience; although this is disputed, there are, I think, quite cogent considerations in favour of it, associated with the thesis that colours are secondary qualities. The

---

[28] William James, *The Principles of Psychology* (2 vols., New York: Henry Holt, 1890), ii. 299.   [29] *AR*, 32–3.

[30] This position is developed by Keith Campbell in *Abstract Particulars* (Oxford: Blackwell, 1990).

interesting question is whether we can use this familiar thesis as a way of establishing the Bradleyan conclusion that no judgements involving such experience-dependent concepts are absolutely true. I cannot, in fact, see any defensible way of developing this point to lead to the conclusion that such judgements are not true at all. But, following Bernard Williams,[31] one might say that the truths in question do not belong to the 'absolute conception' of reality—where the 'absolute conception' is that which is in principle available to any rational being because it does not draw on any resources, such as types of experience, which are species-specific. Now although Williams's use of the term 'absolute' is intended to contrast with the term 'relative' (in that the 'absolute conception' is that which is not *relative* to any limited point of view), rather than to recall Bradley's metaphysics, it may none the less be wondered whether Williams's 'absolute conception' does not provide a way of reinterpreting Bradley's thesis that judgements which involve experience-dependent concepts are not absolutely true.

I think that this turns out in the end to be a mistake. For Williams, the 'absolute conception' is a slimmed-down conception of the world that has been purged of all concepts that are infected by relativity to a specific point of view, although it is also a condition on the adequacy of such a conception that it be possible to explain the existence and structure of these relative points of view with the resources available within the 'absolute conception'. Since this is basically the natural scientist's conception of the world, it is intuitively clear that this is a long way from Bradley's Absolute. The reason for this has much to do with their different attitudes to the issues raised by experience-dependent concepts. Whereas Williams's project implies that these concepts should be excluded from the 'absolute conception' because they are dependent upon our human point of view, Bradley simply takes it that this dependence upon experience makes it impossible for these concepts to yield judgements that characterize all by themselves things just as they are; in order for any judgement to be 'absolutely true', it should be altogether independent of such conditions as the non-conceptual structure of visual experience.

[31] Bernard Williams, *Descartes: The Project of Pure Enquiry* (Harmondsworth: Penguin, 1978).

Hence he holds that in order to obtain unconditional truth, one has to combine the experience with the concept in a way which then transcends judgement and the possibility of truth. Thus, where Williams's 'absolute conception' *excludes* experience in order to avoid relativity, Bradley's Absolute *incorporates* experience alongside conceptual thought in order to attain unconditional truth. Their starting-points, concerning the problematic status of experience-dependent concepts, are somewhat similar; but the reactions of the two philosophers to this problem are entirely different: Williams *subtracts* the experiential component from the situation in order to preserve the possibility of an abstract, detached representation accessible to any rational being, whereas Bradley *adds* this very component to produce a new kind of post-conceptual thought that is anything but abstract and detached, since it is constitutive of reality itself.

It would be a mistake, therefore, to seek to assimilate Bradley's position to that of Williams in order to provide a defensible reconstruction of it. Unlike Williams's aspiration to provide an abstract but all-encompassing representation, Bradley's doctrine rests fundamentally on his Neoplatonist hostility to conceptual thought; he thinks that judgement is inadequate as a representation of reality, because it excludes those aspects which are 'felt' but not 'thought'. Yet the recognition that in some respects our conceptualization of the world is dependent upon the non-conceptual structure of experience simply does not warrant this conclusion; it just implies that in judgement we can incorporate a sensitivity to the non-conceptual structure of experience.

III

The second way in which Bradley acknowledged that one might attempt to avoid his thesis that no judgements are absolutely true was 'by falling back on designation',[32] and this indicates what I regard as his other route to this conclusion, one which rests upon his critical discussion of designation or, as we might now say, reference. The grounds for this second argument are set out in most detail in *The Principles of Logic*. Because Bradley is anxious

---

[32] *ETR*, 230.

in this work not to enter into metaphysics, he does not usually assert here without qualification his thesis that no judgements are unconditionally true, though it does surface in his discussion of analytic judgements of sense,[33] and in his concluding remarks he hints pretty directly at it,[34] adding to these remarks in the second edition a note (n. 25) which connects them directly with the doctrines of *Appearance and Reality* with which I am here concerned. Certainly, too, in his later writings he explicitly connects the thesis that no judgements are true with his views about designation.[35]

The main premiss of this second argument is that there is no context-free, or unconditional, direct reference to particular objects. Bradley usually expresses this as a claim about the *generality* of all ideas; being, as he puts it, 'merely symbols', they are 'general and adjectival'.[36] Let us leave aside for the moment Bradley's reasons for this claim; what needs clarification first is why Bradley can infer from this that no judgements are true. The main extra premiss here is that 'the real is individual',[37] where, as Bradley explains, this does not mean that reality is a bare particular, but only that it is not 'general and adjectival'. For, once this is accepted, the final step seems relatively straightforward, given Bradley's conception of the relationship between truth and reality. Since a judgement is true just where its ideal content is real, if no such 'general and adjectival' contents are real, then, it appears, no judgements can be true.

Actually, this last step is a bit too quick. For even if one accepts that all ideas, and thus all judgements, are inherently general, and that reality is 'individual', why can one not hold that this individual reality has certain general aspects which judgements are capable of capturing truly? Even if, somehow, the nature of judgement rules out particular truths, why should this eliminate also the possibility of any general truths? The response which, I think, Bradley would offer to this objection would be to introduce his holism and argue that since all aspects of reality are interrelated as diverse parts of one unity, one cannot have the general truths without the particular ones. This is certainly the way in which Bradley defends his claim that all 'analytic judgements of sense' (judgements concerning one's present perceptible environment) are

---

[33] *PL*, 100. [34] *PL*, 588 ff. [35] *ETR*, 233–6, 262–5.
[36] *PL*, 45. [37] Ibid.

false.[38] But I want to keep clear of Bradley's holism in this part of the argument, if at all possible, since the holism depends on the account of immediate experience that I have already discussed critically. Moreover, I think this is possible. All that is needed is the thesis that there cannot be general truths without the possibility of particular ones; and this, I think, can be readily defended. If universal and existential instantiation from general judgements always fails to produce true particular judgements, then, by contraposition, it seems that the general judgements themselves cannot be true.

The way in which Bradley introduces and defends the premiss that 'the real is individual' merits some attention. He introduces it as a conclusion drawn from reflections at 'a level not much above that of common sense'.[39] Common sense is supposed to inform us that we 'encounter' reality in 'feeling and perception'; as such, its distinctive features are that it appears in space and time, resists our wills, 'acts' (by which Bradley means that it has causal powers), and 'maintains itself in existence'.[40] By this last condition Bradley means that its existence is not dependent upon anything else, and he singles this out as the most important condition, to the effect that 'the real is self-existent'.[41] This seems close to the traditional conception of *substance*, and Bradley, I think, has this largely in mind when he says that his condition can be re-expressed by saying that the real is 'individual' (a little later he says that the essence of reality is to be 'substantial and individual'[42]).

These claims are not in themselves particularly remarkable; what is remarkable is that Bradley allows himself to rely on the warrant of common sense for them, although he also acknowledges the need for further investigation: 'It is the business of metaphysics to submit these ideas to a systematic investigation. We must content ourselves here with taking them on trust.'[43] But we do not ourselves need to investigate these ideas further; instead, we can turn to his criticism of 'designation' and the

---

[38] *PL*, 94–5.   [39] *PL*, 44.

[40] *PL*, 45. It is noteworthy that Bradley concludes this list of the features of reality by remarking that 'truth has not one of them'; the implication appears to be that truth does not belong to reality—i.e. that no judgements are really true.

[41] *PL*, 45.   [42] *PL*, 46.

[43] *PL*, 45. Bradley in fact devotes the first chapter of Book II of *Appearance and Reality* to a vindication of this account of reality.

related thesis that ideas are inherently general. Bradley's claim is that thoughts cannot *all by themselves* designate, or refer to, particular objects.[44] He does not deny that we do succeed in particular reference. He writes: 'That in fact we are forced to use designation and cannot in life possibly get on without it, I suppose, is obvious.'[45] His claim is just that this success depends on contextual features which cannot be incorporated into judgement in such a way as to provide a context-free guarantee of success.

The straightforward case here is that of demonstratives ('This') and indexicals ('I'); for it is now a familiar point that these secure their reference from their context of use, and that the demonstrative or indexical content of the judgements thereby made is ineliminable. Where Bradley invokes Hegel,[46] we can invoke Perry.[47] Bradley makes two further points here which are worth noting: first, that demonstratives such as 'this' depend upon perception to secure their reference, since demonstration of an object involves *showing* it to one's audience.[48] This point is important for Bradley, in that it establishes a way in which the truth of the judgement depends upon experience. Bradley's second point is that 'the idea of "this", unlike most ideas, can not be used as a symbol in judgement'.[49] This is an obscure remark (Bradley calls it a 'subtle reflection'); but what he has in mind is just that because the reference of a demonstrative depends upon what is demonstrated in each context of use, it lacks a constant reference, and hence cannot be employed 'as a symbol' of any one thing. The demonstrative has a constant *character*,[50] so there is a definite idea of 'this'; but its *content* is variable, so the idea cannot be used as a 'symbol'.

Proper names certainly can be used as symbols in this sense, and present an obvious challenge to Bradley's thesis that there is no context-independent direct reference. Bradley recognizes the challenge here, but his discussion of proper names is brief and rather obscure.[51] He begins by arguing against J. S. Mill's view that names have no connotation, or meaning. Bradley observes

---

[44] For further discussion of this thesis, see Guy Stock, 'Bradley's Theory of Judgement', in A. Manser and G. Stock (eds.), *Philosophy of F. H. Bradley*, 131–54.
[45] *ETR*, 233–4.   [46] *ETR*, 207 n. 1.
[47] John Perry, 'The Essential Indexical', *Nous*, 13 (1979), 3–21.
[48] *PL*, 64–5.   [49] *PL*, 67.
[50] Cf. David Kaplan, 'Thoughts on Demonstratives', in P. Yourgrau (ed.), *Demonstratives* (Oxford: Oxford University Press, 1990), 34–49.
[51] *PL*, 59–61.

correctly that since grasp of a name includes an understanding of the criteria for individuating and reidentifying the object named, proper names certainly do have a meaning. He then moves from this point to the conclusion that, since the use of a name involves in this way grasp of general criteria, 'the meaning of such a name is universal',[52] as if this settled the matter. But this is not enough: Bradley also needs to explain why one could not take the view that, although grasp of a name involves grasp of the relevant criteria, for one who does grasp them, the name functions as a context-free way of denoting its bearer. Bradley's response to this, I think, would be that we have to rely on the context-dependent apparatus of demonstration to introduce us to the particular object thus named; as he would put it, the content of a *synthetic judgement of sense* involving a proper name depends upon that of demonstrative *analytic judgements of sense*.[53] It might be objected that, instead of relying on a demonstrative method of introduction, we could employ spatio-temporal parameters to uniquely identify the object. But to this Bradley replies that spatio-temporal parameters cannot by themselves guarantee uniqueness; for there is nothing in them to exclude alternative, though internally indistinguishable, spatio-temporal frameworks.[54] So 'the mere quality of appearance in space and time can not give singularity'.[55] Instead, 'we find uniqueness in our contact with the real, and . . . we do not find it anywhere else'.[56] Hence even though, thanks to their meaning, proper names are used as symbols to refer to one and the same object in a variety of contexts, the fact that they have the reference they do have is ultimately dependent upon context-dependent judgements involving demonstratives. So they do not, after all, provide a counterexample to Bradley's thesis that 'ideas are inherently general'.

Bradley has a good deal more to say in this connection, for the topic relates closely to his thesis that no judgements are categorical.[57] But there is no need to pursue the matter further, for the basic point is clear enough, and indeed seems correct to me. Yet it only implies that no judgements are absolutely true, if

[52] *PL*, 61.   [53] *PL*, 62–3, 75.

[54] *PL*, 63–4. Despite employing this argument, Bradley subscribes to the principle of the identity of indiscernibles; I am not sure how these points are to be reconciled.   [55] *PL*, 64.

[56] *PL*, 65.   [57] *PL*, 103.

'absolute' truth is taken to be truth without reference to any context; and yet once Bradley's thesis is interpreted in this way, it is no longer immediately problematic. Nonetheless, Bradley uses it as a springboard for the ascent to the Absolute, and I think one can reconstruct his line of argument in support of this conclusion as follows. The critique of designation shows that truth is context-dependent; so if one then introduces Bradley's identification of truth and reality,[58] it should follow that reality is equally context-dependent. But it is not clear what this amounts to, and anyway, it conflicts with Bradley's other thesis, that reality is 'individual'—that is, self-sufficient. So Bradley takes it that, to meet this latter requirement, we should bring together the demonstrative context of judgement with judgement itself, in such a way that we no longer have judgement at all, but a richer mode of experience whose content is no longer context-dependent and can be taken to be definitive of reality itself.

We may well doubt whether the hypothesis of this kind of metamorphosis of experience is coherent. It is indeed remarkable and wonderful that a butterfly can emerge from its pupal larva; but Bradley's Absolute has to be able to surmount logical, as well as empirical, obstacles. The crucial assumption in the argument I have attributed to him is that reality must be such that it can receive a context-free definition, if not from the contents of thought, then from the contents of some higher mode of post-conceptual experience. Yet surely the true moral of Bradley's argument is that this assumption should be rejected. One might say that in hanging on to this assumption, Bradley shows his position to be not so very different after all from that of the scientific realists whom he opposes. For though he will reject their claim that reality is given by the contents of scientific thought, he agrees with them that there is a kind of experience whose content will provide a definitive, context-free characterization of reality—for him it is the Absolute.

Yet what is it to reject Bradley's assumption while accepting his thesis that context ineliminably infects the contents of speech and thought? It appears to me that there is a hard choice here: either one must suppose that reality itself is not, after all, 'individual' and is somehow context-dependent, or one must abandon

[58] *ETR*, 113.

Bradley's internalist conception of reality. It is difficult to make much sense of the first alternative. Even if, say, the identification of space and time has an essential contextual element, the causal structure of space-time is not itself contextual. The contemporary philosopher who seems most ready to embrace the conclusion that the contextuality of truth infects reality itself is Jacques Derrida, as in his slogan that 'there is nothing outside a context' (*il n'y a pas d'hors contexte*).[59] But this turns out to be a crypto-idealist position, and most of us will be unwilling to follow him to this conclusion. Yet perhaps Derrida's 'contextual idealism' is the position for a Bradleyan who has abandoned the metaphysical illusion that there can be an absolute transcendence of contextuality. For the alternative of abandoning the internalist conception of reality as that which is ultimately given through the contents of experience is precisely the adoption of a realist conception of 'brute facts', in the form of the contextual situations of experience which ineliminably contribute to its content whilst escaping incorporation into it. In any particular case, it will of course be possible, at least in principle, to identify the context of a judgement and incorporate this in a higher-order judgement. But, for reasons which Bradley himself well expounds, such higher-order judgements are themselves inevitably infected by contextuality. So the role of brute facts, and thus the realist implication of this alternative, remains uneliminated.

IV

How, then, do things stand overall? I have been discussing the main thesis of *Appearance and Reality*, that thought can only attain its *telos*, truth, by recognizing the limitations of its conceptual structures and, in a happy suicide, combining them with the richer resources of immediate experience. At one level, this is a late Romantic vision of self-fulfilment with which we can all feel some sympathy. There is certainly much in our culture which echoes Bradley's dissatisfaction with a purely intellectual form of

---

[59] The slogan comes from Jacques Derrida's 'Afterword' to his debate with John Searle: *Limited Inc.* (Evanston, Ill.: Northwestern University Press, 1988), 136. The general theme of the contextuality of discourse is prominent in Derrida's discussion of J. L. Austin's work: 'Signature, Event, Context', in *Margins of Philosophy*, trans. A. Bass (Brighton: Harvester Press, 1982), 307-30.

life. But *Appearance and Reality* is not a work of ethics; it is intended to be a contribution to metaphysics, and it is as such that I have been examining its main thesis.

My conclusions are twofold, arising from the two lines of argument that I have attributed to Bradley. One, the line of argument that predominates in Bradley's later *Essays on Truth and Reality*, dealt with questions concerning predication, holism, and the unity of judgement. Very briefly, Bradley's argument, as I construed it, was that judgements cannot be absolutely true, because there is no coherent account to be had at the level of judgement of the way in which a property qualifies an object, or a relation combines with its terms. The problem of universals is insoluble when approached in the terms appropriate to judgement and truth. The solution to this problem, according to Bradley, lies in the resources available within immediate experience, in the holistic unity amid diversity that is exemplified there; but to bring this resource into thought is precisely to transcend thought towards the Absolute. This line of argument, I suggested, does not survive critical scrutiny: we can regard it as a fine example of Neoplatonism, but the hypothesis that the problem of universals receives its solution from the non-conceptual structure of immediate experience seems fanciful.

Bradley's other argument, which predominates in his early work *The Principles of Logic*, arose from questions concerning reference. The core of this argument is that reference is always context-dependent, and thus that there are no context-free truths which can be employed to provide an absolute, or unconditional, definition of reality. Bradley, however, assumes that because reality is 'individual', it must be possible to provide such a definition, and proposes combining the perceptual context of thought with thought itself to achieve this, albeit by thereby transcending thought itself towards the Absolute. I expressed some scepticism about the coherence of this last proposition, and argued that Bradley's argument should instead be regarded as calling into question the assumption that it must be possible to provide a context-free definition of reality. It is unclear what one is then committed to, but this conclusion certainly looks like a way of questioning the metaphysics of the Absolute. So, instead of accepting Bradley's call for thought's suicide, I suggest that we turn his argument against him, and call instead for the death of the Absolute.

4

Bradley's Theory of Truth

RALPH C. S. WALKER

———◆———

Bradley's views on truth are puzzling. He is often said to be a coherence theorist; but some of his remarks make him look like a correspondence theorist; and recently a case has been made out for thinking he holds an identity theory, whereby 'the truth of a judgement consists in the *identity* of the judgement's content with a fact'.[1] Things are not helped when we find Bradley equating truth with the whole of reality, in a manner that feels distinctly alien to us; or when we see that he is firmly committed to holding that, strictly, truth as we ordinarily understand it is not possible at all.

If we are to investigate what Bradley's theory of truth is, it is important to be careful about the expression 'theory of truth'. The various different things he says about truth may turn out to be answers to different questions, and it may be that quite different answers to quite different questions could each be entitled a theory of truth. Certainly this has been so in the philosophical literature since Bradley. It is at least not clear, for example, that Tarski's theory of truth is an answer to the same question, or even the same sort of question, as Austin's correspondence theory, or the redundancy theory in the hands of Ramsey. This is not the place to go into that issue; but an investigation of the various things Bradley says about truth may help us, at least, towards a clarification of some of the various questions that 'theories of truth' may be designed to answer.

---

[1] Thomas Baldwin, 'The Identity Theory of Truth', *Mind*, 100 (1991), 35. References to this article in the text are given simply by page number.

At first sight Bradley's least promising remarks are those that imply there is no such thing as truth, followed fairly closely by those that identify truth with the whole of reality. These sound incompatible, but they belong together, and the incompatibility is soon dissolved. Nowadays we automatically take truth to be a property of sentences, propositions, or something of the sort, and when he takes it in this way—as a property of judgements— Bradley's view is that there is no such thing as truth, strictly speaking. Every judgement limits and abstracts, and therefore distorts, the reality it seeks to capture. No judgement can capture it fully and still be a judgement, though the less a judgement distorts reality, the truer it is. Judgements, or thoughts, can therefore be related to one another as truer and less true, and when Bradley says that truth is the objective of thinking (*AR*, 145) part of what he means is that we seek to make our judgements as true as possible, and that it is of the nature of thinking that we should do so. He does mean more, however. The process of achieving greater truth is the process of capturing reality more effectively in thought. Because (discursive) thought can never capture reality altogether, the process leads to thought's suicide—its transcendence by a higher intuition (*AR*, 151) which is not discursive and does not involve abstraction. This higher intuition, in its completed form—with every abstraction removed and every limitation overcome—must, according to Bradley, be that totality of experience which is Reality itself. Fortunately we need not be concerned here with his argument for that. It provides him, however, with his reason for equating Truth with Reality: Reality itself is the unattainable limit of the series of judgements generated by the relation 'truer than'. Truth in that sense is Reality under another name and not, of course, a property of judgements at all.

BRADLEY AND THE IDENTITY THEORY OF TRUTH

Baldwin and Candlish ascribe to Bradley an identity theory of truth, though Baldwin says that the identity can be seen as the limit of a correspondence relation.[2] If to hold an identity theory

---

[2] Ibid. 35–52; Stewart Candlish, 'The Truth about F. H. Bradley', *Mind*, 98 (1989), 331–48.

is to subscribe to the identity of Reality with Truth in the sense just noted, they are certainly right. But that by itself is not much help towards an account of what it is that makes one judgement more true than another. Baldwin elucidates this in terms of similarity: 'one set of judgements is more true than another if the contents of the former are more similar than the contents of the latter to reality as it actually is' (39). But as Baldwin would no doubt admit, putting it in terms of similarity does not really clarify anything, and it might indeed seem potentially misleading to suggest that a judgement which is more or less true is so because it is *similar* to the state of affairs it describes. The traditional talk of correspondence would do equally well, and would avoid this, though of course it leaves Bradley open to the criticism that we need an account of what the correspondence, or the similarity, amounts to.

Baldwin finds the identity theory not only in Bradley but also in Hegel, the early Moore, and the early Russell. In Moore and in Russell it arises from a repudiation of the thesis that there is anything psychological about the objects of judgement or belief. That thesis they take to be a typical idealist error. In their view, the objects of judgement are real and objective entities, which they call propositions. Propositions exist in their own right, and not just in the minds or in the mouths of people. Some of them are true and some are false: but true propositions just *are* facts, and false propositions are non-actual states of affairs. Baldwin compares these with David Lewis's possible worlds.

Moore and Russell (like Frege, notably in 'The Thought')[3] saw this as allowing them to escape from an idealist argument they evidently considered dangerous, though to us it is more likely to seem simple-minded. This is the argument which goes: all our thoughts are ideas (ideas being mental entities); therefore all we can think about is ideas, and ideas are all we can ever know. Against this it seems adequate to observe that although all our thoughts are ideas in the sense that whenever someone has a

---

[3] G. E. Moore, 'The Nature of Judgement', *Mind*, 8 (1899), 176–93; Bertrand Russell, 'Meinong's Theory of Complexes and Assumptions', *Mind*, 13 (1904), 204–19, 336–54, 509–24, repr. in D. Lackey (ed.), *Russell: Essays in Analysis* (London: Allen & Unwin, 1973), 21–76; Gottlob Frege, 'The Thought', trans. A. M. and M. Quinton, *Mind*, 65 (1956), 289–311, repr. in P. F. Strawson (ed.), *Philosophical Logic* (Oxford: Oxford University Press, 1967), 17–38.

thought, a mental event is going on, it evidently does not follow that the thought is itself about a mental entity. Only complete confusion about intentionality would tempt one to think that it did. Brentano and Husserl use the term 'psychologism' for that confusion. My present thought is that my pen is leaking; it is obviously about my pen, and there can be no harm in calling the fact that my pen is leaking the 'object' of that thought. There is, of course, an issue here over how thoughts are to be individuated, and whether I could still be described as having that same thought if my pen were not leaking, or if I had no pen. But whatever one thinks about that, there is no reason to lose one's grip on the truism that my having this thought now is a mental event. However one chooses to individuate thoughts, if someone else has that thought, his or her thought is a mental event too—a mental event with intentional content. These thoughts cannot *be* the facts that make them true. What leads to unclarity here is partly the opprobrious use of the term 'psychologism', but more importantly the tendency to think of the contents of thoughts—propositions—as entities of a special and mysterious kind. If (say) one takes it that the same proposition is expressed on any given occasion of utterance if the same property is predicated of the same object, it is natural enough to go on and observe that that object's having that property is a fact (or alternatively, perhaps, a non-actual possibility), and then to equate the proposition with the fact or the non-actual possibility. But there is no reason to regard propositions as mysterious entities at all; it is just that two people are said to believe the same proposition if they both hold, concerning that object, that it has that property (or something of the sort). Their believing or thinking is itself psychological, and it is these psychological occurrences, or perhaps the verbal expressions of them, which are in the first instance the bearers of truth-value. Even if we do take such mysterious entities seriously, and ascribe truth-values to them, to equate true propositions with facts is to ignore the key question about truth, which arises just because we can know what somebody thinks without knowing whether it is true or not.

The question about truth is: What is it that makes certain of our thoughts, judgements, or beliefs true? What does their being true consist in? It is because Bradley recognizes this, and because Bradley is one of the people Moore and the others are reacting against, that it is not helpful to see him as a proponent of the identity theory of truth, despite the fact that he equates Reality with the Truth. For Bradley the Truth, so conceived, is not, and could not ever be, a property of judgements, as we saw. Every judgement, he says, has both a logical and a psychical aspect (*ETR*, 388), which is to say that it has an intentional or 'ideal' content, and is made by a particular subject at a particular time. It would be unfair to accuse Bradley of clarity on the status of the ideal content, or the 'what' as he often calls it; but it is of central importance to him that the judgement 'asserts this of something which is other than that content' (ibid.); it is distinct from the 'that', the reality about which the judgement is made.

Judgement is essentially the re-union of two sides, 'what' and 'that', pro-visionally estranged. But it is the alienation of these aspects in which thought's ideality consists . . . so far as in thought this alienation is not made good, thought can never be more than merely ideal. . . . Thought predicates an ideal content of a subject. This idea is not the same as fact, for in it existence and meaning are necessarily divorced. (*AR*, 145, 146, 148)

Certainly, by committing suicide, thought can get beyond this limitation, but thought is then no longer discursive thought: no longer the sort of thought that can be expressed in judgement.

Thus discursive thought, in aiming at truth, points beyond itself, and the ideal of truth can never be fully achieved by any judge-ment; as already remarked, Bradley regards the identity of thought with reality as the ideal limit in the series of higher degrees of truth. Thought is at that stage no longer discursive; one may well find its nature puzzling, but that need not concern us here. What seems to be more than puzzling is the idea of a scale of degrees of truth with this identity at the end of it. Baldwin's inter-pretation in terms of increasing similarity may help us to share Bradley's picture of things, but it does not remove the funda-mental incoherence, simply because identity does *not* stand at the end of a scale of greater and greater resemblance. Identity is not any kind of similarity or resemblance, but something quite different. Bradley would no doubt disagree with this; but his own view of the matter also seems to demand a sharp discontinuity at the point where judgement, or thought in its discursive mode, has gone as far as it can. The step beyond this is not a further step of the same kind. It takes us to something different altogether.

It takes us to a region far removed from Moore's concern, which was to determine the object of judgement, to a region where 'true' no longer functions as a predicate of judgements, but has taken on a life of its own. Bradley's overall position commits him to the view that ultimately, at the end of the dialectic process, all differences must be overcome, and hence thought must become identical with the reality which is its object. Thought, so conceived, is no longer thought as we know it; it is certainly not the thought that we are accustomed to assess for truth or falsity. It is therefore misleading to ascribe to Bradley an identity theory of truth. Truth in the ordinary sense consists in correspondence with reality: it is only at the limit, where thought has gone beyond thought and truth beyond truth, that he can say that 'being the same as reality, and at the same time different from reality, truth is thus able itself to apprehend its identity and difference' (*ETR*, 116).

It is worth noticing that, as Baldwin points out, it is also misleading—'strictly incorrect' (p. 42)—to call Moore's 1899 theory an identity theory of truth. This is because what Moore actually holds, at that point, is that truth is an indefinable property of propositions; reality can then be defined in terms of truth, as the totality of true propositions. Thus, Baldwin says, 'whereas Bradley uses the thesis that truth is identity with reality . . . to define truth, Moore uses it in the opposite direction, to define reality' (p. 42). Moore's theory, therefore, would be better called an identity theory of reality than an identity theory of truth, for it is not truth that he is defining: he is not telling us what truth consists in. The same point would not apply to the early Russell, who on Baldwin's account does think that truth *consists in* identity. So of course does Bradley, on Baldwin's view of the matter. But Baldwin also thinks he can ascribe to Bradley a coherence theory of truth, as people very often do. He observes, of course correctly, that Bradley regards coherence as the *test* of truth. Does Bradley also think that truth *consists in* coherence?

BRADLEY AND THE COHERENCE THEORY OF TRUTH

If the coherence theory of truth is the theory that truth consists in coherence, Bradley is not a coherence theorist. People who have talked and written about 'the coherence theory of truth' have usually taken it in this way, but there are exceptions. Some have taken it to be the theory that coherence is the test of truth. Others, perhaps, have taken it as the view that a judgement is true *if and only if* it coheres in some appropriate way with other judgements or beliefs. But just as it is misleading to describe Moore as holding an identity theory of *truth* just because he accepts that a proposition is true if and only if it is identical with a fact, so it is misleading to describe someone as holding a coherence theory of *truth* simply by virtue of their acceptance of the biconditional. Bradley accepts the biconditional. But he accepts it not because of something about the nature of truth. He accepts it because of something about the nature of reality. Reality is the one fully coherent and comprehensive whole. Our judgements are true just to the extent that they correspond to this reality, and the more adequately they meet the test of coherence, the more fully they will reflect the way things are.

In the rest of this essay I want to do two things. One is to render plausible this interpretation of Bradley. The other is to rebut an important objection: that I am drawing a distinction where there is no difference, in that to say that truth consists in coherence is just the same as to say that a judgement is true if and only if it coheres in the appropriate way. Reversing what may perhaps seem the appropriate logical order, I shall start with the interpretation of Bradley.

In its traditional form, as a theory of what truth consists in, the coherence theory of truth holds that the truth of a judgement or belief consists in its coherence with other judgements and beliefs, and amounts to nothing over and above that. Different versions of the theory have put forward different accounts of what coherence amounts to, but it must be a relationship between judgements or beliefs, and the important thing about these is that the beliefs are held or the judgements made. There are different accounts also of whom they are held by or made by, and under what circumstances: by the individual or the society, and under actual conditions (either now or at the end of enquiry) or ideal conditions, assuming these can be specified in such a way as not to render the theory vacuous. It would be rendered vacuous if they could be specified only as 'the conditions in which people believed all and only what is true'. What is important about the theory, however, is that the truth of a judgement becomes wholly internal to the system of beliefs. It is therefore not only a coherence theory of truth: it is a coherence theory of fact. What makes something a fact is that the corresponding belief is true, and what makes that belief true is its coherence within the system.

It is not inappropriate for a coherence theorist to talk of correspondence between beliefs and reality. Thus I cannot support my claim that Bradley was not a coherence theorist by pointing to the fact that he sometimes writes in this way.[4] For one thing, 'corresponds with the facts' is just a colloquial way of saying 'is true', and used in that common way it carries no loading of theory. For another, any coherence theorist will obviously grant that some of our judgements are true and some false, and that the true ones conform to the way the world is. Coherence with the belief system as a whole determines the way the world is, so that the world itself is not independent of what is believed or judged about it, but is still objective in the familiar sense of being independent of what I happen to think about it at the moment. If my present judgement coheres in the appropriate way, it matches that objective reality, and so stands in a relation to it which can harmlessly be called correspondence. In other words, the coherence theorist can readily accommodate the thesis that p is true if and only if it corresponds with the facts. What the coherence theorist rejects is just the thesis that the truth of p *consists in* its correspondence with the facts, where these are construed as obtaining in their own right and independently of the coherent system of beliefs.

The coherence theory of truth is counter-intuitive. That, of course, is no ground for not ascribing it to Bradley. But it has been found attractive for two reasons, neither of which Bradley seems to have found particularly congenial. One is epistemological. The threat of radical scepticism, represented by the mad scientist or Descartes' *malin génie*, has seemed to some absurd and intolerable; despairing of the standard attempts to defuse it, they have felt it can be removed only by removing the gap that seems to exist between our beliefs on the one hand and the world on the other. The coherence theory destroys that gap, by making our beliefs (or those of society) determinant of the nature of the

---

[4] Though see *ETR*, 118–20, which seems to go rather further.

world. The other reason is semantic. We can ascribe meaning to our assertions, it is held, only in so far as they can be verified. But they can be verified only by establishing their coherence with other beliefs or with experience. Now experience (it is argued) can be relevant only in so far as it takes the form of experiential judgements or beliefs, for it is only between propositions that evidential relations can obtain; so verifying a claim is always a matter of establishing its coherence with other beliefs. Once a belief passes these tests, however, there can be no further question as to its truth, for to suppose that would be to suppose some reality, independent of our judgements and beliefs about it, which could determine its truth or falsity. Such a reality would inevitably be verification-transcendent, and the supposition of it consequently unintelligible. There are steps here, certainly, which not all verificationists would accept; but some would, and these steps constitute a natural route to the coherence theory of truth, a route which Neurath followed, as more recently Putnam and Davidson have done.[5] If one takes this route, of course, one dissolves the epistemological problem of the *malin génie* at the same time.

Bradley thinks that reality is a coherent whole, but his reasons are neither epistemological nor semantic: they are metaphysical. This emerges in three ways. First, he recognizes the *malin génie* problem, and though he thinks that in the end it is not to be taken too seriously, his discussion makes clear that he has to hand no such straightforward dissolution of it as the coherence theory would have offered him. Second, his positive case for thinking of reality in the way that he does derives not from reflections on knowledge or meaning, but from the thought that it *must* be

[5] Otto Neurath, 'Soziologie im Physikalismus', *Erkenntnis*, 2 (1931), 393–431, and 'Protokolsätze', *Erkenntnis*, 3 (1932–3), 204–14, trans. as 'Sociology and Physicalism' and 'Protocol Sentences' in A. J. Ayer (ed.), *Logical Positivism* (Glencoe, Ill.: Free Press, 1959) 282–317, 199–208, and as 'Sociology in the Framework of Physicalism' and 'Protocol Statements' in Neurath's *Philosophical Papers 1913–1946* (Dordrecht: Reidel, 1983), 58–90, 91–9. Hilary Putnam, *Realism and Reason* (Cambridge: Cambridge University Press, 1983); Donald Davidson, 'A Coherence Theory of Truth and Knowledge', in E. LePore (ed.), *Truth and Interpretation* (Oxford: Blackwell, 1986), 307–19; repr. in A. Malachowski (ed.), *Reading Rorty* (Oxford: Blackwell, 1990). However, it is fair to point out that Davidson now denies that his theory is properly a coherence theory at all: see his 'Afterthoughts, 1987', in Malachowski (ed.), *Reading Rorty*, 134–8, and his article 'The Structure and Content of Truth', *Journal of Philosophy*, 87 (1990), 279–328.

like that; and I, at least, find the resulting argument much less convincing than the parallel arguments of coherence theorists like Green and Blanshard.[6] Third, his conception of reality, while in some ways like that of the coherence theorist, is importantly different from it. The nature of reality can never be captured by beliefs or by any relationship between beliefs, because reality consists in feeling.

The first point scarcely requires elaboration. The discussions in *Appearance and Reality* of scepticism and of things in themselves establish it beyond reasonable doubt. The objection to things in themselves is not that they would constitute a verification-transcendent reality; so far as it is not just muddled, it is simply that the hypothesis of things in themselves is redundant. It is also 'a false and empty abstraction', but the reason for saying this is that we have a different, concrete picture of reality which leaves no place for such unknown entities (*AR*, 113–14). The objection to Cartesian doubt is the familiar one that, after all, we have to take something for granted, and that if the doubter insists on pressing the matter, there is no answer that can be provided. It is true that he also says: 'We hold that our conclusion is certain, and that to doubt it logically is impossible. . . . It is impossible rationally even to entertain the question of another possibility' (*AR*, 459); but here the stress is on 'logically' and 'rationally': to someone who suggests that the world may not be a rationally graspable world, there is no answer to be given. There is nothing here to suggest that reality is like this because all it is for something to be real is for the claim that it is real to cohere with the system of beliefs.

The second point no doubt requires more elaboration than I can give it here; but the basic case for Bradley's position is set out in chapters 13 and 14 of *Appearance and Reality*, which start with the need to *assume* that 'Ultimate reality is such that it does not contradict itself' (*AR*, 120), and go on to interpret this in a rather creative way to produce some surprising results. Like Hegel, Bradley has a rationalistic view of the world; but he differs from Hegel in his grounds for it. For Hegel, who is a coherence theorist, it is grounded in the nature of truth: that reality is rational

---

[6] Thomas H. Green, *Prolegomenon to Ethics*, 2nd edn. (Oxford: Oxford University Press, 1884), book 1; Brand Blanshard, *The Nature of Thought* (London: Allen & Unwin, 1939), chs. 25 and 26.

is not an assumption, but a requirement constitutive of truth, and so of rationality itself. For Bradley, as for Descartes, it is an assumption we must make because we have to start somewhere, and no other starting-point looks tenable.

My third point was that Bradley's account of reality is different from, and incompatible with, the coherence theorist's. For Bradley, reality is a concrete totality of sentient experience—of feeling. Its character can never be adequately captured in judgements or beliefs, because judgements and beliefs inevitably involve abstraction. This, as we saw, is why they can never be completely true; truth is only fully achieved by moving beyond judgement, to experience itself. For the coherence theorist, on the contrary, it is judgement and belief that determine truth. There is no way in which reality can lie beyond the limits of what can be judged.

Bradley is therefore best described as holding a correspondence theory of truth—that is, of what truth consists in—though with two qualifications. Truth consists in a match between our judgements or beliefs and the reality they describe. The first qualification is that because of the nature of judgement and the nature of reality, Bradley thinks this correspondence can never be complete, so that no judgement or belief can be wholly true. The second is that Bradley in *not* one of those correspondence theorists who think it possible to give an informative account of what 'correspondence' consists in. Whether or not this can be done is of course a contentious matter; it may not be possible to say more than that the relationship is the one which holds when things are as they are judged to be. But the logical atomists thought it could be done, and when Bradley attacks what he calls the 'copy theory of truth', it is that idea he is attacking (*ETR*, 107–26, 293–309). More exactly, it is a presupposition of that idea. The copy theory holds that the world is divided into a great many discrete facts, corresponding to the very many discrete true judgements we can make. Bradley's objection is just what we should expect, knowing his view of reality. It is not the coherence theorist's objection, that reality is not independent of what is believed about it, but the objection that reality is not articulated in that way. Our judgements always involve abstraction, and therefore always distort. Reality itself is a concrete whole, not a collection of discrete items. Pertinently, Bradley asks how the copy theorist is to cope with disjunctive, negative, and hypothetical judgements

(*ETR*, 109), and that of course was something Russell saw as a difficulty. But Bradley's own view is not that such judgements do not correspond to reality—they do that as much as any other judgements do. His view is that they correspond to reality by capturing aspects of it, but aspects which are necessarily limited and abstract, so that such judgements are never fully and completely true. Nor, of course, are any other judgements, since discursive thought is inevitably condemned to abstraction.

My account has depended, however, on distinguishing between holding that truth consists in coherence (or correspondence) and holding that a belief is true if and only if it coheres (or corresponds with the facts). I mentioned earlier a fundamental objection, but postponed it. It was that there is no such distinction to be drawn. It is not very clear just what is meant by saying that A consists in B, or that A is nothing over and above B, or that B constitutes the nature of A. This is a question with wider implications, of course; philosophers are frequently concerned to promote, or confute, theses of a similar kind—for instance, that physical objects consist in sets of sense-data, or that mental events or mental properties consist in something physical. But it is not always clear what is at issue. This is particularly so with the relation between the mental and the physical, where (for example) it is hard to see what is at issue if one person contends that pain consists in the occurrence of a certain physical state, and another denies it but accepts that there is an unbroken (and non-accidental) concomitance between the two kinds of state.

The thesis that physical objects consist in sets of sense-data has sometimes been argued on grounds of meaning: statements about physical objects are said to be synonymous with, or at least analytically equivalent to, sets of statements about sense-data. This strategy will not do, however, in most of the cases where we want to say that A consists in B. A more plausible suggestion is that what needs to be established, at least to begin with, is not an analytic equivalence, but an equivalence which is metaphysically necessary. 'Heat is the mean kinetic energy of molecules' is metaphysically necessary, or so it is claimed; it gives us the essence of heat; it tells us what heat consists in.

However, there are equivalences that are metaphysically necessary without telling us anything about what consists in what. 'Has a shape' and 'has a size' are necessarily coextensive, and the necessity would seem to be of the strongest kind, though the properties are different; 'is born at *t*' and 'dies at some time later than *t*' are necessarily coextensive predicates, and the necessity must have a good claim to be called metaphysical; but there is no case for saying that being born consists in dying at some later time, or vice versa. The reason is that in each case the two expressions, though necessarily coextensive, pick out different things. They are predicative expressions, and they pick out different properties. Since properties belong to the real world, and are not our artificial creation, I doubt if there are sharp, general criteria to be found for their identity, any more than there are sharp, general criteria to be found for the identity of substances; but it seems necessarily true of properties that the same property can be instantiated at different times, and that properties involving relations to different times—like 'is born at *t*' and 'dies at some time later than *t*.—cannot be identified with one another. On the other hand, 'heat' also picks out a property—of material bodies, for example —but it seems very plausible to hold that 'the mean kinetic energy of molecules' picks out the same property (assuming, of course, that the molecules concerned are those of the thing that is hot).

Truth is a property, likewise, and someone seeking to say what it consists in is therefore seeking an alternative expression for that same property. An alternative expression for it will necessarily be coextensive, provided that it designates the property rigidly, as 'truth' itself does, rather than picking it out by some feature which applies to it only in an accidental way. This is one reason why Tarski's theory cannot be said to give us the nature of truth. It provides a precise specification of a property which is coextensive with truth within a given (artificial) language. But an account of what truth consists in would have to tell us something much more general than this. The concept of truth applies to sentences of all sorts of languages, actual and possible, and arguably to beliefs which are not linguistic at all.

To say that truth consists in (a certain sort of) coherence is to say that truth and (that sort of) coherence are the same property, but it is also to say more than that, for to say that A consists in B is to claim that there is something more fundamental about B than there is about A. This is sometimes put by saying that B is ontologically prior to A, or that B is metaphysically basic in a way that A is not; but care is needed here. Since the expressions

'A' and 'B' refer to the same property, the difference can only
be between the two ways of expressing it. The property itself
cannot be metaphysically more basic under one description than
another. The point is rather that one description is more illumin-
ating than the other, and also perfectly adequate on its own to
designate the property rigidly. We can say that heat consists in
the mean kinetic energy of molecules, because the latter description belongs to a wider physical theory; it places heat within the
context of this theory, and through being perfectly adequate to
designate heat, it enables us to see that there is nothing more to
heat than the theory provides for. Similarly, in trying to show
that truth consists in a certain kind of coherence amongst beliefs
or judgements, the coherence theorist hopes to make us see that
there is nothing more to truth than just this relationship amongst
beliefs or judgements, and thereby to illuminate what we are doing
when we call a judgement true.

Bradley has no such intention. For him, coherence is the test
of truth—but only the test.[7] He never claims that truth is identical with any relationship of coherence. Certainly, he holds that
judgements are true if and only if they cohere, and that this biconditional is necessary. But it holds not because of the nature of
truth, but rather because of the nature of reality. Reality is a
rationally coherent whole. One could perhaps distinguish Bradley
from the coherence theorists by saying that they are committed
to holding that if there were no judgements or beliefs, there would
be no such thing as truth: that property would not be instantiated. This might be so if there were no minds sufficiently complex to make judgements or hold beliefs—for a judgement, in the
sense in which Bradley and the coherence theorists use the term,
is always a mental act. Bradley is committed to no such conditional. Reality does include judgements, and given that assumption,
the class of true judgements and the class of coherent judgements
are necessarily coextensive (because reality is necessarily coherent).
But if it had not included judgements, that would not have meant
that there was no such thing as truth, though there would of
course have been no true judgements (and no doubt no true beliefs
either). For things would still have been *the case*, even though
there was no judging that they were.

---

[7] *ETR*, 202, 219. Here I am in agreement with Candlish, 'Truth about F. H.
Bradley', 337.

This way of putting it may be objected to, however. Metaphysicians, including Bradley, often seem committed to holding that reality *necessarily* takes the form that it does; so that to envisage a situation in which there were no judgements would be to envisage something impossible (or, as he would say, 'contradictory'). Such radical counterfactuals may be regarded as objectionable in any case, even (or perhaps especially) by those who lack such strong metaphysical sympathies. But the point does not need to be expressed in any such fashion. All that matters is that the two properties, being true and cohering in the appropriate way, are distinct properties for Bradley, even if they are necessarily coextensive; just as for many traditional theologians, being true and being believed by God are distinct properties, even though necessarily coextensive.

One may feel slightly reluctant to leave it at that, but this is because of the insidious idea that property identity is simply an arbitrary matter, or because of the equally insidious (though even less plausible) idea that property identity is fixed by language. If property identity were fixed by language, analytic equivalence would be the mark of it, and if that were so, heat could not *be* the mean kinetic energy of molecules. Properties, in any case, must be as real as the things they are properties of; it could not be that God made the substances, and left it to us and to our linguistic practices to determine what the substances were like. Since they are real entities, it must at least be intelligible to ask questions about their identity which are not automatically answered by our use of words. It is perfectly possible, no doubt, that certain issues concerning their identity might turn out to be arbitrary, as arguably it is arbitrary whether we identify the original ship of Theseus with the ship kept by the Athenians, which now contains none of the original timber, or with the ship reconstructed out of the original planks after they were removed, one by one, to be replaced. But it is evident that not all issues of property identity could be arbitrary, for an arbitrary decision can be made only in the light of something, and there must therefore be some facts about what things are like (and therefore about which things share what properties), in order for arbitrary decisions to be even possible.

Just because properties are real, and property identity is not determined (at least in general) by us, there is no reason to expect neat criteria by which questions of property identity can be settled.

Squareness as felt is so regularly concomitant with squareness as seen that it is obviously reasonable to put forward the hypothesis that there is one single property, squareness, which is both seen and felt. But this remains a hypothesis, though an eminently plausible one: the hypothesis that one single property of things is responsible for two different sorts of perceptual experience. The situation is much the same in principle when it comes to the identification of mental properties with physical or neurophysiological properties. If a regular and reliable concomitance were established between a certain type of neurophysiological state and feeling tired, or being in pain, or sensing a green quale, in each case the question would be whether it was not reasonable to hypothesize that there is one single property which we can be aware of in different ways—by neurological means, or just by having it. In none of these cases, of course, is it relevant to appeal to the content of the different concepts involved, because in none of them is it claimed that the concepts are equivalent—only that the properties they pick out are the same. Similarly with truth and coherence: the coherence theorists' hypothesis is that truth and coherence are one property, Bradley's that they are two. There is no automatic procedure for deciding between these different hypotheses, either in the case of truth or in the case of the mental and the physical. One can only consider the merits of the alternatives. What Bradley takes to be the merits of his own alternative I have already tried to indicate.

CONCLUSION

As I said at the start, different people mean different things by the words 'theory of truth', and that causes confusion. Sometimes they are concerned with analysing our ordinary use of the word 'true', as Austin and Ramsey were; what Bradley would have said about this we do not know, for he never attempted it. Sometimes they are concerned with the nature of truth, with saying what truth consists in. If the coherence theory of truth is a theory about what truth consists in, Bradley does not hold it. Nor does he hold the identity theory, if that is taken to be a theory about the nature of truth in the ordinary sense—the sort of truth that our judgements can have. On the other hand, if to be a coherence theorist is just to hold that coherence is the test of truth, then Bradley is a coherence theorist. If to be a coherence theorist is to claim that truth and coherence are necessarily coextensive properties, without claiming that truth consists in coherence, then again Bradley is a coherence theorist. And if to hold the identity theory is to make his peculiar claim about the ultimate identity of that very special thing he calls truth, with reality, then he is an identity theorist too.

Is he a correspondence theorist? I have called him one; but I have also pointed out that he firmly repudiates the attempts of those, like Russell, who seek to give an account of the correspondence in terms of relationships between discrete judgements and discrete facts. If a correspondence theorist is taken to be someone who holds that an informative account of the correspondence relation can be provided, then I think Bradley is not a correspondence theorist. But the correspondence theory is often taken to be the claim that the truth of a judgement consists simply in things being as that judgement says they are, and if that is what it is, then Bradley is a correspondence theorist.

5

The Wrong Side of History: Relations, the Decline of British Idealism, and the Origins of Analytic Philosophy

STEWART CANDLISH

———◆———

> Sherlock Holmes closed his eyes, and placed his elbows upon the arms of his chair, with his finger-tips together. 'The ideal reasoner', he remarked, 'would, when he has once been shown a single fact in all its bearings, deduce from it not only all the chain of events which led up to it, but also all the results which would follow from it.'
>
> A. Conan Doyle, 'The Five Orange Pips'

INTRODUCTION: THE SIGNIFICANCE OF RELATIONS

Even to philosophers with no special interest in the monistic idealism which so marked British philosophy in the late nineteenth century and beyond, it is perhaps no longer news that the picture of those idealists bequeathed to us by Moore and Russell stands in need of correction. But how distorted is that picture, and what should take its place? I doubt that there would be much agreement even among specialists on any detailed answer to these questions: there are still confusing factors at work. Many of these belong to that Moore–Russell legacy, such as the effect of their presenting the idiosyncratic Bradley as representative of so-called Hegelians in general. This effect can take two forms. What is rightly attributed to Bradley, we may wrongly attribute to other idealists. But it has been more common to attribute to Bradley what is true only of others. So for many years we had a picture of Bradley which was liable to mislead us about not only him but everyone else as well. The potential for confusion is compounded by the picture's power and simplicity, and by the fact that there is textual support for crucial parts of its detail, so that it seems to survive an independent check. As well, there is its constant availability in writings far more accessible and readable than those of the idealists themselves—for example, *The Problems of Philosophy*.[1]

We can add to this the persisting bad habit among commentators of treating Bradley's writings as presenting a philosophical position unchanging over time; while there might be a certain pleasing irony about that, and although he clearly was not the restless spirit that Russell was, it is asking for trouble just to assume, for example, that what he thought about relations near the end of his career in 1924 was straightforwardly the same as he had thought when writing the 1883 *Principles of Logic*.[2] Finally, there is another part of the Moore–Russell legacy: this is that certain anti-idealist conceptions characteristic of analytic philosophy (e.g. that of the black/white character of truth and falsity) became so deeply embedded in the common philosophical consciousness that some idealist doctrines important to the intelligibility of their views looked so obviously illegitimate that they became almost invisible to readers looking for rational argument.[3]

---

[1] Some indication of the influence of this book on generations of undergraduates is the fact that the library in my own university, never especially lavishly funded, has for decades had *eight* copies on its shelves.

[2] An illustration of movement in Bradley's thought, if any be needed, is his remark to Russell in a letter dated by Russell as November 1908 (now in the Russell Archives, McMaster University, to which I owe thanks both for a copy and for permission to quote), 'I do not now hold the view which I accepted from Hegel that any truth can be developed into all truth by us through its own dialectical incoherence'. The point is made less succinctly in the 1909 essay 'Coherence and Contradiction'; see *ETR*, 223–4.

[3] I owe this last observation (though he should not be blamed for my way of putting it) to Peter Hylton's magisterial *Russell, Idealism, and the Emergence of Analytic Philosophy* (Oxford: Clarendon Press, 1990). The present essay would no doubt have been completed had it not been completed in first draft before I saw this book. Hylton's view of Bradley is so much like my own, as expressed both here and in earlier publications, that there are many specific points of consonance which appear to have been arrived at quite independently. These, unlike points I have actually taken from Hylton, I have not noted individually.

I take it for granted that Bradley cannot be regarded as a typical idealist or Hegelian. But because Moore and Russell wrote as though a refutation of Bradley would be a refutation of idealism, any answer to our original questions full enough to engage with the detail of their arguments will involve comparison of analytic philosophy's inherited picture of Bradley with the original. Now significant parts of that picture concern the subject of relations, and include such claims as these: first, Bradley was opposed to relations, because he assumed the only possible propositional form to be subject–predicate; secondly, his attempted *reductio* of relations treats them illegitimately as objects; thirdly, he believed that all relations are internal, and what this means is that all relations are reducible to properties, or alternatively, that no relation holds contingently; fourthly, he held this view of relations as an axiom or dogma. This last ingredient may have been added in order to explain away Bradley's not recognizing that he had been refuted; presumably he was not open to argument on the matter.[4]

There is much in what Bradley says about relations which seems to fit the summary presented in the previous paragraph,[5] and the initial purpose of this essay is to evaluate its accuracy. This is a historical matter of some significance, for something like that summary has been important to analytic philosophy's self-image, an image which depends upon contrast with that of a benighted and vanquished predecessor, idealism. And one of the battlegrounds on which it did indeed seem for many years that idealism had decisively lost was that of relations. Many of us, at least of my generation, absorbed this story as undergraduates. And where the story has not been absorbed by younger philosophers, this will not usually have been because it has been questioned, but because they were left ignorant of it, perhaps through the confidence of their teachers that the battle could never be rejoined, perhaps through that contempt for history, especially of the non-canonical sort, which has so disfigured much analytic philosophy. Only in such a way, it seems, can one explain the near disappearance of the issue,

---

[4] The provenance of these elements of the picture is given in sect. 2 of my 'The Truth about F. H. Bradley', *Mind*, 98 (1989), 331–48. But they recur in surprising places: e.g. the second appears in Blanshard's 'Bradley on Relations', in A. Manser and G. Stock (eds.), *The Philosophy of F. H. Bradley* (Oxford: Clarendon Press, 1984), 215.

[5] We should note that Moore and Russell may have read Bradley in the way they did because it was easy to do so.

despite its having been central to the idealist criticisms of empiricist accounts of knowledge and experience, and despite the fact that Russell thought a correct account of relations to be critical for the vindication of mathematics. This disappearance is particularly striking when seen in the light of the persistence in recent philosophy of other characteristically Russellian themes, such as proper names, definite descriptions, and acquaintance. But that very centrality to idealism of its treatment of relations must also be part of the explanation for the disappearance in the twentieth century not merely of any serious discussion of relations, but also of idealism itself, and even of the early realism which was its immediate successor. For it was principally the topic of relations over which the idealists differed from their empiricist predecessors—after all, they shared Berkeley's hostility to the independence of the physical world, to the point that nineteenth-century arguments for idealism could seem mere perfunctory repetitions of Berkeley's own—so that once *monistic* idealism had been made to seem wrong about relations, the natural reaction would have been to reopen the possibility of an *atomistic* idealism, rather than to move to realism. The eventual result was, as we know, a return, via a brief detour into Moore's and Russell's early realism, to the empiricism which Bradley had so much despised. Both disappearances are graphically illustrated by subsequent events. As Manser has pointed out, although Russell in 1924 could still describe the question of relations as 'one of the most important that arise in philosophy, as most other issues turn on it',[6] the symposiasts at a 1935 Joint Session already 'found the doctrine of internal relations absurd'. (It is not insignificant that these symposiasts were Ayer and Ryle, both with many years of influence ahead of them.) And the infrequent subsequent commentators have found it hard to understand what all the fuss was about, as Bradley seems so obviously in the wrong. Yet as soon as one

---

[6] Anthony Manser, *Bradley's Logic* (Oxford: Blackwell, 1983), 120; *idem*, 'Bradley and Internal Relations', in G. Vesey (ed.), *Idealism Past and Present*, Royal Institute of Philosophy Lecture Series 13 (Cambridge: Cambridge University Press, 1982), 182. 'Bradley and Internal Relations' is only negligibly different from ch. 7 of *Bradley's Logic*. Manser is a welcome exception to the habit of treating Bradley's writings as exhibiting no change in view over time. I shall have occasion to refer to Manser's work on Bradley again, but to save space shall confine my references to *Bradley's Logic*, pp. 119–34 of which correspond to pp. 181–95 of *Idealism Past and Present*.

begins to read the original texts, it is hard to retain the artificial clarity of hindsight; this was surely one of the most baffling disputes in the history of philosophy. One of the reasons for this is that the participants themselves appear to have been confused about what is at stake.

I intend to sort this matter out for good and all. Yet it might be thought that this task is impossible. For example, Hylton (p. 11) says: '[I]t is . . . absurd to suppose that we can discuss the dispute over relations while leaving the nature of truth as an open question, to be resolved later.' But this remark is almost ludicrously pessimistic as it stands. (What further questions must be resolved before we can discuss differences over the nature of truth? And where do we stop?) Even were we to substitute 'settle' for 'discuss', the claim is still an exaggeration, for there is much about this dispute that can be settled, and even settled in Bradley's favour while baulking at his notion of truth. And the claim is contrary to Hylton's own practice, for he himself believes, rightly, that Russell did not succeed in straightforwardly refuting Bradley's view of relations. Of course, what Hylton was probably after was the more plausible idea that we cannot, as it were *sub specie aeternitatis* and in isolation from other philosophical commitments, answer the question 'Who was right about relations, Bradley or Russell (or neither)?' But the trouble with this question is merely that it is too coarse-grained: it can be treated as a compound of several others which may not all get the same answer, and as we shall see in what follows, some of them at least can be settled. To say this, of course, is not to deny what I shall try to show: that in order to *understand* Bradley's views on relations, one has to take into account some of his views about truth.

I begin with the question of whether Bradley did in fact hold that all relations are internal. (So far this is little more than a slogan. But it *is* a little more, for it at least contains a quantifier; practised readers of Bradley will appreciate that this imports a precision to the doctrine which could easily be lacking in any original. However, what exactly it comes to, and whether it was indeed an axiom or dogma for Bradley, are secondary to this question.) It appears to be clear that at least in the later part of his life he did not, as several remarks indicate.[7] The unfinished

---

[7] e.g. *ETR*, 239 and 312, from 1909 and 1911 respectively.

essay of 1923–4, 'Relations' (*CE*, 628–76), is perhaps the most outspoken. Referring to the very notion of the reality of internal relations, he says, for example (p. 642): 'The idea, I would add, that I myself accept any such doctrine as the above seems to myself even ludicrous.' Awareness of this fact has now begun to filter through into the literature. For example, Thomas Baldwin's *G. E. Moore* (1990), in its treatment of Moore's early retreat from idealism, contains a very fair and non-stereotypical account of Bradley's views on relations which acknowledges the problems in supposing that Bradley adhered to the doctrine of internality; but even there, the notion that there was some commitment on Bradley's part to internal relations still survives.

MANSER'S BRADLEY

The idea persists too even in work whose avowed purpose is to make us rethink our opinion of Bradley. A striking example is Manser's *Bradley's Logic*, in which the chapter to which we have already referred opens: 'It is generally accepted that Bradley believed that all relations were internal. To many recent philosophers this has been enough to show that he was either confused or silly.' Manser, although he regards his task as one of showing that Bradley was neither confused nor silly, does not go on to dispute this acceptance, but instead appears to concur with it. What he does do is to distinguish between two interpretations of the doctrine, an initial 'logical' view of how judgements are to be analysed which finds expression in the first (1883) edition of *The Principles of Logic*, and a later 'metaphysical' interpretation, associated with *Appearance and Reality*, which Manser describes as 'a falling away from the interesting and probably correct analysis of the nature of judgement and language which he gives in the *Principles*' (*Bradley's Logic*, 134).

According to Manser, then, there are two doctrines of internal relations in Bradley's writings, the first of which, that of the first edition of *The Principles of Logic*, is a sensible one concerning the analysis of the proposition. But, as we have seen, Bradley appeared at the end of his life to disclaim any adherence to internal relations. What, then, was he dissociating himself from at this stage? If we are to believe Manser, it could have been either or both of the logical and metaphysical doctrines. But the later essays give us no reason to believe that it was anything specifically logical—as opposed to metaphysical—at that later stage. What are we to make of this? Had Bradley forgotten about the earlier doctrine? Manser suggests that he had lost interest in logical issues by this stage; but another possible diagnosis is that there was no such earlier doctrine at all.

So let us have a look at the pages in which it is supposed to appear. Manser cites page 21 of *The Principles of Logic* as a crucial text (and one could add, using Bradley's own index, pages 10–11 and 22 as well). It is true that Bradley uses the phrase 'internal relation' on page 21. But I think that it is pretty clear that any impression that there is a commitment on Bradley's part here to anything which could in any interesting sense be called a doctrine of internal relations is merely the result of a kind of linguistic accident.

To see this, we should ask first what Bradley himself thought of what he had done. One way to come at this is via the index to the *Principles* (which he compiled himself for the second edition; there is none to the first). This contains a separate entry under 'Relations, internal', and this sole entry refers to a footnote belonging only to the second edition of 1922 and expressing the sort of view which Manser has described as a 'falling away'. The references in the index to the sort of view which Manser praises are under the heading 'Relation, in judgement'. This leads to my second point: that the two occurrences of the phrase 'internal relation' on page 21 are both in the context of a discussion of the relations holding among the material contained *inside the judgement* (not the reality about which the judgement is made, but the ideal matter, as Bradley himself calls it, the kind of intermediary between language and reality whose existence Moore and Russell came to deny in their early writings[8]). That is, the force of 'internal' in this context is no more than to distinguish between, on the one hand, relations within the judgement and, on the other, relations of the ideal matter to things outside the judgement. The same is true of the other occurrences of the word cited in the previous paragraph. In other words, the fact that Bradley uses the

[8] The theory of denoting concepts which we find in *The Principles of Mathematics* is an exception to this denial; but it is just that—an exception, brought in to deal with difficulties arising for the principal doctrine.

phrase 'internal relations' here indicates nothing at all about what sort of analysis of the proposition he is offering. It is a phrase which with equal justification and the same sense could have been used by the authors of the Port Royal *Logic*, by Mill, by Frege, by Russell—indeed by any of those with whom we might regard Bradley as in actual or potential disagreement over logical matters.

We have seen that if we search in the text of the first edition of *The Principles of Logic* for a doctrine of internality that is restricted to judgement, we find nothing that is identified as such. The same holds if we search for a denial of external relations in judgement. For example, in discussing analysis and synthesis in inference, Bradley says (*PL*, 471–2): 'In one case the whole precedes and is followed by its internal relations; but in the other case external relations come first and so produce the whole.' And in an endnote (*PL*, 494 n. 5) glossing this remark, he adds: ' "External relations." "External" means here "not falling within our *datum*." '[9] Even much later in his career Bradley continued on occasion to use 'external' and 'internal' in this non-technical sense, especially when speaking of judgement; and sometimes it takes very careful reading to discern this fact. Two significant examples, which seem to be universally unnoticed for what they are, occur on page 26 of *Appearance and Reality*, right in the middle of the famous chapter on relations![10] It would be hard to imagine a more effective way of causing confusion. I shall say more about this chapter later.

On the other hand, if we start to look in the *Principles* for a doctrine on relations which is not restricted to judgements, practically the first thing that we find (on p. 96) is an early version of Bradley's argument against, not the *externality* of relations, but the *reality* of relations (with no restriction as to type), in a full-bloodedly metaphysical version:

If relations are facts that exist *between* facts, then what comes *between* the relations and the other facts? The real truth is that the units on one side, and on the other side the relation existing between them, are nothing

---

[9] This too is clearly what 'external' means on p. 488. There are in *PL* other uses of the phrase 'external relation' that are more reminiscent of Bradley's later 'metaphysical' aspersions on externality; but these are hardly relevant to a claim to find a special logical doctrine of internality in that book.

[10] One must also read the beginning of p. 27 to get absolutely clear about these. Another example (where one has to consider the footnote as well as the text to get the intended sense) is at *ETR*, 326, in an essay of 1911.

actual. They are fictions of the mind, mere distinctions within a single reality, which a common delusion erroneously takes for independent facts.

In the light of this, it is perhaps no surprise that Manser says, 'There is a sense in which the doctrine of internal relations can be seen as a denial of relations' (*Bradley's Logic*, 129), for this remark expresses concisely a confusion between two different theses about relations which have both been attributed to Bradley: namely, that all relations are internal, and that all relations are unreal. And in doing this, it grafts on to the second thesis a controversial interpretation of its meaning. As we have seen, the second thesis is certainly expressed in the *Principles*, although not in the passages which Manser refers to; while the first, construed as 'the issue of the internality or externality of relations, as far as Bradley was concerned at this time of his life' (*Bradley's Logic*, 127), is simply not an issue at all.[11]

If we are going to identify how a 'metaphysical' question of the internality of relations ever arose for Bradley, we must look elsewhere. Certainly, when Manser comes to the question of how the later doctrine arose from the earlier logical point, he can find nothing better than 'a confusion between sense and truth' (*Bradley's Logic*, 132).

There is of course an objection to the points I have made so far in this section. It is that I have been making a lot of fuss about what is essentially a verbal issue. What does it matter, one might say, what label we apply to Bradley's theory of judgement? The point is surely that he had such a theory, and that it worked by denying that judgements are made by relating distinct ideas. It is this which is of philosophical interest and which Manser has got hold of. Whether we choose to call this a doctrine of internal relations or something else is essentially trivial.

There is some justice to this objection. Nevertheless, the matter is not trivial. For if we think of Bradley's theory of judgement in terms of internal relations, we are likely to assume, as Manser himself did, a more general commitment to internality, when (as I shall show) Bradley's relation to that doctrine was at least problematic. And we may start looking, as Manser did, for a way in which the earlier doctrine could have developed into some later

[11] If additional confirmation is needed, it can be found in Manser's further remark on p. 127: 'It is not explicitly "relational" propositions that Bradley is talking about, but any possible proposition.'

doctrine which might with more justice be thought to be one of internal relations, whereas, as we saw, one must attribute grossly fallacious reasoning to him in order to maintain that what is thought to be his later doctrine grew out of the supposed earlier one. Moreover, thinking this way is likely to lead us to misunderstand the earlier doctrine, which in fact is more obscure than the claim that the ingredients of a judgement are internally, rather than externally, related. Indeed, it is on the face of it hard to see how this claim could be an expression of Bradley's central assertion about judgement: namely, that in a judgement, 'The relations between the ideas are themselves ideal' (*PL*, 11); whereas, reminding ourselves that Bradley is consciously working with two senses of the word 'idea' (opposing the conception of the idea as a psychological entity to that of the idea as a logical unit), and remembering that he opposes the ideality of the logical unit to reality (this, in one version or another, is a constant theme in his writings over most of his life), it is much easier to see how this assertion amounts to a suggestion that, in a judgement, there are no real relations, internal or external, between independent logical units. This is what is right about Manser's view, but we shall always be tempted to misunderstand its significance if we think of it in terms of internality rather than unreality. The account of judgement in the early pages of the *Principles* is in fact just an early appearance of the later doctrine of the unreality of relations and of their terms applied to the ingredients of judgement. Its later extension beyond the ingredients of judgement needs no particular explanation. Indeed, given Bradley's commitment to the identity theory of truth, already evident in the *Principles*,[12] he could hardly have drawn the distinction between judgement and fact which Manser's distinction between the logical and metaphysical version of the doctrine of internality requires. What needs explaining is the initial confining to judgement, and the explanation is that Bradley was, as he said, trying to write a book on logic without getting involved in metaphysics.

But the problems with thinking of Bradley's theory of judgement in terms of internal relations do not stop there. For *clear and*

---

[12] I have discussed Bradley's identity theory of truth in 'Truth about F. H. Bradley'. The point I make here requires an emphasis on the presence of the identity theory of truth in *PL* which may seem inconsistent with what I said in that article about Bradley's attitude in *PL* towards the correspondence theory. This issue is taken up in an appendix to the present essay.

unequivocal expressions of the doctrine of internality, whether in an application restricted to judgement or not, are not common in his writings; and, lacking them, in our efforts to gain understanding, we naturally turn to the interpretations of Bradley's remarks which have become established in the literature as both demonstrating the presence of the doctrine and simultaneously giving its nature. These interpretations have some, at least, of their roots in hostility to the doctrine—they are presentations of it as ripe for refutation—and if we then understand Bradley's theory of judgement in their light, the theory may in consequence become as obscured as his position on relations has been.

I have discussed this issue at some length. This is because Manser's is the first concerted attempt to secure Bradley a place in analytical philosophy's pantheon; not only must it thus stand as exemplary, but any errors it makes increase the risk that previous misapprehensions about Bradley will simply be replaced by new ones.[13] And if Bradley is eventually going to be reinstated as a philosopher whom we can argue with, rather than merely wonder at, it is important that this should proceed on a secure basis.

INTERPRETING THE DOCTRINE OF INTERNAL RELATIONS

I remarked a moment ago that Bradley's position on relations has been obscured. This brings us to a matter I can postpone no

---

[13] e.g. the admirable Bradley scholar James Allard has not only accepted Manser's view of the treatment of internal relations in *PL*, but has gone on to use it as part of the basis for posing an 'antinomy' between Bradley's theory of judgement and his theory of inference, since, according to Allard, his theory of inference requires some judgements to contain more than one distinct idea, while his theory of judgement requires that judgements all contain only one distinct idea. But Allard's own description of the problem reveals that it can be posed without bringing in the notion of internal relations at all, arising as it does from the conflicting requirements that judgements are to have no relations inside their content and that they are to have some such relations. See James Allard, 'Bradley's Intentional Judgments', *History of Philosophy Quarterly*, 2 (1985), 475, and *idem*, 'Bradley on the Validity of Inference', *Journal of the History of Philosophy*, 27 (1989), sect. 2, esp. nn. 8 and 12.

Thomas Baldwin, in his elegant and insightful article 'Moore's Rejection of Idealism', in R. Rorty, J. B. Schneewind and Q. Skinner (eds.), *Philosophy in History* (Cambridge: Cambridge University Press, 1984), 357–74, finds in Bradley's thought a distinction in some respects analogous to Manser's, between essentialist and semantic holism, suggesting that the former is based on the doctrine of internality of relations, the latter on that of their unreality. I do not think the distinction is so neat. There are some hints as to why in my final section.

longer: namely, the question of how the doctrine of internal relations should in fact be understood. There are two standard interpretations in the literature. One is that to assert the internality of all relations amounts to asserting that no relational statement is contingently true; and this in turn is treated as entailing that all are necessary. This version is usually associated with Moore, but Russell too (in a letter to Bradley of 9 April 1910[14]) interpreted Bradley as making this claim. Given that any subject–predicate statement can be cast in the form of a relational statement, and that, as might well have been assumed at the time, there are no other irreducible propositional forms, this version amounts to the assertion that there are no contingent truths at all, and hence that all truths are necessary. The other interpretation, this time associated solely with Russell, has it that the doctrine is that apparent relations are reducible to properties. (This is connected with Russell's often-repeated charge that, for Bradley, the only possible propositional form was subject–predicate, a charge which sits uneasily with another standard Russellian allegation that Bradley's arguments sometimes rested on the 'trivial confusion' of subject–predicate statements with identity statements—i.e. the former are interpreted as the latter.)

There are remarks in *Appearance and Reality* which can seem to express a commitment to the doctrine of internal relations in general, and then more specifically in both these senses. Moore, for example, begins his famous and influential essay 'External and Internal Relations' by quoting from its index, 'Relations are all intrinsical', which looks hard to gainsay[15]—it is perhaps the clearest

---

[14] The complete text is reproduced in *The Collected Papers of Bertrand Russell*, vi: *Logical and Philosophical Papers 1909–13* (London: Routledge, 1992), 349–51.

[15] Though in my 'Scepticism, Ideal Experiment, and Priorities in Bradley's Metaphysics', in Manser and Stock (eds.), *Philosophy of F. H. Bradley*, 266, I had a determined try at gainsaying, and what I claimed there about Bradley's real view I still stand by. (The present essay is, in part, an attempt to make out what that real view is and how it relates to the doctrine of internality.) In n. 14 to that essay I simply asserted without argument or illustration that the references which we find under the index heading on which Moore relied so heavily do not state or even imply the doctrine. I was there anxious, perhaps over-anxious, to shake the common beliefs on the subject of Bradley and internal relations; and what I then said should be regarded as superseded by the more balanced account given here. Nevertheless, the reasons I originally gave for attaching little weight to the index of *AR* still stand.

apparent commitment to the doctrine of internality to be found in Bradley. While it is worth noticing, in view of what I said earlier about the interpretation of the word 'internal' in the chapter on relations in *Appearance and Reality*, that none of the references under this index heading is to that chapter, we do find, when we pursue them, such remarks as these:

That which exists in a whole has external relations. Whatever it fails to include within its own nature, must be related to it by the whole, and related externally. Now these extrinsic relations, on the one hand, fall outside of itself, but, upon the other hand, cannot do so. *For a relation must at both ends affect, and pass into the being of its terms.* (AR, 322; emphasis added)

Now this lends itself to the Russellian interpretation: first, its special subject-matter seems to be external relations, and secondly, it can be read as entailing the reducibility of relational propositions to subject–predicate propositions, in that version where the subject is one or other of the related items. It is also possible to find (e.g. on pp. 125–6) remarks which make it appear that the subject should really be the complex whole formed by the related objects taken together in their relation. On the other hand, the Moorean interpretation is obviously supported by such claims as this: 'There is a like self-contradiction in absolute chance. The absolutely contingent would mean a fact which is given free from all internal connexion with its context. It would have to stand without relation, or rather with all its relations outside' (ibid. 347).

One thing that may strike us here is that these two accounts seem not to amount to the same thing, for on the face of it a subject–predicate statement that a certain object has a certain property can be just as contingent as a relational statement. In order to make them the same thing, one would apparently have to maintain also that every property of a thing belonged to it essentially, something which it is difficult to hold without some elaborate justificatory machinery such as we find, for example, in Leibniz. And even Leibniz attempts to draw back from the consequence that contingency is an illusion, 'our ignorance set up as reality' (to use Bradley's words from *AR*, 517). But in so far as they are present in Bradley, he seems to move from one to the other quite indiscriminately, as though he himself saw no significant difference between the two (this is evident, e.g., as one continues to read down p. 347 from the quotation already cited), and he is openly hostile to the notion of contingency.

Perhaps the first thing that needs to be said at this point is that even if Bradley thought that any relational proposition is logically equivalent to some subject–predicate proposition—and we should recognize that attribution of such a thought is itself likely to be anachronistic (depending on our criterion of logical equivalence), and in precision goes well beyond anything that he actually does say—this would not have meant that he believed that relational propositions were reducible to non-relational ones; for he thought that subject–predicate propositions themselves involved relations between subject and predicate, so that any problems with relations would hardly be solved by attempting to eliminate them in favour of subjects and predicates.[16] Noting this important qualification, let us assume for the sake of argument that remarks like those just quoted are an expression of a commitment to some sort of equivalence between relational and subject–predicate propositions.

Given his hostility to contingency, then, did Bradley think at this time that every property of a thing belonged to it essentially? Alas, the situation is much more complicated than that, and to understand what it is, we must begin by examining note B to the appendix to *Appearance and Reality*. There is much in this note that is helpful for understanding Bradley's position on relations, but also much that is downright confusing, and we shall have to handle it very delicately. In it, he considers the claim that spatial relations are external. His examples are a man and a billiard-ball, and he imagines an opponent urging that it is just common sense

---

[16] See e.g. *AR*, 17, and *ETR*, 239; the apparent conflict between this and his *PL* account of judgement is merely apparent, for the account of judgement is an account of the status of those relations, as ideal not real. This is just another example of the perpetual difficulty encountered in giving any exposition of Absolute Idealism to a readership which does not share its assumptions, of saying what a denial of reality is if it is not to amount to a flat denial of existence. I have more to say about this in the next section, inspired by the most profound single remark on the subject, that of Wittgenstein, *Philosophical Investigations*, trans. G. E. M. Anscombe (Oxford: Blackwell, 1958), sect. 402: 'For *this* is what disputes between Idealists, Solipsists and Realists look like. The one party attack the normal form of expression as if they were attacking a statement; the others defend it, as if they were stating facts recognized by every reasonable human being.'

that these are unaffected in themselves by a mere alteration of place. His response is of the first significance for our topic:

But an important if obvious distinction seems here overlooked. For a thing may remain unaltered if you identify it with a certain character, while taken otherwise the thing is suffering change. If, that is, you take a billiard-ball and a man in abstraction from place, they will of course—so far as this is maintained—be indifferent to changes of place. But on the other hand neither of them, if regarded so, is a thing which actually exists; each is a more or less valid abstraction. But take them as existing things and take them without mutilation, and you must regard them as determined by their places and qualified by the whole material system into which they enter. And, if you demur to this, I ask you once more of what you are going to predicate the alterations and their results. The billiard-ball, to repeat, if taken apart from its place and its position in the whole, is not an existence but a character, and that character can remain unchanged, though the existing thing is altered with its changed existence. Everything other than this identical character may be called relatively external . . . but absolutely external it cannot be. (*AR*, 517–18)

It is very hard to assess this reply: conflicting pictures of the nature of the world are in play, and it may be that nothing more can be said *in argument* by either side to resolve the stalemate.[17] But one point can be made, if not exactly in Bradley's favour, then at least helping to make his view intelligible. It is this. What for him is at stake is the justifiability of the linguistic categories in which the common-sense advocate of external relations unhesitatingly conducts his discussion. Of course, this advocacy implicitly relies on those categories, such as term, subject, predicate, relation, attribute, and so on, so that its points, which are in effect points about how those categories work, will appear so obviously true as to make scepticism concerning their applicability ludicrous. But for this very reason the victory is hollow. To be worth having, it must be attained using a vocabulary which is neutral between the disputants, one which will at least allow Bradley to make himself understood. But there is no such vocabulary: we simply have no words for a billiard-ball, or a man, taken *not* 'in abstraction from place' (or from some other background).

---

[17] On a closely related dispute showing similar characteristics, and its eventual negative significance for Bradley's metaphysics, see sect. X of my 'Scepticism, Ideal Experiment'.

And this is no accident which could be remedied by the introduction of technical terms, for the difficulty is systematic, and the examples given are merely representative.[18] The stalemate, then, amounts to this: that one side attempts to conduct the argument in terms whose very legitimacy the other side is questioning, while the other side is unable to provide any other terminology in which the question can be framed non-self-defeatingly.

It is sometimes suggested[19] that Bradley's reply is fallacious, moving from the essentiality to a material object of some spatial relations or other to the essentiality of the particular relations it happens to be in. What I said in the foregoing paragraph may be regarded as a rejection of this charge. Bradley's claim, which the English language itself hinders him from making clearly, is that to think of the total particular situation in terms of *a billiard-ball* is already to have abstracted without argument, to have

---

[18] There are, of course, some terms which play a limited role of this sort in our language, like 'father', 'the current Premier of the State of Western Australia', and so on. But such terms are only partial redressings of the systematic linguistic shortcoming which Bradley is indicating, and they are relational. Neither should we forget that Bradley argued in *PL* that all language necessarily remains at the level of universals, and cannot without appeal to extra-linguistic resources enable the completely unambiguous designation of individuals. What I am saying about Bradley's procedure shows up a striking contrast (pointed out to me by Terry Diffey) between him and Collingwood: 'My reason for adopting this terminology is, chiefly, that it stands nearer than any other to everyday speech, and therefore begs fewer questions. The philosopher who tries to "speak with the vulgar and think with the learned" has this advantage over one who adopts an elaborate technical vocabulary: that the use of a special "philosophical language" commits the user, possibly even against his will, to accepting the philosophical doctrines which it has been designed to express, so that these doctrines are surreptitiously and dogmatically foisted upon every disputant who will consent to use the language: whereas, if the language of every day is used, problems can be stated in a way which does not commit us in advance to a particular solution. This gives the user of common speech an advantage, if what he wants to do is to keep the discussion open and above-board and to get at the truth. For a philosopher whose aim is not truth but victory it is of course a disadvantage; he would be wiser to insist at the start upon using a terminology so designed that all statements couched in it assume the contentions he is anxious to prove. And this in effect is what those philosophers are doing who profess themselves unable to grasp the meaning of this or that statement until it has been translated into their own terminology. To insist that every conversation shall be conducted in one's own language is in men of the world only bad manners; in philosophers it is sophistry as well' (R. G. Collingwood *The Principles of Art* (Oxford: Clarendon Press, 1938), 174).

[19] e.g. by Thomas Baldwin, *G. E. Moore* (London: Routledge, 1990), 314 n. 34. It should be noted that Baldwin's page references are to the old Allen & Unwin edition, whose pagination is very different from the Oxford edition now more commonly used.

divided the total situation into object plus (possibly unmentioned) surroundings. Once we have made that abstraction, then of course some relations will be external to the object; but unless we do, none can be singled out in any principled way as external. But the crucial point is that the very process of abstraction involved in thinking this way itself relies upon some relations being external to the object; for without such externality, no conception of an object, at all, is possible. As an argument for the externality of some relations, this appeal to common sense is plainly circular.

Now that we have observed Bradley's distinction between existences and characters, we are in a position to say something useful about the connection between the two interpretations of internality. For there is such a connection, and it is given in that distinction. How? Well, suppose that relations are indeed reducible to properties. The question I asked earlier is: Why should these properties be any more essential to their terms than the original relations were? And the answer is, of course, that they need not be; but this lack of necessity depends on a division of the properties of the object in question into essential and non-essential. And to make the assumption that this division is possible is already to employ Bradley's *bête noire*, abstraction, and to treat the object 'as a character', not as an existence. (It is worth comparing Bradley's hostility to the analytic/synthetic distinction, already evident in *PL*.) If we refuse to make this division, then we can plausibly be supposed to be committed to the denial of contingency (though it should also be added that we are equally committed to the denial of necessity, at least in any of its common understandings). And there is no doubt that Bradley does so refuse—albeit with a vital qualification whose significance we have yet to make clear.

The qualification is this: as Bradley insists again and again, he is not opposed to such division for practical purposes; he is just not prepared to regard it as the final truth about things.

THE DEVELOPMENT OF BRADLEY'S
VIEWS ON RELATIONS

We have seen that, of the two interpretations of the doctrine of internal relations, Russell's is unjustified, and that the remarks which appeared to justify it support, at best, a claim of equivalence between some relational statements and others, a claim which cannot amount to reducibility, but instead is closely connected to the Moore interpretation. The Moore version does at least seem to reflect Bradley's hostility to contingency. What we have yet to see is that Bradley rejects the doctrine, why he does, the way he does so, and, given that we have found passages which appear to express a commitment to it, what his relation to it actually was.

My thesis, briefly expressed, is this. Bradley does appear to be explicitly committed to the doctrine in the first and second editions of *Appearance and Reality* in 1893 and 1897.[20] We have seen reason to suppose that this commitment does not begin until after 1883, the year of publication of the first edition of *The Principles of Logic* (although a general hostility to separateness, which can be regarded as later finding expression in the doctrine of internal relations, is already present in *Ethical Studies*, published in 1876).[21] By the time we get to the essays of the period 1909–11 which make up a substantial part of *Essays on Truth and Reality*, whatever commitment there was is over, and the doctrine is rejected (*ETR*, 190, 238–9, 290–1, 312), albeit in qualified fashion, and this rejection is maintained until the end of his life, as the unfinished essay on relations in *Collected Essays* shows (see e.g. *CE*, 641, 646, 665, 667–8). Further, I shall argue that Bradley's commitment to the doctrine was based to a significant extent on a confusion with another doctrine about relations which he did hold to from 1883, at the latest, until the end of his life: namely, the doctrine of the unreality of relations; that in *Appearance and Reality* he moves from one to the other and back again, and perhaps was never clear that he had done this; that this confusion is understandable in the light of the genuine logical relationships between the two doctrines; and that it is over-attention to *Appearance and Reality* which, from Moore and Russell onwards,

---

[20] Hylton's more extreme suggestion, that 'Until he comes to defend himself against criticism, however, Bradley makes no real use of this distinction' (*Russell, Idealism*, 54), seems to me to need careful weighing against some of the remarks in the first edition of *AR*. (One would like to know what 'real' is being opposed to here.) But, as will become clear, in the end it hardly matters whether this commitment is merely a matter of appearance or not.

[21] See sect. 8 of my 'Bradley on My Station and its Duties', *Australasian Journal of Philosophy*, 56 (1978), 155–70.

has given Bradley the reputation of being the archetypal theorist of internal relations. (Though we should not forget the effect produced by controversy: Bradley, holding Russell to be committed to the reality of external relations, criticized him for this.[22] It would be only natural to infer from this criticism some commitment on Bradley's part to the doctrine of internality.)

We have already seen that in *The Principles of Logic* there is no commitment to a doctrine of internal relations, even in the sanitized form devised by Manser, and that the impression that there is, is based on a pun, but that matters look importantly different in Bradley's next major publication, the first edition in 1893 of *Appearance and Reality*. Yet the chapter of that book which is normally assumed to be an argument for the doctrine of internality, chapter 3, is in fact not easy to read that way. To begin with, it is not a treatment of relations and terms in general at all; rather, it arises directly out of the previous chapter's argument that reality is not captured by the attribution of adjectives to substantives, and argues further that the situation is not improved by dropping the substantives and treating reality as consisting of qualities in relation. (The terminology in the original exhibits this sort of fluctuation between language and the world.) However, Bradley himself occasionally substitutes 'term' for 'quality', so there is some justice in generalizing his argument and taking it to be a reflection of what he would say about terms and relations without specification of what the terms are, and I shall not press this point.

So, allowing that Bradley's discussion may be treated as one of relations and terms, we can turn to my second point, which is that most of what he says is about relations in general, without qualification.[23] The following remark, when read in context, is surely definitive:

The object of this chapter is to show that the very essence of these ideas [sc. 'the arrangement of given facts into relations and qualities'] is infected and contradicts itself. Our conclusion briefly will be this. Relation presupposes quality, and quality relation. Each can be something neither

---

[22] See e.g. *ETR*, 237 n. (from 1909).

[23] As I noted previously, there are two occurrences of the phrase 'internal relation' on p. 26, but, as can be clearly seen by going on to read the first four lines of p. 27 if it is not already obvious, both reflect the pun we have already observed in *PL*.

together with, nor apart from, the other; and the vicious circle in which they turn is not the truth about reality. (*AR*, 21)

However, in the middle of the discussion we already see signs of confusion about what it is supposed to be proving:

It is possible for many purposes to accept and employ the existence of processes and relations which do not affect specially the inner nature of objects. But the very possibility of so distinguishing in the end between inner and outer, and of setting up the inner as absolutely independent of all relation, is here in question. (*AR*, 23)

The first sentence in this second quotation suggests that it is external relations which are in question, and that the conclusion is going to be that all relations are internal; but in the second sentence we immediately return to part of the original issue: whether there can be terms without any relations at all.[24] If we read carefully, though, we can see that the main theme here is that there is something in principle wrong with the whole distinction between the external and the internal. He never resiles from this suggestion, and it recurs in his writings right up to his death. But it needs to be carefully separated from one easy to confuse with it: that there is such a distinction, but necessarily all examples fall on one side of it.

Unfortunately, such care is not always exhibited by Bradley himself, as for example in the following passage:

But the 'this' certainly is used also with a negative bearing. It may mean 'this one', in distinction from that one and the other one. And here it shows obviously an exclusive aspect, and it implies an external and negative relation. But every such relation, we have found, is inconsistent with itself (Chapter iii). For it exists within, and by virtue of an embracing unity, and apart from that totality both itself and its terms would be nothing. And the relation also must penetrate the inner being of its terms. (*AR*, 201)

And this looks like an unequivocal affirmation of the doctrine that all relations are internal, via the assertion of the inconsistency of *external* relations. Moreover, it refers to the very chapter

---

[24] I think that the idea of terms without any relation at all is hard for a present-day reader to keep in mind, because it is a question that for us seems not even to arise; so it is easy to overlook Bradley's opposition to it. The clue to its occurrence in his writing is phrases like 'the mere "And"'. On the intelligibility of the idea itself, see Hylton, *Russell, Idealism*, 26.

of *Appearance and Reality* which specially dealt with relations as proving this. Given the index entry that we have already noted as introducing Moore's classic paper, it is hardly surprising that Bradley was credited with the doctrine by both followers and opponents.

Any lingering doubts would now surely be removed by reference to the 1897 note B to the appendix, where Bradley not only is explicitly hostile to external relations (and does not remind us that this hostility might be based either on the belief that all relations are internal or on the belief that there is something wrong with the internal/external distinction, for he seems at this point himself to have lost sight of the difference between these alternatives[25]), but also comes out with the notorious assertions about the red-haired man, assertions which seem to go even further than Holmes's remarks about the ideal reasoner in my epigraph, and which look as though they amount to the claim that starting from, say, one's own red-hairedness, one would, in principle, be able to infer every other truth about the universe, which implies that everything is internally related to everything else.

But in later years Bradley becomes clearer about what he wants to say. In a letter to Russell of 28 January 1901 he insists that 'I don't hold *any* relational system can be consistent', and at least from 1909 onwards, he resolutely adheres to the view, most vehement and explicit in the 1923–4 essay 'Relations', that his hostility to externality is based on a rejection of the external/internal distinction, so that now he is openly hostile to internality as well:

Criticism therefore which assumes me committed to the ultimate truth of internal relations, all or any of them, is based on a mistake. (1909; ETR, 239)

Mere internal relations, then, like relations that are merely external, are untenable if they make a claim to ultimate and absolute truth. But taken otherwise, and viewed as helpful makeshifts and as useful aids in the pursuit of knowledge, external and internal relations are both admissible and can be relatively real and true. (1923–4; CE, 645)

---

[25] In fact, the latter belief does emerge briefly at *AR*, 513, but is immediately swamped by concerns about externality. My suggestion that Bradley was confused in *AR* is borne out by one of his own later remarks concerning what seems to have been a dialectical form of the doctrine of internal relations in that book, where he says 'I have perhaps fallen in places into inconsistency' (1909; *ETR*, 224 n.).

No relation is *merely* intrinsic or external, and every relation is both. (1923–4; *CE*, 667)

In other words, Bradley might even accept the view of, for example, Ayer in *Russell and Moore: The Analytical Heritage*, that relations are external or internal according to how a thing is described.

It is in the light of such remarks as those I have just quoted that we need to view claims like the following:

And Pluralism, to be consistent, must, I presume, accept the reality of external relations. Relations external, not relatively and merely in regard to this or that mode of union, but external absolutely must be taken as real. To myself, such relations remain unthinkable. (1909; *ETR*, 237)

The odd thing about Ayer's comments is that he seems to take himself to be offering a view which is a rival of Bradley's. Perhaps the explanation of this is that Ayer, unlike Bradley, would not have committed himself to the unreality of all relations, a view which, as we have now finally seen confirmed, Bradley held from the publication of *The Principles of Logic* in 1883 until the end of his life. But what does this doctrine amount to?

I take it that no one these days would suppose that it amounts to the claim that no relational statement is true (and we have Wittgenstein to thank for helping us to get clear about this). Or at least, if one wants to suppose that, then one has to do so on the basis of general considerations about metaphysics, which, as we shall see, will have the effect of condemning rival pluralist views as much as Bradley's, though Russell's anxiety over relations and their importance for mathematics may still have been based on some such idea, even if we associate it with Moore. Rather, Bradley's claim of unreality is simply that relations are not substances (*PL*, 52, 71, 187; *AR*, 9; *ETR*, 227 n., 289–90). (It is worth mentioning here that it would be no criticism of Bradley to suggest that no ordinary thing can be a substance either, for Bradley would of course accept that suggestion. For him, only the Absolute itself is substantial, so a successful attack of this kind would have to reject the legitimacy of the notion of substance itself. This possibility was not open to Russell, for his own views on particulars in 'The Philosophy of Logical Atomism' require that legitimacy, as he himself made plain.) As relations are not substances, there are no names of relations. This far, Bradley and the early Wittgenstein might be regarded as being at one over relations: 'Not "The complex sign 'aRb' says that a stands to b in the relation R", but rather, *that* "a" stands to "b" in a certain relation says *that* aRb' (1921; *Tractatus*, 3.1432, my trans.). Wittgenstein's remark concerning how relations are to be symbolized is one expression of the idea as applied to external relations,[26] and the Tractarian view that internal relations are shown and not said (4.122–4.125) is another expression of it in the other application. The big difference, of course, is that for Bradley terms are as unreal as relations (1914; *ETR*, 151 n.); and that is one of the reasons why Wittgenstein was a pluralist and Bradley a monist.

All this said, however, it remains that Bradley was more sympathetic to internal than to external relations, and he was careful to deny only their *ultimate* reality. The following remark reveals this: 'As to what has been called the axiom of internal relations, I can only repeat that "internal" relations, though truer by far than "external", are, in my opinion, not true in the end' (1911; *ETR*, 312). In view of this lingering sympathy, and of Bradley's own inclination to confuse the doctrine of internality with that of unreality, one may wonder whether there is some close logical connection between the two doctrines. Indeed, Baldwin, in discussing this question (*G. E. Moore*, 32–4), begins by quoting an explicit rejection of the doctrine of internality, and ends by alleging that Bradley is committed to both doctrines. What is the explanation of this?

In a metaphysical system one of whose governing concepts is that of reality in the sense of substantiality, the doctrine of internality is an inherently unstable position. It is unstable because things that are internally related do not have—by definition—the kind of independence that is logically required of substances, and yet without such independence they cannot be thought of as related *things* at all. Russell, in 'The Philosophy of Logical Atomism',[27] reminds us that each of his particulars 'stands entirely

---

[26] There is an interesting and entertaining, but ultimately unsuccessful, attempt to spell out Wittgenstein's point by Nicholas Denyer, *Language, Thought and Falsehood in Ancient Greek Philosophy* (London: Routledge, 1991), 118–26.

[27] B. Russell, 'The Philosophy of Logical Atomism', Lecture II, in *Logic and Knowledge*, ed. R. C. Marsh (London: Allen & Unwin, 1956), 201–2, and in *The Collected Papers of Bertrand Russell*, viii: *The Philosophy of Logical Atomism and Other Essays 1914–19* (London: Allen & Unwin, 1986), 179.

alone and is completely self-subsistent', having 'that sort of self-subsistence that used to belong to substance', so that 'each particular that there is in the world does not in any way logically depend upon any other particular'. There are, broadly speaking, two ways in which such independence can be achieved. One is the logical atomists' way: extrude complexity from objects into facts, so that complexes lose their status as objects and the substances are independent in virtue of their simplicity. Another is Bradley's: absorb complexity, so that the eventual sole substance has its independence in virtue of there being nothing else. (There are, of course, also attempts to have it both ways, such as Leibniz's.) But the point is that what systems of both kinds agree on is that internal relations not only are unreal themselves, because all relations are, but that they also undermine the reality of their terms, even if not everyone would like this idealist way of putting it. (It took Russell many years to come around to acknowledging this even implicitly, and even then it was Wittgenstein's influence, not Bradley's, that brought about Russell's change of mind on the reality of relations. Russell never acknowledged that Bradley had been right: the account of relations in the 1924 essay 'Logical Atomism'[28] is quite different from that of *The Principles of Mathematics*, and in that essay Russell, recounting Bradley's criticisms of his earlier views as though they were directed towards those of 1924, simply conceals the change of mind, and wrongly implies that Bradley misrepresented him.)

Once we see that the internality of relations entails their unreality, it need no longer surprise us that Bradley was more sympathetic to internality than externality, for internal relations wear the unreality of themselves and their terms on their faces, so to speak, because their necessary mutual connectedness precludes independence; nor that he was at one stage inclined to confuse the two, and sometimes seems indifferent as to whether he is trying to show that relations are internal or that they are unreal. For the former is but an indirect route to the latter. It should be

---

[28] 'Logical Atomism', in *Logic and Knowledge*, 321–43, and in *Collected Papers of Bertrand Russell*, ix: *Essays on Language, Mind and Matter 1919–26* (London: Routledge, 1994), 160–79. See esp. p. 336 (p. 173): immediately after quoting a Bradley criticism, without remarking that the criticism appeared in 1910 and concerned *The Principles of Mathematics*, Russell says: 'With regard to external relations, my view is the one I have just stated, not the one commonly imputed by those who disagree.'

no surprise either that he eventually became clear enough on the point to be able to make it explicit that the rejection of the claim that there are external relations did not commit him to the doctrine of internality, and that, when rejecting the doctrine of internality, he did so by stipulating carefully that it does not express the 'ultimate truth' about things, is not true 'in the end'. Even when, as we saw, he dismissed as 'ludicrous' the idea that he would accept the doctrine of internality, the doctrine is described as that of 'a relation which is asserted to be real ultimately and internal merely' (CE, 642).

An analytic philosopher is likely to get irritated around this stage, and ask brusquely, 'Does Bradley maintain that all relations are internal or not?' But the only accurate answer here, when we are dealing with his mature beliefs, would have to be: 'He does and he doesn't.' He does on a superficial level, as having a greater *degree* of truth than 'All relations are external', a rarely held view which does on occasion feature in Bradley's writings as the target of his attack. But he doesn't, if the comparison is with 'Some relations are external and some are internal', for this last expresses something about the realm of common sense which is not even in the same race as the doctrine of internality—the comparison itself is ill-judged. Nor does he maintain it if the comparison is with this genuine rival: 'The division of relations into the external and the internal is not exclusive and exhaustive.' He says these things himself—for example, 'No relation is *merely* intrinsic or external, and every relation is both' (CE, 667)—but we are blind to such remarks, or dismiss them as unintelligible, frustrating, or evasive. Yet, when we are not being philosophers, we allow such manœuvres without hesitation. Few of us, for example, would find it difficult to rank 'France is hexagonal' higher than 'France is triangular' in terms of degrees of truth; but who would want to say that either was completely accurate?

So it is hard for those of us reared in the analytic tradition, who probably absorbed without question the assumption that the truth/falsity distinction is a matter of black and white,[29] to keep

---

[29] It is easy for us to forget that this assumption is not obvious to those who have not received a twentieth-century philosophical training. Here, e.g. is Beatrice Webb's perceptive comment on one of the forces behind the assumption: 'Bertrand Russell's nature is pathetic in its subtle absoluteness: faith in an absolute logic, absolute ethic, absolute beauty, and all of the most refined and rarefied type. His

in mind in more than a token way the fact that the idealist
account of truth includes such a doctrine of partial and temporary truths which suffice for the business of daily life and for
the practice of science, logic, and mathematics, but which may
nevertheless be metaphysically inadequate in that they lead to
contradiction when fully thought through. And even an idealist
would hardly have embraced a metaphysics which treated the
statements 'Australia is chronically short of potable water' and
'Australia is not chronically short of potable water' as both just
plain false, with nothing to choose between them when it comes
to making a practical decision on, say, immigration policy. Thus
Moore's saying that it is just obvious that there are contingent truths,
and even Russell's demonstration that propositions expressing
transitive asymmetrical relations are irreducible and essential for
mathematics, are neither of them direct refutations of Bradley's
considered views on relations. Baldwin (*G. E. Moore*, 34–5) tries
to maintain that Bradley can, nevertheless, be condemned on the
basis of his methodology's coming into conflict with common
sense and lacking independent support. But to this it can be said,
first, that Bradley's methodological requirements grow naturally
out of those which common sense and scientific practice take for
granted;[30] and second, that, as we have seen, he is careful to take
steps to ensure that his metaphysics is not in competition with
common sense or any of the disciplines.

All the same, as soon as one leaves the level of common sense
and gets into metaphysics at all, some doctrine which has the
same purpose as this idealist one of partial truth is going to have
to be brought into play somewhere. Russell pretended to believe
that it was just plain false 'that there are no relations and that there
are not many things, but only one thing', jibing that 'Idealists
would add: *in the end*. But that only means that the consequence

---

abstract and revolutionary methods of thought and the uncompromising way in
which he applies these frightens me for his future and the future of those who
love him or whom he loves. Compromise, mitigation, mixed motive, phases of
health of body and mind, qualified statements, uncertain feelings, all seem unknown
to him. A proposition must be either true or false; a character good or bad, a
person loving or unloving, truth speaking or lying' (*Diaries*, ed. Norman and Jeanne
MacKenzie (4 vols., Cambridge, Mass.: Belknap Press of Harvard University Press,
1982–5); ii. 252–3; quoted in Nicholas Griffin (ed.), *The Selected Letters of Bertrand
Russell*, i: *The Private Years (1884–1914)* (London: Allen Lane, 1992), 249).

[30] For the argument for this, see my 'Scepticism, Ideal Experiment'.

is one which it is often convenient to forget'.[31] But thus hunting with the hounds of common sense, he could have had no realistic expectation that he would be allowed to run with the hare of metaphysics himself, and *in the end*, he too, who said 'I do not believe in complex entities of this kind', a kind exemplified by 'all the ordinary objects of daily life',[32] had to face the task of giving an account of their status that would preserve (at least many) ordinary truths about them while discarding ordinary falsehoods. And I think it may fairly be said that the programme of logical constructions has proved, in the long run, no more satisfactory a working philosophical tool than the idealist notion of partial truths. But things must have looked different at the outset, and the eclipse of the latter by the former must be explained at least in part by the notion of the logical construction's at least appearing to offer a workable programme, which its predecessor did not, completely lacking as it did a metric with which even a rough estimate of the degree of truth of an individual proposition might be reached. (The example concerning the shape of France involves merely ordering two easy cases, and anyway cannot readily be generalized. But it must not be forgotten that things may have looked different to an idealist. Here is Bradley on Hegel: 'No one who has not seen this view at work, and seen it applied to a wide area of fact, can realize its practical efficiency' (1909; *ETR*, 223).) And the long run is always arguably not yet over, so that even today the crucial test for the programme of logical constructions, the one which was supposed to demonstrate unequivocally the power and superiority of the new method—that is, the logicist account of arithmetic—and which was so spectacularly failed right at the outset, still seems to many philosophers merely to await the overcoming of a few difficulties for success to be attainable. (Even radical logicians like the paraconsistentists are inspired by the hope of rescuing this account from the paradoxes.)

---

[31] Bertrand Russell, *My Philosophical Development* (London: Allen & Unwin, 1959), 56–7. Russell is quoting there from his Aristotelian Society paper of 1907 in which he discussed Joachim's book *The Nature of Truth*. The relevant part of the paper is reprinted as 'The Monistic Theory of Truth', in Russell's *Philosophical Essays* (London: Longmans, 1910; repr. in 1966 by Allen & Unwin). On Russell's treatment of idealist writings on truth, see my 'Truth about F. H. Bradley', and Thomas Baldwin's 'The Identity Theory of Truth', *Mind*, 100 (1991), 35–52.

[32] 'Philosophy of Logical Atomism', in *Logic and Knowledge*, 190, and in *Collected Papers*, viii. 170.

BRADLEY'S ARGUMENTS FOR THE UNREALITY OF RELATIONS AND THEIR TERMS

Finally, I turn to what is, after all, the real issue, to which all that I have said until now is merely preliminary. This is the question of how good Bradley's arguments on the subject of relations and their terms are. I have left myself little space for this; my defence is that, without removing the undergrowth of confusion first, what is at stake here could never have been clearly identified, and that, once it is identified, matters can then be seen to be far more straightforward than the accumulation of commentary would have led us to expect. But I cannot hope, in the little space I have left, to do more than shift the burden of proof. As we have observed the doctrine of internality to be of secondary significance, we can concentrate on the question of the doctrine of unreality.

It is important to remember that Bradley's various arguments on this subject are a team effort. No one of them on its own is meant to show conclusively the unreality of relations or of terms, but each closes off one of the possible positions which an opponent might adopt. The systematicity this allows is most evident in chapter 3 of *Appearance and Reality*; but the presentation there is marred by the confusions already mentioned (though other versions are less tidily arranged). And it is important, too, to bear in mind that the question always lurking more or less visibly behind Bradley's arguments is: Are relations and their terms real? I have mentioned already that this question is the same as: Are relations and their terms substances?, and that the linguistic counterpart of this question, for him at least, is: Do names of relations and their terms figure in a language which accurately mirrors reality?

Bradley's most notorious argument, which, as we have seen, occurs as early as 1883 and is repeated in *Appearance and Reality* (27–8) as well as later writings, is the second member of a pair which works by excluding in turn each component of this disjunction: either relations essentially relate their terms (in the sense that there can be no such thing as a term-free relation, a 'floating idea'), or they do not. The first member alleges that if they do, then they do not exist independently of their terms, and are thus obviously unreal. The second member alleges that if, on the other hand, we try to deny this conclusion and insist that relations are real, then they would be themselves extra terms which would require further relations in order to link them to the terms which they were supposed to be relating (and so on *ad infinitum*). Given the technical sense which Bradley attaches to 'real', it seems to me that he is unanswerably correct in this contention, whether it is taken as a point in the philosophy of language about the analysis of propositions—that apparent names of relations are in principle eliminable—or as a point in metaphysics about the constituents of the world—that relations are not substances. Our modes of expressing relations are not names, and the relations themselves are not objects, and that is that. Even if one wants to say that nothing is, or could be, a substance in the required sense, it remains true that relations fall far shorter of the mark than do, say, material objects. Anyone who studies the debate of 1910–11 between Bradley and Russell in the pages of *Mind* (both sides of which are now available in Volume vi of *The Collected Papers of Bertrand Russell*), and compares the ontological extravagance of *The Principles of Mathematics* with the eventual parsimony of the 1924 essay 'Logical Atomism', can hardly disagree, and it is a source of continual wonder to me that Bradley can still be blamed for treating relations illegitimately as objects, when it is just that treatment that he is disputing. It has taken us too long to notice that when, for example, Russell wrote, 'Bradley conceives a relation as something just as substantial as its terms, and not radically different in kind', he was writing in 1927[33] from the comfortable position of having abandoned not only the ontology of *The Principles of Mathematics*, but also the 1910 theory of judgement, in both of which relations are just so conceived. No wonder that Russell, having surreptitiously switched sides to become the new champion of the insubstantiality and unreality of relations, could make his long-standing opponent appear, *ex officio* as it were, to have subscribed to their substantiality and, via this, to the denial of ordinary facts. (Notice too that Russell managed to change sides without apparently encountering any catastrophic consequences for mathematics.)

[33] Bertrand Russell, *An Outline of Philosophy* (London: Allen & Unwin, 1927), 263.

There is a standard reply to this regress argument which originates with Russell and is endorsed by Wollheim.[34] It is that the regress is indeed endless, but not vicious, being merely one of implication, and not requiring the actual completion of an infinite series before anything can actually be related. (Thus 'A and B are alike' implies 'A is like something which is like A', which in turn implies that 'A is like something which is like something which is like B', and so on, *ad infinitum* but unworryingly.) I think this reply, if it is to be effective, must be based on the idea that the goal of the argument is to prove the internality, rather than the unreality, of relations. (This is particularly obvious in Wollheim's treatment of the matter; though Russell is clear that Bradley's argument is against the reality of relations, his reply is so bound up with confused conceptions of meaning that it is hard to know what to make of it.) If we keep it in mind that the question at issue is whether or not relations are real, we can see that the argument's point is that an infinite series of actual *objects* is generated, not just an infinite series of possible names, so that even if the argument does not prove there to be a vicious infinite regress, it still threatens to show that the reality of relations requires an ontology embarrassing to anyone less easygoing than the Russell of 1903. But to see what the argument succeeds in demonstrating, let us take a familiar analogy. Suppose I am given the task of making a chain out of some loose metal rings, and when I come to join any two of them, I assert that we need a third ring to do the job, so that the most I can achieve is just

---

[34] See e.g. Russell, *Principles of Mathematics*, para. 99, and Richard Wollheim, *F. H. Bradley*, 2nd edn. (Harmondsworth: Penguin, 1969), 114. On my claim concerning the ontology of *The Principles of Mathematics*, consider the following extracts: 'Among concepts, again, two kinds at least must be distinguished, namely those indicated by adjectives and those indicated by verbs. . . . the latter are always or almost always relations' (sects. 48). '[T]he theory that there are adjectives or attributes or ideal things . . . which are in some way less substantial, less self-subsistent, less self-identical, than true substantives, appears to be wholly erroneous, and to be easily reduced to a contradiction. Terms which are concepts differ from those which are not, not in respect of self-subsistence' (sects. 49; the rest is irrelevant to the present purpose). What Bradley *was* guilty of in this debate was not doing justice to the details of Russell's own extended, albeit unsuccessful, attempt in *Principles of Mathematics* to reconcile the idea that concepts are terms with his recognition of the unity of the proposition. (On this attempt and its successors, see my 'The Unity of the Proposition and Russell's Theories of Judgement', in R. Monk and A. Palmer (eds.), *Bertrand Russell and the Origins of Analytical Philosophy* (Bristol: Thoemmes, 1996), 103–35.)

the addition of more rings to the collection. It is quite clear that no matter how many rings I add, I shall never get a chain unless I do something 'radically different in kind' from merely collecting more rings, something that I could just as well have done with the first pair of rings as with any of those subsequently added. Now as long as we think of relations as real—that is, as substantial in the sense which was common ground between Russell and Bradley (see the remarks from 'The Philosophy of Logical Atomism' which I quoted in the last section)—we are in an analogous situation. A relation needs to be something 'radically different in kind' from its terms.

A parallel analogy can be constructed to pacify those who want to protest with Wollheim (*F. H. Bradley*, 114) that things are in fact related, and that the problem is not to relate previously unrelated things, but to understand actual relational facts: suppose I have a chain and I want to understand its principle of construction. It is clear that I am already barking up the wrong tree if I begin by pointing out that the two end rings of an existing chain are linked by the intervening ones, for this account of linking does *nothing at all* towards explaining how two adjacent rings are linked; and if I try to pretend that there is some further ring intervening between adjacent ones, once more an infinite regress appears.

For the life of me, I can see no good reason why this argument has had such a bad press.[35] (There are, of course, historical reasons, some of which I have brought into the open here and elsewhere.) It should now be obvious that it would be an *ignoratio* to suggest that the argument ignores the fact that it is a matter of sheer common sense that there are related things in the world; for this is not in contention. What *is* in contention is

---

[35] The conventional wisdom on this matter is so entrenched that, e.g. Nicholas Griffin feels able to write of Bradley's arguments concerning relations, without further explanation: 'The defects of these arguments are by now well-known' ('What's Wrong with Bradley's Theory of Judgment?', *Idealistic Studies*, 13 (1983), 199). Compare too these remarks from Reinhardt Grossmann's book *Meinong* (London: Routledge, 1974), 67, where a true sentence is used as a licence for concluding a false one (I have italicized the revealing phrase): 'What Bradley's argument shows is, in the last analysis, that relations behave quite differently from non-relational entities when it comes to being related to something. Bradley, *needless to say*, is comparable to someone who concludes from our glue and board example that there simply can be no glue at all.' This conventional wisdom persists, in somewhat more vestigial form, in Leonard Linsky's 'The Unity of the Proposition', *Journal of the History of Philosophy*, 30 (1992), 273.

a philosophical account of the world's variety and relatedness, a fact obscured by the same word, 'relation', having to do double duty as identifying *both* the problem *and* an unsatisfactory solution to it. (It is hard to overemphasize the importance of that point, for the phenomenon is a widespread source of philosophical confusion.[36]) But even if this argument continues, perversely, to be rejected, Bradley has others on the subject which seem to me to have been underestimated or even ignored.

One of them is very close to the regress argument I have just sketched, and is directed against an assumption he claims to find in Russell's *The Analysis of Mind*, that 'every mental fact can be analysed in the sense of being shown to be a relational complex —where, that is, it fails to be an atomic unit whether as a sensation or a relation' (1923–4; *CE*, 656). Bradley takes this assumption to entail that all complexity must be treated relationally. And he asks, what of the relations themselves? They cannot be simple, for then they could have no internal provision for relating two or more objects; so they must be complex. Yet, if they are complex, they must themselves be analysable relationally; but then the same question arises, and so on, *ad infinitum*. The point resembles that which Wittgenstein made in the *Notes on Logic* against Russell's conception of logical forms in the period immediately prior to the production of the aborted manuscript 'Theory of Knowledge', a conception that was supposed to get around the problems posed by Russell's 1910 theory of judgement, but which required the forms to be both simple and complex. And both criticisms illustrate Russell's constant difficulties with the problem of unity and diversity, and his continuing attempts to resolve them by finding extra objects of acquaintance to do a job which no object, however peculiar, could possibly do.[37]

---

[36] A recent and telling example is described by Rai Gaita, *Good and Evil: An Absolute Conception* (London: Routledge, 1991), 74.

[37] For Wittgenstein's criticism, see the discussion by David Pears in 'The Relation between Wittgenstein's Picture Theory of Propositions and Russell's Theories of Judgement', *Philosophical Review*, 86 (1977), 177–96. Russell's tendency to try to solve problems by introducing objects of acquaintance to do the job, and Wittgenstein's opposition to this, extend far beyond the analysis of the proposition. See e.g. my ' "Das Wollen ist auch nur eine Erfahrung" ', in R. Arrington and H-J. Glock (eds.), *Wittgenstein's Philosophical Investigations: Text and Context* (London: Routledge, 1991), 203–26.

So far, these arguments have concentrated on relations them-selves, and their conclusion is that relations are unreal. This means that they do not constitute elements out of which complex wholes are constructed, but instead are 'abstractions' from those wholes, creatures of intellectualization. Provided we do not forget that this conclusion is not that reality contains no differences, but merely that these differences are not to be understood in the way that some philosophers have supposed, it can, and should, be accepted with equanimity. The same is not true, however, of another argument, one which appears first in *Appearance and Reality* (25–7), recurs in *Collected Essays* (634–5), and is intended to prove the unintelligibility of related terms. (It is again the sec-ond of a pair of arguments whose first member is a proof of the unintelligibility of terms devoid of relation. I take it that this first one needs no special attention, if only because any two terms whatever are related by similarity or dissimilarity.) My grasp of the argument is too tenuous for me to give more than a rough presentation of it, and I am afraid that rough presentations are all we ever get from Bradley himself. The key claim is that 'in order to be related, a term must keep still within itself enough character to make it, in short, itself and not anything diverse' (*CE*, 634). The point is, I think, this. Imagine two numerically different objects of which the same relational predicate holds true. By virtue of their diversity, they must differ in some other respect. (Bradley, at least as long as one is dealing with things at the term–predicate–relation level, held to the identity of indiscern-ibles.) That is, each term must have some other predicate holding true of it which the other term lacks. (This other predicate, although it may itself be relational too, must hold independently of the original relational one, or the terms would have no char-acter of their own.) But then the question of the relation between the relational predicate and the other predicate arises, and a famil-iar regress begins: an endless multiplicity of relations breaks out within the term itself. Of course, this way of putting the argu-ment is very careless about use and mention, but not in any way that affects the question of its soundness. (Rather, I have tried to make clear that Wollheim's criticism (*F. H. Bradley*, 115) of this argument, that the regress does not even begin because there is no relevant diversity internal to the term, is wrong.)

This attacks the reality of terms, albeit, as Bradley himself saw, using the attack on the reality of relations as a model (so that the significance of the issue of relations itself could easily be over-estimated), and its consequences are more far-reaching than those of the attack on the reality of relations. One could compare the logical atomist attack on the reality of complex objects; but the comparison will only take us so far, for the logical atomists were content with simple objects, while Bradley rejected these too. But notice again that the reality of relations eventually became a non-issue for Russell, after his surreptitious switch of sides on the question, as though he had come round to the view that mathematics and logic can survive on the reality of terms alone. Of course, a threat to the reality of terms would equally be a threat to Russell's class-based account of number (a threat which would have persisted despite all the twists and turns in that account in reaction to the discovery of Russell's paradox: monism and the axiom of infinity are not natural bedfellows); and this, together with the idea that mathematical truths are at best less than wholly true, should have been the primary focus of his hostility, which, in its early concentration on relations, misidentified its target. It is, I think, on the rejection of the reality of terms, rather than that of relations, let alone on his muddled and temporary commitment to the doctrine of internality, that we should regard Bradley's more extravagant monistic conclusions as being based.

Even on its most conservative interpretation, the outcome of the attack on the reality of terms will be that a language which tries to be faithful to reality by restricting its names to those of substances will have no such names. It will resemble the language which results from the application of Quine's version of the theory of descriptions, with the word 'reality' playing for Bradley roughly the same formal role as the universally quantified variable does for Quine.[38] But regardless of whether or not this particular analogy will take us very far, the point I want to stress is

---

[38] A point which, incidentally, shows the unfairness, at least on more recent conceptions of meaning, of Russell's charge, in *A Critical Exposition of the Philosophy of Leibniz* (London: Allen & Unwin, 1900; new edn. 1937, 50 n.): 'Mr. Bradley, in attempting to reduce all judgment to predication about Reality, is led to the same view [sc. that "substance remains, apart from its predicates, wholly destitute of meaning"] concerning his ultimate subject. Reality, for him, is not an idea, and is therefore, one must suppose, meaningless.'

that, as Manser tried to prove, this is a game which analytic philosophers know how to play in philosophical logic, just as their debates in the philosophy of science still often concern the reality of space and time, even if the vocabulary has changed. This, though, makes the near total, if gradual, collapse of monistic idealism start to look puzzling.

To explain this collapse, we have to look beyond the arguments. In case what I have said so far is not sufficiently convincing as an illustration of this necessity, it may help to add some brief reminder of how unsatisfactory even the best known of those arguments are. Consider, for example, Moore's famous article 'External and Internal Relations'. Quite apart from the issue on which I have laid so much stress, that of whether Moore even chose the right target in attacking the doctrine of internality, in the whole paper Moore's only *direct* argument against this doctrine was this: 'It seems quite obvious that in the case of many relational properties which things have, the fact that they have them is *a mere matter of fact*: that the things in question *might* have existed without having them.' (Similarly, Moore's sole direct argument against idealism in the 1903 article 'The Refutation of Idealism' was: 'I am suggesting that the Idealist maintains that object and subject are necessarily connected, mainly because he fails to see that they are *distinct*, that they are *two*, at all.'[39] It is not always observed that the tendency to question begging so noticeable in 'A Defence of Common Sense' and 'Proof of an External World' was there in 1903 as well.[40]) Or again, one might look at the well-known allegation of Russell that Bradley could not reduce asymmetrical relations to predicates. We can see from what I have already said that this allegation involves an *ignoratio*, and

[39] G. E. Moore, 'External and Internal Relations', *Proceedings of the Aristotelian Society*, 20 (1919–20), 40–62, and *idem*, 'The Refutation of Idealism', *Mind*, n.s. 12 (1903), 433–53, both repr. in T. Baldwin (ed.), *G. E. Moore: Selected Writings* (London: Routledge, 1993), 79–105 and 23–44 respectively. The first quotation is from p. 88, the second from p. 32, of *Selected Writings*. Bradley's unpublished notes reveal that he held Moore (as a philosopher) in contempt. Baldwin, *G. E. Moore*, 24–8, contains a useful and sympathetic brief study of Moore's relations paper, and assesses its achievement.

[40] These articles, originally published in 1925 and 1939 respectively, were reprinted in G. E. Moore, *Philosophical Papers* (London: Allen & Unwin, 1959). They can now most easily be found in Baldwin (ed.), *G. E. Moore: Selected Writings*, 106–33 and 147–70.

Bradley pointed this out himself. (Not so well known are the overwhelming problems which non-symmetrical relations posed, ironically, for Russell himself.[41])

Looking beyond the arguments demands an essay to itself, and all I shall do here is mention a couple of crucial factors. One is what seems to have been a genuine *fear* of idealism on Russell's part. This comes out again and again—for example, in passing remarks to the effect that any philosophy which deals in ideas will impose a veil between us and the world. Another is, as I have already stressed, that idealism had no particular veneration for mathematics, regarding it as just one human activity amongst others, and its truths, like all others, as merely partial. Compare that with this extract from one of Russell's letters (written in December 1901):

The world of mathematics . . . is really a beautiful world. It has nothing to do with life and death and human sordidness, but is eternal, cold and passionless. To me, pure mathematics is one of the highest forms of art; it has a sublimity quite special to itself, and an immense dignity derived from the fact that its world is exempt from change and time. I am quite serious in this. . . . And mathematics is the only thing we know of that is capable of perfection; in thinking about it we become Gods. This alone is enough to put it on a pinnacle above all other studies.[42]

Because of his general influence, Russell's *feelings*—not only his fear of idealism, but also his regard for mathematics—and his consequent loathing of a metaphysics which threatened to undermine the basis of that regard must be high on the list of causal factors in idealism's decline. It is tempting to see his arguments about mathematical relations as mere rationalizations; but however this may be, it is certainly true that the characteristic language of idealism is a vague, windy, moralizing rhetoric, almost intolerable to those whose standards of clarity are derived from

[41] For Bradley's response to the problems with asymmetrical relations, see 'Relations', *CE*, 670-2 n. 14. For Russell's difficulties, see Russell, *Theory of Knowledge: The 1913 Manuscript*, in *The Collected Papers of Bertrand Russell*, vii, ed. E. R. Eames (London: Allen & Unwin, 1984), esp. 85-9 and 134-5.

[42] Griffin (ed.), *Selected Letters of Bertrand Russell*, i. 224. The quotation is from a letter to Helen Thomas, dated 30 Dec. 1901. For an excellent brief account of the complex logical relationships between the vindication of mathematics and the refutation of idealism, see Hylton, *Russell, Idealism*, 167-70. (The account is developed at length in the subsequent pages.) My point here concerns not these relationships, but historically effective causes.

mathematics and logic, or from the painstaking efforts of G. E. Moore. Even if idealism's subject-matter is timeless, its style quickly became hopelessly dated. Another factor I have in mind is the gradual fading of the need for a substitute for religion. It is a familiar observation that conventional Christian belief waned under the impact of Darwinism. A less familiar observation is that idealism, providing a natural outlet for vague spiritual longings, waxed at the same time.[43] Once the lessons of Darwin had been fully absorbed, the need itself began to wane. Not independent of this is the impact of the Great War, after which it was harder to believe in the spirituality of the universe. And connected in turn with this impact is the decline of British imperialism, whose moral and spiritual mission had been justified by idealist philosophers, and undertaken by their pupils.[44] Those who rejected the imperialist destiny were unlikely to accept the views claimed to underpin it; while even those more sympathetic to imperialism might in the aftermath of the war look askance at a metaphysics seemingly tainted by association with the ideology of the Prussian state.

We, decades later, are in the fortunate position of being more detached from these causal influences, so it is easier for us to assess the arguments on their own merits. My verdict is that,

[43] David Stove, *The Plato Cult* (Oxford: Blackwell, 1991). This book manages the rare combination of being marvellously funny, impressively scholarly, and philosophically acute. Especially relevant here are the two chapters entitled 'Idealism: A Victorian Horror Story', and also the chapter 'The Jazz Age in the Philosophy of Science'. *Horror victorianorum*, which Stove suggests lies behind the philosophy of Karl Popper, is another factor which should be borne in mind when considering the decline of idealism. It is easy for us to underestimate the influence of such things, partly because they sit uncomfortably with the dignity of philosophy (and philosophers), but also because it is difficult now to recover what it was like to be in an intellectual climate in which the immateriality of the universe could be taken for granted. Some idea of the degree to which idealism had a grip upon the minds of educated people can be obtained from this remark by Thomas Hardy (who, it can be seen from the context, in this case is not speaking for one of his characters) in ch. 1 of *Tess of the d'Urbervilles* (1891): 'The world is only a psychological phenomenon.' Quotation in isolation cannot show, however, what makes the remark so striking and revealing when read in its original context, even allowing for the possibility of irony: its casualness, as though to make such an observation at that time were the merest commonplace.

[44] Cf. Heinz Gollwitzer, *Europe in the Age of Imperialism* (London: Thames and Hudson, 1969), ch. 12, and Anthony Quinton, 'Absolute Idealism', Dawes Hicks Lecture on Philosophy, British Academy, 1971 (Oxford: Oxford University Press, 1972).

whatever one thinks about the soundness of Bradley's arguments on relations terms and, it is clear that they were not refuted at the time, and that if his place in analytical philosophy's pantheon is any longer to be disputed, this must be on grounds of style rather than substance. But if we should begin to suspect that they might be sound, the consequences for metaphysics will be dramatic. No longer will it be possible merely to invoke, as, for instance, Armstrong does on more than one occasion, Hume's doctrine of distinct existences as though this sufficed to prove a point,[45] and the comfortable pluralism now so often just taken for granted by philosophers will have to be argued for all over again. No matter how much we would like to think otherwise, philosophy is always at risk of subversion by doctrines which reappear from the wrong side of its history.[46]

APPENDIX

Near the end of the second section I made a point which relied on the claim that Bradley was committed to the identity theory of truth in *The*

---

[45] See e.g. his *A Materialist Theory of Mind* (London: Routledge, 1968), 106–7.

[46] I thank the organizers for inviting me to the F. H. Bradley Colloquium, 1993, and the Australian Research Council and the British Academy for helping me to get there. But I also owe so much to Tom Baldwin that I can't help feeling it unfair that a philosopher's indebtedness to a colleague should so often express itself in criticism. James Allard supplied helpful written comments on an early draft, which I made use of in revision. Michael Morris pointed out serious omissions in an initial oral presentation of these themes at the University of Sussex, omissions which I hope are remedied here. Another earlier version was delivered as the Don Mannison Memorial Lecture, at an annual conference of the Australasian Association of Philosophy held at the University of Queensland. The affection and regard which Don Mannison inspired in so many people made it an honour to be asked to give this lecture, and I am grateful to Mary Mannison and to the Department of Philosophy of the University of Queensland for the invitation. The rewriting required to meet the reflective nature of the occasion led to many improvements. A subsequent draft included clarifications in response to comments of the late David Stove, while this final version has taken some account of comments at the Bradley Colloquium itself, especially those of Ralph Walker. I cannot neglect to mention my own university, The University of Western Australia, which has maintained, despite external pressures, leave policies without which it would now be hard to write anything at all, and also the University of Illinois at Urbana-Champaign, than whose administrative, library, and secretarial staff none could be more helpful, which gave me unrestricted use of its facilities during the period in which I wrote the first draft. I dedicate this paper to the memories of Don Mannison and David Stove, colleagues and friends.

Principles of Logic, and promised a discussion of whether that claim is defensible in the light of the account of Bradley's views on truth given in my 'The Truth about F. H. Bradley' (*Mind*, 98 (1989), 331–48; unless otherwise stated, page references in this appendix are all to this article). As we shall see, the significance of this question goes well beyond the matter which prompts it.

In that 1989 paper I argued, following a proposal of Thomas Baldwin's, that Bradley's theory of truth in his later writings was not the coherence theory, as is commonly believed, but one which could appropriately be termed an identity theory. I also said that truth was 'a subject on which [Bradley] changed his mind' (p. 335), and that Bradley's theory of truth in *The Principles of Logic* was the correspondence theory (p. 336). These last two assertions have been disputed (e.g. by Baldwin himself, 'The Identity Theory of Truth', *Mind*, 100 (1991), 35–52), but to defend them would seem to undermine the point made in the second section above.

It is natural to read my remarks as implying the suggestion that Bradley changed his mind over the nature of truth, moving from a correspondence to an identity theory. And critics have surely been right to reject this suggestion. Indeed, what I wrote even looks incoherent: having said that Bradley's theory of truth in *The Principles of Logic* was the correspondence theory, I then added that the book contained a series of objections to the correspondence theory of truth which 'amount to a kind of roll-call of the kind of problems for the correspondence theory to which only the theory of truth-functions eventually provided a solution (if even then)' (p. 341).

But the incoherence, if any, lies in Bradley's own text, and what is wrong with any suggestion of a change of mind lies in the implication that Bradley first held one view and then held another. As I went on to make clear, the correspondence and the identity theories are present at the same time in *Principles*; but while the correspondence theory is presented as the theory which is presupposed in logic—which, after all, is what the book is about—it is never advocated by Bradley as the ultimately correct account of truth.

But arriving at an ultimately correct account is, Bradley thinks, the business of metaphysics, whereas the concern of *Principles* with logic, whose presuppositions may include theories which he would regard as ultimately indefensible (however necessary they may be for the practice of argument), allows him to work in terms of the correspondence theory. For this reason, the presence of the identity theory of truth in *Principles* does not imply the absence of the correspondence theory. But the full ambivalence between logic and metaphysics, an ambivalence which pervades the book and affects far more in it than just the question of the nature of truth, appears with great clarity in the following passage, which stands as a corrective to what I wrote previously:

An idea is symbolic, and in every symbol we separate what it *means* from that which it stands for. A sign indicates or points to something other than itself; and it does this by conveying, artificially or naturally, those attributes of the thing by which we recognize it. A word, we may say, never quite means what it stands for or stands for what it means. For the qualities of the fact, by which it is recognized and which correspond to the content of the sign, are not the fact itself. Even with abstracts the actual case of the quality is hardly nothing but the quality itself. The ideas and the reality are presumed to be different.

It is perhaps an ideal we secretly cherish, that words should mean what they stand for and stand for what they mean. And in metaphysics we should be forced to consider seriously the claim of this ideal. But for logical purposes it is better to ignore it. It is better to assume that the meaning is other than the fact of which the meaning is true. The fact is an individual or individuals, and the idea itself is an universal. (*PL*, 168)

Here we see how wrong it is to imply a 'change of mind' on Bradley's part over the nature of truth, for this passage shows that he was not *minded* to hold the correspondence theory at all, at least as an account of complete, rather than merely partial, truth. But it also displays the correctness of the more important claim: that 'there is an "official" correspondence theory in *The Principles of Logic*, for the temporary purpose of suiting the presuppositions of logic' (p. 336), even if Bradley himself did not wish to endorse it as the last word on the matter. Bradley makes this clear in one of the notes added to the 1922, second edition of *Principles*:

The attempt, made at times in this work for the sake of convenience . . . to identify reality with the series of facts, and truth with copying [sc. correspondence]— was, I think, misjudged. It arose from my wish to limit the subject, and to avoid metaphysics, since . . . I was not prepared there to give a final answer. But the result of this half-hearted attempt was an inconsistency, which in this Chapter is admitted. (*PL*, 591–2)

The inconsistency to which Bradley refers is one which arises between metaphysics and logic. What we are to make of a metaphysics which claims that theories whose truth is necessary for the practice of reasoning are ultimately indefensible is a question which, while unavoidable in any assessment of the overall coherence of Bradley's views, is fortunately beyond the scope of a mere appendix. On the face of it, of course, the metaphysics has to give way, since its conclusions appear to undercut the arguments which get us to those very conclusions. One way in which Bradley can attempt to evade this obvious difficulty is by exploiting his doctrine of degrees of truth, which is meant to do justice to the claims of logic, science, and common sense, while denying them ultimate truth. In the present essay I have tried, amongst other things, to show how important to Bradley's metaphysics that doctrine is. If that is right, then

the claim made here (a claim made previously by Wollheim, and by Hylton, though it is not clear that either saw quite how dee that the doctrine appears to provide not even an approximate the estimation of degrees of truth in any particular case, is, if mortal blow to that metaphysics.

6

Did Russell's Criticisms of Bradley's Theory of Relations Miss their Mark?

NICHOLAS GRIFFIN

———————•———————

In *The Principles of Mathematics*[1] Russell considers two ways in which it might be supposed that relations could be eliminated in favour of intrinsic properties.[2] The first, which he calls 'the monadistic theory', attempts to eliminate relations in favour of intrinsic properties of their terms taken individually. On the monadistic theory, the relational proposition '*aRb*' is to be replaced by a pair of propositions '*ar*$_1$' and '*br*$_2$', 'which give to *a* and *b* respectively adjectives supposed to be together equivalent to *R*' (p. 221). The other theory, 'the monistic theory', 'holds that every relational proposition *aRb* is to be resolved into a proposition concerning the whole which *a* and *b* compose—a proposition which we may denote by *(ab)r*' (p. 224). Of these two views, he goes on to say, 'the first is represented by Leibniz and (on the whole) by Lotze, the second by Spinoza and Mr. Bradley' (p. 221). Russell goes on to produce cogent refutations of both theories. My concern here is not with his refutation, but merely with his remark that the monistic theory was Bradley's.[3]

---

[1] Bertrand Russell, *The Principles of Mathematics* (London: Allen & Unwin, 1964; 1st edn. 1903), 221–6; subsequent page references are given in parentheses in the text.

[2] An 'intrinsic property' is any property ϕ such that no contingent claim can be inferred from '$\phi(a)$', without other premises, about any term *b* distinct from *a*.

[3] Russell repeats the attribution in *My Philosophical Development* (London: Allen & Unwin, 1959), 54.

In assessing Russell's remark, two things are obvious: (i) that Bradley rejected relations; (ii) that many significant judgements are, at least putatively, of relational form. It follows from this that Bradley must have thought that there was some way in which what was expressed by the putatively relational judgements could be expressed without the use of relations. And this, in turn, suggests the need for some mechanism for eliminating relations. The question I am concerned with is whether Russell was right to think that the mechanism Bradley favoured was the monistic theory of relations. Several commentators have argued that it was not.[4]

Russell's monistic theory, as an account of Bradley's theory of relational judgements, may be objected to on three grounds. In the first place, it may be objected that Bradley sought to reduce all judgements to a single form in which an 'ideal content' was predicated of a single subject, the Absolute, the same for all judgements. This objection may be emphasized by pointing out that for Bradley, as a monist, there is only one logical subject, whereas on the monistic theory there will be as many subjects as there are *n*-tuples of related terms.

Secondly, it may be objected that the subjects which Russell supposes the monistic theory to require are not at all of the same type as Bradley's Absolute. In modern terms, it is entirely appropriate to think of the subjects which Russell has in mind for the monistic theory as the mereological sums of the terms of the relation—for example, that Russell's expression '(*ab*)' denotes the mereological sum of *a* and *b*. Bradley, on the other hand, did not regard the Absolute as merely a mereological sum.

The third objection is that on Bradley's theory of judgement the 'ideal content' which is predicated of the Absolute is the entire original proposition. Thus the relational proposition '$R(a,b)$' is to be read as 'The Absolute (or Reality) is such that $R(a,b)$',

---

[4] Among Russell's critics on this point are Timothy Sprigge, 'Russell and Bradley on Relations', in G. W. Roberts (ed.), *The Bertrand Russell Memorial Volume* (London: Allen & Unwin, 1979), 151–3, 156–9; and John Watling, *Bertrand Russell* (Edinburgh: Oliver and Boyd, 1970), 40–1. A notable exception, which I discovered after I had written this essay, is Fred Wilson's 'Bradley's Impact on Empiricism', in J. Bradley (ed.), *Philosophy after F. H. Bradley* (Bristol: Thoemmes, 1996), 251–81. In my *Russell's Idealist Apprenticeship* (Oxford: Clarendon Press, 1991), 320, I noted Sprigge's objection without comment.

which can be presented '(A) [R(*a*,*b*)]'.[5] Russell's account of what
is predicated on the monistic view is quite different. In his statement of the theory at *Principles*, 224, he does not specify what
it is, but on p. 221 he says that the theory 'regards the relation
as a property of the whole' (*ab*). This last, however, cannot be
quite right, for the relation requires two terms, whereas (*ab*) offers
only one. Presumably what Russell meant is that *r* is a property
associated with the relation *R*; perhaps (to use terminology that
Bradley often resorted to) *r* is the property of being qualified by
the relation *R*.

Of these three criticisms only the first is really serious. The
other two arise merely because Russell was trying to state a
generic type of reduction theory for relations, of which Bradley's
theory would be one brand. Naturally a good deal of Bradleyan
detail is lost in the process—but this loss does no damage to
Russell's case. Russell's monistic theory is intended to be the
lowest common denominator of all theories of this type. The exact
nature of the subject (*ab*) and the exact nature of the property
predicated of it are not at issue. Against the second objection,
Russell can concede that Bradley will wish to impose further
conditions on (*ab*) than those that are required for its being the
mereological sum of *a* and *b*. Bradley will want to regard (*ab*),
and still more the Absolute, as a whole or unity. He is far from
explicit about what conditions must be imposed to ensure this,
but, whatever they are, Russell can readily admit them. It is plain
from Russell's subsequent discussion of the monistic theory that
he intends to admit the case in which (*ab*) is what Bradley would
regard as a whole, but it is also plain that a Bradleyan whole is
at least a mereological sum. Henceforth, I shall simply assume
that whatever I call a 'sum' meets the conditions (whatever they
are) that Bradley thinks must be met by anything which is to
qualify as a whole or a unity. The third objection is met similarly. Russell is certainly far from explicit as to what is predicated on the monistic theory—and this is quite intentional,
given that he aims to describe a generic theory. While, as we have

---

[5] The clearest statement of this comes in the second of the Terminal Essays
added to the 2nd edn. of *PL*, 626–41. See also *ETR*, 253–4. But for a passage
which Russell would have known before writing *Principles of Mathematics* see
PL, 13.

seen, it cannot be the relation itself that is predicated, there is no reason to suppose that it cannot be a Bradleyan ideal content.

The chief issue to be considered, then, is whether Bradley's insistence that ultimately all judgements have the Absolute as their subject is consistent with Russell's characterization of the monistic theory. One further preliminary point remains to be made. Bradley's system, as is well known, is strongly stratified, and doctrines that are true on one level do not necessarily remain true on neighbouring levels. In general, therefore, it is essential in interpreting any remark of Bradley's to know what level he is talking about. Clearly the stage at which the Absolute appears as logical subject is the highest in the system. At lower stages the subject is what Bradley sometimes calls a 'selected reality': that is, 'a limited aspect and portion of the Universe'.[6] Evidently, Russell's statement of the monistic theory fits more naturally these lower-level accounts. But this is not to say that it excludes Bradley's highest-level account. In this context, it is important to note that *all* judgement for Bradley, at *whatever* level, involves some degree of abstraction, and therefore of falsification. Thus, even the predication of an ideal content of the Absolute cannot, for Bradley, be wholly true.

Bradley himself thought that Russell had misunderstood his treatment of relations, but the monistic theory was not his cause for complaint. He did not object to Russell's ascription in the notes he made on *The Principles of Mathematics*;[7] nor was it one of the many points which he took up with Russell in their correspondence just after the *Principles* was published. In a later letter he did say:

I do *not* believe that a monistic view (or any other view) can reconstitute intelligibly a given relational whole or indeed any given whole. And I entirely reject the idea that the relation of subject and attribute is in the end intelligible or satisfactory.[8]

But the context of this discussion was Bradley's claim that analysis involves falsification, and it is not even clear that 'the monistic

---

[6] *PL*, 629.

[7] His notes are in his Notebook IB19 kept among his papers in Merton College Library, Oxford.

[8] Bradley, letter to Russell, 11 Mar. 1907, in Russell Archives, McMaster University.

view' which Bradley refers to is what Russell called 'the monistic theory of relations'. It seems more plausible to suppose that Bradley was referring to his monistic metaphysics. Bradley's main point in this letter was that he did not regard any judgement as completely 'intelligible or satisfactory', and that no relational fact (and, for that matter, no subject–predicate fact either) could be 'explain[ed] or reconstitute[d] . . . rationally in *any* way'.[9] In short, no judgement was wholly true.

There is no reason to suppose that Russell was ignorant of this doctrine of Bradley's when he wrote *The Principles of Mathematics*, but he explicitly included reference to it when he repeated the attribution of the monistic theory to Bradley in his later essay 'The Nature of Truth'. There Russell distinguished two versions of what he called 'the axiom of internal relations', 'according as it is held that every relation is really *constituted* by the natures of the terms or of the whole which they compose, or merely that every relation has a *ground* in these natures'.[10] This time Bradley objected explicitly: 'I don't see how the "constituted" view could be attributed to myself. And do you think that "internal relations" *must* mean that relations are adjectives of the terms? I fail to see how this follows.'[11] My main concern in what follows will be roughly to show that Russell had good reason for thinking that, if relations were to be eliminated, it did mean this.

But the effort of trying to identify the reasons which Russell may have had in mind is only worthwhile if we can be sure that Russell understood what Bradley's theory of judgement was. A far simpler explanation, very popular with Russell's critics, is that Russell was simply ignorant of Bradley's views about the ultimate nature of judgement. Fortunately, here the textual record is very clear.

Russell knew perfectly well that for Bradley there was ultimately only one logical subject for all judgements[12] and that that

[9] Ibid.; emphasis added.

[10] Bertrand Russell, 'On the Nature of Truth', *Proceedings of the Aristotelian Society*, n.s. 7 (1907), 38; repr. in Russell, *Philosophical Essays* (New York: Simon and Schuster, n.d.; 1st edn. 1910), 141.

[11] Bradley, letter to Russell, 4 Oct. 1907, in Russell Archives, McMaster University.

[12] Cf. 'The Classification of Relations' (1899), in *The Collected Papers of Bertrand Russell*, ii: *Philosophical Papers 1896–99*, ed. N. Griffin and A. C. Lewis (London: Hyman Unwin, 1990), 142.

subject was 'Reality as a whole'.[13] He repeated the point in writings that he published. In his book on Leibniz, for example, Russell complains about Bradley's attempt to 'reduce all judgement to predication about Reality';[14] and in *The Principles of Mathematics* itself he writes as follows:

[T] he most logical adherents of the dogma [that there are no relations]— e.g. Spinoza and Mr. Bradley—... have asserted that there is only one thing, God or the Absolute, and only one type of proposition, namely that ascribing predicates to the Absolute. (p. 448)

This evidence poses a problem for those who think that Russell was mistaken to include Bradley among those who held the monistic theory. For if Russell knew what Bradley's theory was, and Bradley's theory was not a form of the monistic theory, why should Russell have ascribed the monistic theory to Bradley? The fact is that Russell knew his Bradley rather well, and Bradley as good as states the monistic theory in a passage entirely overlooked, so far as I know, by Russell's critics:

Although some judgements present two or more subjects in relation, yet all can be reduced to the affirmation of a connection of content within one subject. In 'A is to the right of B', the whole presentation is the subject, and the spatial relation of A and B is an attribute of that.[15]

Now against this passage we can certainly provide others which seem directly to contradict it, though Bradley did not retract the passage in his notes for the second edition of *Principles of Logic*. In *Appearance and Reality* Bradley writes: 'For the relation hardly can be the mere adjective of one or both of its terms; or, at least, as such it seems indefensible'[16]—a remark amplified in a footnote:

The relation is not the adjective of one term, for, if so, it does not relate. Nor for the same reason is it the adjective of each term taken apart, for then again there is no relation between them. Nor is the relation their common property, for then what keeps them apart? They are now not two terms at all, because not separate.[17]

[13] 'An Analysis of Mathematical Reasoning' (1898), in *Collected Papers of Bertrand Russell*, ii. 168.

[14] *A Critical Exposition of the Philosophy of Leibniz* (London: Allen & Unwin, 1975; 1st edn. 1900), 50 n. See also *Our Knowledge of the External World* (London: Allen & Unwin, rev. 1926, 1st edn. 1914), 48, and *An Outline of Philosophy* (London: Allen & Unwin, 1961; 1st edn. 1927), 262.

[15] PL, 180.   [16] AR, 27.   [17] AR, 27 n.

Why did Russell apparently overlook the passage from *Appearance and Reality*? In the first place, Russell, as a neo-Hegelian, was more strongly influenced by Bradley's *Principles of Logic* than by *Appearance and Reality*, and was apt to read the latter in light of the former. This may have been unfortunate, since Bradley warned Russell that in his *Principles of Logic* he had not expressed himself well.[18] But even with this warning Russell was, I believe, right to take the passage from *Principles of Logic* more seriously than the one from *Appearance and Reality*. It hardly needs to be pointed out that the reasons Bradley gives in *Appearance and Reality* for rejecting the monistic theory are extremely weak. The fact that *A* and *B* have some common property does not imply that they are not distinct terms: distinctness does not presuppose, as Bradley seems to assume, complete separation.

There were, however, more important reasons than these for Russell's ascription of the monistic theory to Bradley. Whether or not Bradley adopts the monistic theory at some intermediate stage in his treatment of judgement, it is clear that he holds that, ultimately, all judgements have the Absolute as their only subject. Now, as Bradley told Russell in his letter of 11 March 1907, he did not think that even at this last stage the judgement could be reconstructed in an entirely intelligible or rational way. No judgement, for Bradley, was wholly true, even in its final form. But this is not, I think, important. When Russell ascribed the monistic theory to Bradley, there is no need to suppose that he ascribed to him the view that relational judgements analysed according to the monistic theory were ever wholly true. Russell was well aware of Bradley's views about degrees of truth, and mentioned them in 'The Nature of Truth' in conjunction with his account of the monistic theory. All we need suppose is that Russell thought that Bradley believed that relational judgements when treated monistically were more true than when the relation was treated as external, and further, that when the subject of the judgement was the Absolute, the judgement was truest of all. The sole question of importance here is whether Bradley's view, that the ultimate subject of the relational judgement $R(a,b)$ was the Absolute, can be reconciled with Russell's claim that in the

[18] Bradley, letter to Russell, 9 Dec. 1904, in Russell Archives, McMaster University.

monistic theory its subject was (*ab*). It seems to me that Russell had good reason for thinking that Bradley's theory was merely a special case of the monistic theory, and that if his arguments against the monistic theory were any good, they would thus be equally effective against Bradley's position.

Russell states the monistic theory explicitly for dyadic relations only, but he presumably intended the same account to hold for *n*-adic relations. Now Russell had a trick by means of which any proposition involving an *n*-adic relation could be replaced by an equivalent proposition involving an *n* + 1-adic relation. He mentions it in 'The Philosophy of Logical Atomism',[19] but he had it long before that. He explained it in a letter in 1904:

> Given any statement $\phi(x,y)$ combining two variables, and any constant *a*, there will be a statement $\psi(x,y,a)$ which, for all values of *x* and *y*, will be equivalent to $\phi(x,y)$. Thus we should infer that *every* relation of two entities is really a relation of three. Similarly every relation of three entities would be really a relation of four, and so on.[20]

Thus, if there is some upper limit *n* to the adicity of the relations one is prepared to countenance, then every proposition can be expressed as a proposition involving an *n*-adic relation. This is important because, if *R* and *R'* are two *n*-adic relations, then it is possible to form an *n*-adic relation, R^*, such that $R^* (a_1, \ldots, a_n) \equiv R (a_1, \ldots, a_n) \,\&\, R' (a_1, \ldots, a_n)$.[21] Thus, if *n* is the highest adicity of any relation one will ever need, as for example if *n* is the total number of items in one's universe of discourse, then it is possible to frame a complete description of one's universe of discourse by means of a single *n*-adic relation. If the monistic theory of relations worked, this proposition could be expressed as a subject–predicate proposition in which the subject was the sum of all the elements in the universe of discourse.

---

[19] 'The Philosophy of Logical Atomism' (1918), in *The Collected Papers of Bertrand Russell*, viii: *The Philosophy of Logical Atomism and Other Essays 1914–19*, ed. J. Slater (London: Allen & Unwin, 1986), 183. The technique is better known in the semantic form in which Tarski used it to define 'satisfaction': cf. Alfred Tarski, 'The Concept of Truth in Formalized Languages', in *Logic, Semantics, Metamathematics* (Oxford: Oxford University Press, 1956), 191.

[20] Russell, letter to A. B. Kempe, 15 Oct. 1904, copy in Russell Archives, McMaster University, original in West Sussex Records Office.

[21] Bertrand Russell and Alfred North Whitehead, *Principia Mathematica* (3 vols., Cambridge: Cambridge University Press, 1925–7; 1st edn. 1910–13), *23.36.

The connection between this and Bradley's theory of judgement is now easy to see. For this comprehensive judgement, as construed on the monistic theory, looks very much like the sort of judgement which Bradley thinks has the highest degree of truth: a judgement in which a single comprehensive content is predicated of the Absolute. It is reasonable to think of Bradley's Absolute as at least incorporating everything real. There will be, if Cantor-style paradoxes are to be avoided in the Absolute, some definite (though not necessarily finite) number of items which compose the Absolute.[22] Let N be this number; we may think of N if we like as the cardinality of the Absolute. Then, at the highest level of Bradley's system, we are to regard judgements as involving the predication of ideal contents of the Absolute, which is a whole consisting of N items. But judgements, so construed, are merely a special case of the situation Russell has already covered by the monistic theory. Consider a particular example from the Bradleyan point of view. Suppose we have an ordinary relational judgement '$R(a,b)$' about two terms a and b. Suppose Bradley denies that we can properly regard this as a judgement in which a property r is predicated of the whole comprised of a and b, or claims that any such reformulation of the judgement, though an improvement, still fails to give us the highest degree of truth. Bradley's alternative is to enlarge the subject of the predication until it is the Absolute itself. But we can see now that Russell has already taken care of this case. For the Absolute as a subject of judgement is itself a whole, though one with N members rather than two. In this case, Russell can replace the original dyadic relation by an N-adic relation. Then, by a direct application of his formulation of the monistic theory, we would replace the resulting relational proposition by a subject–predicate proposition in which the subject was the whole composed of the N terms of the relation. The result will subsume Bradley's theory of judgement as a special case of the monistic theory. Bradley's theory, therefore, will not be saved by claiming that it falls outside the monistic

[22] The stratification of these items into orders (in some appropriate way) will serve to bar Cantorian paradoxes, to which Bradley's Absolute would otherwise seem to be subject. What should be done about them is an important question for Absolute theory (not so far tackled, to my knowledge), but one which would take us too far afield here. Of the plausible options, stratification and limitation of size would satisfy the cardinality requirements mentioned above; but paraconsistency, a third alternative, need not.

theory of relations, and thus outside the scope of Russell's arguments against the monistic theory. Bradley's theory can be saved only if it can be shown that Russell's objections to the monistic theory are invalid. And that, I think, is a much harder task.[23]

---

[23] The main arguments in this paper were arrived at in the course of discussion with Evlyn Gledhill. The research was supported by the Social Sciences and Humanities Research Council of Canada.

7

Bradley and Floating Ideas

DAVID HOLDCROFT

———•———

It is a fundamental tenet of Bradley's metaphysics that every idea in some sense qualifies reality.[1] Yet *prima facie* there are many ideas which do not, so that it could be argued that:

> When an idea is taken as false it may even be repelled and denied. And, apart from this, ideas may be recognised as merely imaginary, and, taken in this character, they float suspended above the real world. The same thing happens wherever we deal with questions, with ideal experiments, and again with those suggestions which we merely entertain without pronouncing on their truth. And how, when you do not know that an idea is true, or when you even know that it is not true, can you say in such a case that the idea qualifies reality? In such cases the idea, it is plain, can do no more than float. (*ETR*, 29)

As we shall see, Bradley's examples by no means exhaust the types of floating ideas that there are; but the list is more than long enough to be going on with.

However, before we discuss the examples in detail, two key terms call for comment: 'idea' and 'qualify'. The first of these is potentially misleading, but in the event not seriously so. The crucial point is that one of Bradley's central theses is the primacy of judgement. According to this, ideas taken to be constituents of judgements, which is the most commonly understood sense of the

---

[1] See, *AR*, 324: 'to hold thought so to speak, in the air, without a relation of any kind to the Real, in any of its aspects or spheres, we should find in the end to be impossible'. But the argument is much clearer in *ETR* (esp. chs. 3, 7, and 12), and in the Terminal Essays to *PL*.

term, can only be understood in terms of their role in judgements;[2] ideas in this sense are not independently identifiable. So, because they are not independently identifiable, the question whether ideas in this sense can float reduces to the question of whether judgements can do so. But what, then, is it to float?

The denial that ideas can float is, according to Bradley, equivalent to the claim that all ideas (and, *a fortiori*, judgements) qualify reality. However, the term 'qualify' is very general; there are many different ways in which one thing can qualify another, just as there are many different ways in which one thing can depend on another. So the key question is whether there is any one way, or a circumscribed related set of ways, in which *all* ideas qualify reality. To the extent, and only to the extent, that he has an answer to that question can Bradley explicate in detail his claim that no ideas float—that is, that all ideas qualify reality.

Now not only might it be argued that ideas can float, but Bradley himself has so argued in his *Principles of Logic*: 'We have a judgement which is either true or false, because it implies a relation to a fact. But imagination is without this reference. . . . what it wants is a point of identity to fasten in on to the "this" ' (*PL*, 75). But later, under the influence of Bosanquet, he abandoned the view that there could be an idea that was 'held before the mind without any judgement' (*PL*, 76). There were many reasons for doing so. For one thing, the existence of floating ideas is not consistent with the development of an idealist metaphysics according to which reality is a single experience which contains 'in the fullest sense everything which is' (*ETR*, 246). Second, their existence might seem to undermine the claim that coherence is the test of truth; for if ideas can float, are we not free at will to construct systems of ideas more embracing than the 'true' one? Third, Bradley came to be more aware of the varying uses to which ideas might be put, and so of different ways in which they could qualify reality. So his later metaphysics tries to show that the *prima-facie* counterexamples are no such thing, and to describe how in each case they qualify reality.

Obviously, it is not possible in a short essay to discuss how he deals with each case, in part because their treatment is not uniform, but also because, arguably, there are a number of threads

---

[2] See Anthony Manser, *Bradley's Logic* (Oxford: Blackwell, 1983), ch. 4.

to Bradley's argument, some of which are more radical than others. Instead, my aim is to give an overview of a number of Bradley's arguments which underpin his rejection of floating ideas in general, to discuss some of the apparent counterexamples in more detail, and finally to discuss briefly the view of reality that Bradley argues for.

I

A key conception for Bradley's argument which leads to the rejection of floating ideas is that of my real world.[3] This has to be distinguished from reality, which embraces it but is not exhausted by it. How, then, is my real world constituted, and how is it to be distinguished from reality?

The centre of my real world is, Bradley maintains, my body, for

It is . . . the universe of those things which are continuous in space with my body, and in time with the states and actions of that body. My mental changes form no exception, for, if they are to take their place in time as 'real' events, they must, I think, be dated in connexion with my body. (*ETR*, 460)

This spatio-temporal universe is not simply given; though its starting-point is experience, it is something which has to be constructed. The principles guiding the construction are that, relative to my experience, it should be as comprehensive and coherent as possible—an important point, as we shall see, for Bradley's theory of truth.

The fact that the world is mine might indeed suggest that the self has a privileged position. But that is not Bradley's view: 'in truth neither the world nor the self is an ultimately given fact. On the contrary each alike is a construction and a more or less one-sided abstraction' (*ETR*, 247). Immediate experience, the starting-point for the construction, does not involve a distinction between the self and its objects. It is an experience in which

---

[3] See *ETR*, 30, 46, 208, and ch. 16. The conception is ably discussed in Guy Stock's 'Bradley's Theory of Judgement', in A. Manser and G. Stock (eds.), *The Philosophy of F. H. Bradley* (Oxford: Clarendon Press, 1984), 131–54, and in T. L. S. Sprigge's 'The Self and its World in Bradley and Husserl', ibid. 285–302.

there is no distinction between my awareness and that of which it is aware. There is an immediate feeling, a knowing and being in one, with which knowledge begins; and though this in a manner is transcended, it nevertheless remains throughout as the present foundation of my known world. (*ETR*, 159)

There is no space here to examine further Bradley's account of the construction of an enduring self, since it is a subject for an essay in its own right;[4] the important point for present purposes is that for him it clearly is neither a datum nor constructed in such a way that it is a source of self-authenticating knowledge. Judgements about myself are corrigible:

if in such a judgement as 'I am here and now having a sensation or complex of sensations of such or such a kind' by 'I' is meant 'a self with such or such a real existence in time, then memory is involved, and the judgement at once, I should urge becomes fallible'. (*ETR*, 205)

Moreover, the perceptual judgements I make are, Bradley argues, also fallible. To be sure, it is not possible that *all* the judgements of perception and memory that I make could be corrected: 'I cannot, that is, imagine the world of my experience to be so modified that in the end none of these accepted facts should be left standing' (*ETR*, 209). But that does not mean that the construction of my real world rests on a foundation of perceptual judgements which are incorrigible. That construction, as we saw, aims to be as systematic as possible—that is, to be as comprehensive and coherent as it can be. But it may be that by revising a judgement which I have hitherto taken to be true, my construction can be made more systematic:

If by taking certain judgements of perception as true, I can get more system into my world, then these 'facts' are so far true, and if by taking certain 'facts' as errors I can order my experience better, then so far these 'facts' are errors. And there is no fact which possesses an absolute right. (*ETR*, 210)

So, though in virtue of the role allotted to experience, Bradley's epistemology is that of an empiricist, it is not foundationalist; even judgements of perception are in principle revisable.

---

[4] For a subtle account of Bradley's views on the self see Sprigge, 'Self and its World'. James Bradley's discussion of Bradley's theory of immediate experience is extremely helpful: see James Bradley, 'F. H. Bradley's Metaphysics of Feeling and its Place in the History of Philosophy', in Stock and Manser (eds.), *Philosophy of F. H. Bradley*, 227–42.

II

One way in which Bradley tries to show that ideas which apparently float in fact do not can be illustrated by his treatment of negation. Suppose that I judge of something which is part of my real world that it is P, where 'P' is a predicate like 'is red' whose application to a subject S excludes that of the remaining predicates within a given domain (e.g. colours). Then supposing my judgement is true and that 'Q' is a predicate from the same domain as P, then it follows that S is not Q. Now, if I have judged that S is P, I will so construct my real world that it is true of it that S is P. But what of the judgement that S is not Q? Is that also part of the construction?

The function of negation in a judgement is a topic that much exercised Bradley. His central claim, which has led to much debate, is that negation must be grounded: 'The positive quality of the ultimate reality may remain occult or be made explicit, but this, and nothing else, lies always at the base of a negative judgement' (*PL*, 120). However, it is not easy to understand precisely what he meant by this claim. In his paper on negation Ayer interpreted Bradley as saying that negative judgements are parasitic on positive ones, and correctly denied that this is so:

From the fact that someone asserts that it is not raining one is not entitled to infer that he has ever supposed, or that anyone has ever suggested, that it is, any more than from the fact that someone asserts that it is raining one is entitled to infer that he has ever supposed, or that anyone has ever suggested, that it is not.[5]

But true though this is, the view criticized is not Bradley's. Returning to the topic in his Terminal Essays, he tried to clarify his claim that negation is grounded. A crucial step in his argument is the claim that every judgement is selective and makes a distinction 'singled out from the Universe' (*PL*, 662). If I characterize something in a certain way, I am in effect excluding other characterizations of it. This is not to say that I explicitly deny what my judgement excludes:

When in an early judgement I say 'Here is this', and so select one feature from the universal mass, I do not of course explicitly deny that

---

[5] A. J. Ayer, 'Negation', in *Philosophical Essays* (London: Macmillan, 1954), 39. For an interesting discussion of these issues see Manser, *Bradley's Logic*, ch. 8.

which my judgement neglects. . . . On the contrary I emphasize one element in my whole while disregarding the residue. But this residual mass, none the less, is there, and is actually experienced. (*PL*, 663)

Talk of a mass and a residue taken literally is of course puzzling. The term 'mass' usually has connotations of something undifferentiated and nebulous; but that is not how Bradley thinks of it. The point he wants to insist on is rather that the kind of selection involved in predication cannot involve a distinction without a difference, so that it is a selection from a structured whole:

There is no such thing as a distinction which, merely adventitious, supervenes wantonly, or is superimposed in the absence of a ground. And thus distinction and negation determine and qualify, even if in the end we can not show how precisely they do so. (*PL*, 664)

This is so, Bradley seems to argue, because to distinguish—that is, to predicate something of a thing—I have to make a selection from a group of predicates which stand opposed to each other in a variety of ways, so that if P and Q are members of such a set, it follows that if S is P, then S is not-Q. Moreover, he does not, I think, regard the sets of opposed differences which these predicates distinguish as simply given; rather, it is I who 'have to turn my experience into a disjunctive totality of elements which, according to the conditions, explicitly imply and negate one another' (*PL*, 665). So it is, it seems, a condition of judgement that in characterizing something positively I thereby implicitly negate other possible ways of characterizing it.

Put this way, Bradley might seem to be giving positive judgements a special status; but that is clearly not his intention. Rather, what he wants to say is that the same set of disjunctive elements which make it true that if S is P, then it is not-Q, also make it true that if S is not-Q, it is either P, or R, or S:[6] 'Negation everywhere has a ground, not on one side merely but on both sides' (*PL*, 664). So I take it that his point is that one cannot give any logical precedence to positive judgements; for I cannot judge that S is P unless it is also possible for me to make a negative judgement: namely, that S is not-Q.

---

[6] e.g., if S is red, then it is not-green; but if it is not-green, then it is either red, or orange or yellow . . .

III

Returning to the topic of my real world, the question asked, it will be recalled, was whether if I judge that S is P and thereby characterize my real world, I thereby also characterize it as one in which S is not-Q. This question is interesting only in so far as there is reason to think that Bradley thought that my real world was to be characterized positively, since in that case that S is not-Q is not part of the description of it, any more than a painting's depiction of something as red is a depiction of it as not-green. But even if Bradley did think this, though I can find no evidence that he did, the account of negation just given leaves little temptation to say that 'negative' ideas float. What makes it true that S is P—namely, some feature of S, together with the system of oppositions and differences on which the possibility of classing S as P rests—also makes it true that S is not-Q.

The real interest of Bradley's treatment of negation is, rather, the role played by the system of oppositions and differences, which are for him ideal constructions, on which the possibility of classification rests. For this opens up the possibility of a distinction between my real world and a wider conception of reality which includes those ideal constructions. My real world is part of reality in this sense, but does not exhaust it, since it is, as it were, but a selection, from a much wider set of possibilities: 'Negation in short implies at its base a disjunction which is real, and its goal is to set before us reality as a systematic and explicit totality of complementary differences' (*PL*, 666).

Now because my judgement that S is P always involves a selection from a range of alternatives, I have to be aware of other possibilities which, though excluded by my judgement, are not excluded by judgements that others might wish to make. So if someone judges that S is Q, I can understand what it is that he judges to be the case—namely, that S is Q—even though I know that S is P. But to do this, I have to understand it as a judgement about a world, our real world if not mine. In short, though I do not endorse the judgement, I cannot treat the content as floating.

But, it might be argued, if in cases which involve another's judgement there is little temptation to say that an idea floats because I do not endorse it, there is a temptation to say this in cases in which I myself entertain the possibility that S is Q, believing it to be P. I cannot be judging that S is both Q and P; so if the idea that S is Q qualifies reality, this is not because it is judged to do so by someone or other.

The kind of answer that Bradley would give at this point is, I think, that bare entertaining is not possible: that it is always for some purpose or other that I entertain a possibility, and that in each case the purpose involves a judgement of one kind or another which 'refers' the idea to my world, in some way or other, so that it does not float: 'There is not and there can not be any such thing as a *mere* idea, an idea standing or floating by itself' (*PL*, 640). So, for instance, if I wonder how things are, I might entertain a number of possibilities; but then I am doing so in order to see which are true or false of my real world. In this connection, what Bradley has to say about questions is instructive.[7] A question involves a demand for further knowledge which

is addressed to another mind, or even secondarily to our own, or again to material nature. The further knowledge (of which we have the idea) is absent from our known fact. But on the other hand this knowledge, the answer to our question is not fetched from nowhere. We take it to be truth which already is there and which in some sense exists. (*ETR*, 36)

In other words, questions are just as much about my real world as are affirmations, though in a different kind of way. They are, as it were, invitations to pick out from a range of judgements the one which is true.

There are many other examples which could be given of ways in which ideas which *prima facie* float turn out to be in some sense 'about' my real world on closer examination. For instance, ideas expressed by imperatives express a wish that my real world should have features which it currently lacks.[8] Whilst, to take another example, suppositions do not start from a *tabula rasa*, but from known features of my real world, so that the question is: What can we infer from the supposition and these features? In other words, what difference would it make to my real world if the supposition were true? Even imaginary ideas have a relation

---

[7] I am aware that finer distinctions than are made here could, and probably should, be: e.g. between direction of fit and affirmation.

[8] See Bradley's paper 'The Definition of Will', *Mind*, n.s. 49 (1904), 4–5.

to my real world: 'facts of sense are called imaginary or erroneous, when in their offered character they do not belong to [a person's] "real" order in space or time' (*ETR*, 208). Hence, the imaginary has to be defined in relation to my real world, since it is 'qualified by exclusion from real existence, and apart from that exclusion it loses its character' (*ETR*, 46). So, paradoxical though it may seem, 'The existence of the imaginary depends upon my real world' (*ETR*, 47).

I suggest, therefore, that a modest thread in Bradley's argument consists of trying to show that whilst we need a wider conception of reality than that of my real world for an adequate account of negation and disjunction, many ideas that apparently float are dependent on, or are 'about', however indirectly, some aspect of, or are what they are because of some relation they stand in to, my real world. In relation to that, they do not float; which is what one might expect Bradley to want to demonstrate.

Moreover, a position like this does seem to provide a possible basis for a solution to at least one of the problems that the apparent existence of floating ideas presented Bradley with: namely, that their existence might seem to undermine the claim that coherence is the test of truth. If ideas can float, are we not free at will to construct systems of ideas more embracing than the 'true' one? But within the framework just sketched, it seems that Bradley has a reply. For the test of coherence is not simply a logical one, amounting to no more than a question of what is the largest conceivable set of consistent judgements. If that were the test, then the set would doubtless contain much that is imaginary. But the test proposed is more complicated: 'The question with me everywhere is as to what is the result to my real world' (*ETR*, 213). No doubt I can in any particular case accept 'mere fancy' rather than accepted fact. But that is not to say that it could be a principle that I should do so as a rule, even though it led me to reject what I remembered to be so, and what others attested to. The trustworthiness of memory and the reliability of testimony, unless I have special reasons to doubt them, are the principles on which I construct my real world. 'And because by any other method the result is worse, therefore for me these principles are true' (*ETR*, 213).

Given that the construction of my real world is constrained not simply by logic, but by the need to account systematically for immediate experience and perception, for memory, for the testimony of others, and so on, Bradley's defence of the coherence theory has some plausibility. But, as we shall see, some of the consequences of other threads in his argument about floating ideas are not obviously consistent with the defence just sketched.

IV

A feature of the position we have been discussing, which is the first and most modest thread in Bradley's argument, allots a privileged role to my real world. This seems not unreasonable, since it is in relation to it that floating ideas apparently float; so that, prima facie, what has to be shown is that this is not in fact so. But can my real world really have the privileged position that the argument just sketched gives it?

Recall that it is a construction which has its origins in experience, but that it does not rest on a foundation of self-evident judgements; even perceptual judgements are revisable, and the self is no more a given fact than is the world (*ETR*, 247). That is not to say, as we have seen, that anything goes, since the construction aims to bring facts 'before my mind harmoniously and fully' (*ETR*, 461). Further, 'This arrangement is practical since I act on it, and since I must act on it if I am to continue what I call my "real" life' (*ETR*, 460). So it is no part of Bradley's argument that I could or should not take my real world seriously. But what makes it special from a metaphysical point of view remains a question.

Note that the construction is radically incomplete. If we think of it as akin to telling a story,[9] then the story will be relatively rich in detail about the time and space which I currently occupy and the times and spaces I have occupied. Moreover, the principle of accepting testimony unless there is special reason to doubt it means that my real world is likely to be harmonized in many ways with that of my family and my neighbours; after all, much that I take to be the case rests on their testimony. But as I move further away from here and now, the story becomes patchier and

---

[9] The idea of each self or finite centre telling a story I have taken from Sprigge, 'Self and its World', 288.

patchier, until it has nothing to say. Thus, it tells us about 'the merest fraction of the universe' (*ETR*, 464); and though the story never claims to be complete, so the implication is that there is much more to be said, which is also answerable to the test of coherence and completeness, no one person could say it all.[10]

Now, since there are many possible starting-points for such constructions, may there not be genuine alternatives to my real world? Bradley thought that there could be: 'The contention that our waking world is the one real order of things will not stand against criticism. It is a conclusion which in short is based on ignorance which chooses to take itself for knowledge' (*ETR*, 464). In so far as no waking person's construction is or could be complete, Bradley's argument seems inescapable; for though respect for testimony will tend to harmonize different constructions, given that the test of truth is coherence and completeness, there is no reason to suppose that this can always be done, in which case the constructions have to be treated as alternatives.

Such a conclusion does not, I think, mean for Bradley that I should take *my* real world anything other than seriously. For I presumably will believe that my construction is as good as any other on offer; and though I know that future experience may well call for revision of parts of it, relative to my experience it seems to me to give the fullest and most harmonious account possible. Bradley would not, I think, have demurred from Quine's claim that it is when

we turn back into the midst of an actually present theory, at least hypothetically accepted, that we can and do speak sensibly of this and that sentence as true. When it makes sense to apply 'true' is to a sentence couched in terms of a given theory and seen from within the theory complete with its posited reality.[11]

But though I can accept that ideas which are not true in my real world are true in the worlds of others, without losing my confidence in my own construction, accepting this opens up the possibility of yet another way in which ideas which apparently float may not. For some at least of these will be true of other possible worlds, and hence of other posited realities.

---

[10] The continued answerability to experience, coherence, and comprehensiveness is, I take it, the 'realist' constraint on Bradley's construction.

[11] W. V. O. Quine, *Word and Object* (Cambridge, Mass.: MIT Press, 1960), 24.

In so far as the other possible worlds are the posited realities of the constructions made by other waking selves, starting from the same basis and applying the same tests of coherence and so forth, this seems not unreasonable. But may it not be the case that there are ideas which in light of the waking sober constructions of all of us are rejected? Bradley thought not: the claim that 'Because there are many worlds, the idea which floats suspended above one of them is attached to another' (*ETR*, 32) is just as true of what I hope, desire, or dream to be so as it is of the ideas of the madman and the drunkard:

> There are in short floating ideas, but not ideas which float absolutely. Every idea on the contrary is an adjective which qualifies a real world, and it is loose only when you take it in relation to another sphere of reality. (ibid.)

V

In this context, Bradley's discussion of the imaginary is instructive. There are two main points which he insists on: first, that the imaginary depends on my real world, in that it has to be defined in terms of exclusion from it: 'it is by exclusion from this real world that the imaginary is made' (*ETR*, 47). So if one night we all dreamt the same thing, this would still be imaginary, because of its lack of continuity with the real world.

The second feature is that my real world depends on a felt quality. As we saw, my real world is what is continuous in space with my body and in time with its actions. But what is my body?

> If we insist on an answer we have to reply that my real body means my waking body, and that this means my present body. It is simply the body which is for me here and now as I am asking myself this question. The whole centre and foundation of what I call my 'real' scheme is the body which to me is mine at this here and this now. (*ETR*, 461)

In short, my scheme rests on my ability to designate something as this, a particular moment as now, a particular place as here, and so on.[12]

---

[12] For a discussion of the issues raised here see Guy Stock, 'Bradley's Theory of Judgement', and Anthony Quinton, 'Spaces and Times', *Philosophy*, 37 (1962), 130–47. *ETR*, ch. 9, contains an important discussion also.

However, that ability is not a guarantee of the truth of any judgement that I make: 'That which I designate, is not and cannot be carried over into my judgement' (*ETR*, 207). Judgement is inherently general, and so is liable to error; granting that I have succeeded in uniquely designating something 'so far as it is placed in a special construction and vitally related to its context, to the same extent the element of interpretation or implication is added' (ibid.). If, for example, one tries to make explicit what it is one has uniquely designated, then one would try to identify its place uniquely within a series of spatially related objects. But of course, no such series is simply given on Bradley's account; it, too, is a construction. Moreover, he argues that it is a mistake to think of space and time as ' "principles of individuation", in the sense that a temporal or spatial exclusion will confer uniqueness on any content' (*PL*, 63). So if I try in general terms to uniquely individuate what I have designated by 'this', by identifying its place within a series, for all I know there is more than one series which fits the description, one of which, for instance, coincides with my real world in which Caesar crossed the Rubicon, and one which does not, and in which he did not do so (*ETR*, 265).

Another reason why I cannot distinguish my real world from an imaginary one by appeal to designation is, Bradley argues, that it, like all its other apparently distinguishing features, is not unique to my real world. After all, just as there is within my imaginary world a distinction between what is real and what is imaginary—in that I can imagine myself imagining something—and one between what is actual and what is possible (*ETR*, 702), so within my imaginary world there is a distinction drawn between here and there, this and that, now and then, and so on. So the felt quality on which my real world ultimately rests, the sense of something given, is not only not a descriptively distinguishing feature of it, but it is not unique to it, and so cannot distinguish it from other possible worlds.

Similarly, Bradley argues, just as here and now in my waking state my real world seems to me the most comprehensive and orderly, so may my dream world seem to me as I dream to be the most comprehensive: 'suppose that in hypnotism, madness or dream, my world becomes wider and more harmonious than the scheme which is set up from my normal self—then does not, I ask, what I dream become at once a world better and more real?'

(*ETR*, 464). In short, any attempt to make my real world special fails.

So the second, and less modest, thread to Bradley's theory of
floating ideas is that ideas may indeed float, but they do so only
relatively, since 'Every possible idea . . . may be said to be used
existentially, for every possible idea qualifies and is true of a real
world. And the number of real worlds, in a word, is indefinite.
Every idea therefore in a sense is true, and is true of reality' (*ETR*,
42). Reality, or the Absolute, then, contains all these possible
worlds; and my real world is but one of them.

VI

It is not easy, it must be said, to see how the position developed
in the second thread of Bradley's argument is meant to relate to
the first, or how they can be woven together to make whole cloth.
So it is perhaps worth noting that whilst at times Bradley defends
a very strong version of the claim that all ideas are true of some
possible world or other, at other times the claim is qualified in
ways which simply fall back on the first thread identified. For
instance, in 'Floating Ideas and the Imaginary', one of the key
sources for his thought on this point, he says that a floating idea
may hold of a 'distinct world, or may be a residue more or less
unspecified. It may be this or that province of the ideal, or it may
be no more than the undefined space which falls beyond what
we distinguish as fact' (*ETR*, 36). But the second alternative distinguished here requires no more than the wider conception of
reality described earlier, which includes ideal constructions of
quality spaces.

Further, when it comes to the point, Bradley does not seem to
say, for instance, that there are possible worlds in which it is true
that there is a round square, or one in which the idea of 'nothing' is true.[13] What he says in the first case, for example, is that
I can have the thought of a round square either by dropping out

---

[13] The point made about 'nothing' is that it qualifies reality in the sense that
it 'admits presence in a field of distinction taken within reality. And I answer further that "nothing", being always relative, can always qualify such a field' (*ETR*,
41 n.). Perhaps the point is that if, e.g., I say that no men were at the party, I
thereby exclude a possibility: viz. the presence of men on that occasion.

of view 'the special meaning of these words', or by dropping out of view 'the identity of the space which these adjectives are to qualify'. But '[t]he moment, however, that I suppress the diversities and make the space really one, a collision takes place and the round square is destroyed' (*ETR*, 271). So an apparent conception of a round square turns out to be a defective conception.

Second, since floating ideas are very diverse, it is not obvious that a unified account should be expected; so it is intelligible that Bradley should from time to time fall back on a position which combines features of both the threads we have distinguished, as in the quote above.

Third, some of the arguments which Bradley uses to motivate the acceptance of a plurality of possible worlds seem to get perilously close to conceding the objections to the coherence theory discussed earlier, which I suggested might be rebutted from the standpoint developed by the first thread of Bradley's argument. The nub of the objection is that a purely imaginary world could be at least as coherent as, and more comprehensive than, my real world. To which Bradley's response was that this would not be so if the imaginary world had to take into account one's experience, including memories, the testimony of others, other's fancies, and so on (*ETR*, 214). But the arguments used to motivate the existence of a plurality of possible worlds seem to allow that among these are imaginary worlds which are more detailed and richer than my real world. Hence, unless there is a way of distinguishing my real world as the only real world, which Bradley himself argues there is not, then these worlds have a better claim to truth.

Finally, while the notion of a plurality of worlds undoubtedly catches one feature of reality which Bradley's metaphysics was concerned to capture, there is another feature which it seems not to illuminate at all. The first feature is the appearance of an enormous variety of different aspects of our existence, which do not seem to be reducible to each other. The second feature, which the model seems not to illuminate, is the fact that none of these aspects is self-sufficient, so that, in some way which we do not understand, they are all aspects of, and immanent in, Absolute Reality. Different possible worlds, on any account, remain distinct from each other.

VII

However, it may be that a further thread to Bradley's account has to be introduced at this point. For as well as worlds which are commensurable with my real world, in that they are spatio-temporal constructions relating things in space and events in time, in Bradley's view there are also worlds which are not commensurable in this way. So that, as well as a horizontal axis along which worlds of the same kind can be compared, as we have been doing, there is, as it were, a vertical hierarchy, along which is strung worlds of very different kinds. As well as the sensible sphere on which we have been concentrating our discussion, and the 'unreal' worlds of hope, desire, madness, and drunkenness, there are also 'the worlds of duty and of religious truth, which on the one side penetrate, and on the other side transcend the common visible facts' (*ETR*, 31). Moreover, above the sensible sphere rises

the whole realm of the higher imagination. Both in poetry and in general fiction, and throughout the entire region of the arts and of artistic perception, we encounter 'reality'. Things are here in various ways for us incontestable, valid and 'true', while in another sense of the word 'truth' these things could not be called true. But this multiplicity of our worlds may perhaps be taken as a fact which is now recognised. (*ETR*, 31)

The complication is, of course, that this seems to reveal yet another way in which my real world is not privileged. It is not simply that it may not be the most comprehensive and detailed spatio-temporal construction, but that since it is at bottom no more than an abstraction, we can 'comprehend how something may at once offer itself as in comparison fuller and more true, and yet in reality cover and contain less of what works and counts in the whole of things' (*PL*, 690). Thus, Bradley imagines a Christian arguing that the historical events relating to Christ

are something on the other side whose essence and life is elsewhere. Identified with what is beyond, they are no mere occurrences in time or things in space. They represent, and they are the actual incarnation of eternal reality, and for the least of them a man might feel called on to die. (*PL*, 690)

But if worlds constructed according to different principles from those underlying my real world may better articulate the nature of reality, then there is indeed a third thread to Bradley's argument, which would have to be the subject of another essay.

8

The Multiple Contents of Immediacy

DAVID CROSSLEY

———•———

Early in *Appearance and Reality* Bradley asserts the following:
'Feeling, if taken as immediate presentation, most obviously gives
features of what later becomes the environment. And these are
indivisibly one thing with what later becomes the self' (*AR*, 90).
This passage raises two questions: first, if immediacy is a non-
relational unity of some sort, then in what sense can feeling, or
a feeling, have 'features'?[1] and second: what does it mean to say
that these features are 'indivisibly one' with what later becomes
the self, which presumably means 'one' with a finite centre?

What is at issue here, for empirical justification, is how to characterize sensory apprehension. One plausible reading of the claim
that the features presented in feeling are 'indivisibly one' with
the finite centre of the experience is that these experiences are
to be given something like an adverbial interpretation. Adverbial

———

[1] Bradley employs the terms 'feeling' and 'immediate experience' in several senses.
One of these indicates the primordial unified condition logically presupposed by
certain activities, such as judgement, but which at the same time is never fully or
finally transcended. In this sense it reflects something like a doctrine of substance.
This 'substance as substratum' posit has been argued for by James Bradley: see
his 'F. H. Bradley's Metaphysics of Feeling and its Place in the History of
Philosophy', in A. Manser and G. Stock (eds.), *The Philosophy of F. H. Bradley*
(Oxford: Clarendon Press, 1984), 227–42, and his 'The Transcendental Turn in
Bradley's Metaphysics', in W. J. Mander (ed.), *Perspectives on the Logic and
Metaphysics of F. H. Bradley* (Bristol: Thoemmes, 1996), 39–59. A second appears
in contexts in which the referent is an individual, non-cognitive act of sensing
or apprehension by a finite centre. Bradley acknowledges this sort of systematic
ambiguity in *AR* (198, 405 ff.). Since I am concerned only with Bradley's views
on empirical knowledge, I am dealing solely with 'feeling', or immediacy, in the
second of these senses; and more specifically yet, with its use in describing direct,
non-cognitive sensory apprehensions.

theories analyse sensory acquaintance as a non-cognitive mental state (one which is not a propositional attitude) which is non-conceptual and non-judgemental. This is also true of a Bradleyan immediate experience: it is non-cognitive in the sense of not having a propositional object—or indeed any object[2]—and it is a pre-theoretic, preconceptual experiencing, since it excludes, for example, the kind of relational distinctions established by judgements.[3]

Contemporary examples of adverbial theories are found in the works of Ducasse, Sellars, and Paul Moser, among others. In immediate apprehensions we have, in Moser's view, direct experiences of attention-attraction which have special epistemic import because they are involuntary and thereby putative candidates for the foundational experiences which mark our contact with the as yet unconceptualized external world. Moser interprets these direct apprehensions adverbially, as ways or manners of sensing; he thereby takes them as being objectless, although still having content.[4]

(In passing, it must be noted that Bradley does not present an explicit, developed adverbial account of sensory apprehension. This leaves open the question of whether his views of sensory apprehension should be given an adverbial reading. Since what is crucial is that sensory apprehension not involve whatever mental operations are entailed by judgements, it seems important that the logically primitive level of sensory acquaintance, at which empirical data are presented, only be non-cognitive, or, as it might be put in more contemporary terms, that it be a form of non-epistemic perception or a non-doxastic state. However, the adverbial analysis of sensory acquaintance seems to fit Bradley's general position, since it retains an idealist flavour by construing sensations as types of experiences, or modifications of the conscious

---

[2] Cf. *ETR*, 159.   [3] Cf. *ETR*, 194, 196, and 247.

[4] Adverbial analyses oppose act–object analyses of immediate sensory acquaintance. In addition to avoiding the ontological commitments which may go along with an act–object account, adverbial theorists want to avoid what might be taken to be an implication of that view: that the acts of sensory awareness depend on mental operations such as designation or focusing of attention. If successful, an adverbial analysis preserves for sensory attention-attraction the preconceptual, pre-theoretic element requisite for candidacy as the locus of the given or presentational input essential for empirical knowledge. Adverbial theorists who are foundationalists, as Moser is, also hope to stop the regress of justifications at this point; for if immediate apprehensions are not cognitive states with propositional content, they may not themselves require justification. See Paul Moser, *Empirical Justification* (Dordrecht: Reidel, 1985), ch. 5.

perceiver. This is not the place to discuss this issue, and I have dealt with it elsewhere,[5] but it is worth mentioning, if only to warn us that more must be done to establish fully the interpretation of Bradley's account of empirical knowledge which I am presupposing here.)

However, adverbial theories face several problems. The main one is unpacking the notion of 'content' as applied to immediate sensory acquaintance.[6] And in explicating that concept, adverbial theories face a special difficulty once it is admitted that these apprehensions could have a plurality of features. This problem arises for Bradley when we ask how a feeling can have elements or features, how *one* immediate experience can have content*s*?

We can see this difficulty by considering Bradley's example of a pleasant feeling of warmth (*AR*, 91).[7] Here we supposedly have one feeling with at least two characteristics or features.[8] If the warm sensation is not interpreted in the act–object way to give us a conscious subject presented with an object-like content, but rather as a case of sensing warmly (a manner or mode of experiencing), then we can begin to get a handle on what it means to say that this feature of the immediate experience is 'indivisibly one' with the finite centre having it. But if the one immediate feeling of warmth, the feeling warmly, also has the characteristic of being pleasant, we now have multiple contents that are distinct in some sense yet contained within a non-relational unity. In effect, we face the sort of difficulty posed for adverbial theories of sensation by the Many-Property Problem.

---

[5] I have sketched such an interpretation in my 'Justification and the Foundations of Empirical Knowledge', in J. Bradley (ed.), *Philosophy after F. H. Bradley* (Bristol: Thoemmes, 1996), 307–29.

[6] One question is whether these apprehensions yield determinate contents or not. If they do not have determinate content, and thereby amount to mere sensory stimulation, then we have not got anything usable in the justificatory process. Both Bradley and Moser recognize this (cf. *ETR*, 204, and Moser, *Empirical Justification*, 166 ff.). On the other hand, if direct apprehension gives us determinate contents, this must be explained without introducing mental processes such as individuation. The danger is that immediate experience, if it involves mental operation, will fail to provide unmediated access to the extra-theoretic given.

[7] Cf. the example at *ETR*, 205, of a 'complex feeling'.

[8] The point Bradley wants to establish in this context is that this feeling, at the level of immediate apprehension, does *not* present us with one aspect (the pleasant sensation), which can be taken as representing the self, opposed to another aspect (the sensation of warmth) taken as representing an object for, or an adjective of, the self. I am not concerned with that issue here.

In discussing the multiple contents of feeling, Bradley some-times talks of them as 'conjoined' or presented together,[9] even though they have not yet been conceptualized or made the tar-gets of judgements and inferences—that is, they have not yet been 'connected' to render a systematic intelligible unity. But how is this to be interpreted given the official Bradleyan view that, at least for the sphere of empirical knowledge, immediate experi-ences are non-cognitive mental states—or experiencing events within a finite centre—which lack objects with relational pro-perties? That is, how will Bradley deal with the Many-Property Problem?[10]

The Many-Property Problem was first identified in these terms by Frank Jackson in a symposium in 1975.[11] Suppose we grant that an after-image, for example, can have several features, such as being red and triangular, or could even involve the simul-taneous apprehension of a red triangle and a green square. The problem is to provide a perspicuous adverbial analysis of these experiences which, in the latter case, gets all the properties linked up in the right way and which, in the former case, gets the adver-bial modifiers attached so that normal implications hold.

Jackson poses a dilemma for adverbial analyses. Suppose 'S has a sensation of a red triangle' is translated conjunctively as 'S

[9] e.g. *AR*, 199.

[10] One can, of course, understand what Bradley is after in respect of empirical knowledge. If the justificatory enterprise is predicated on the realist assumption of an independent external world and on the plausible thesis that our beliefs about that world are justified only if they are truth-conducive in the sense of repre-senting that world, then there must be a point of contact with that world. And where could this point of contact be except in the involuntary and unmediated confrontations of sensation? If there is nothing given in sensation, and no other possible point of contact between our belief system and the empirical world, then Bradley's avowedly coherentist account of justification would fall prey to the isola-tion objection. Moreover, if we are to avoid 'subjective' epistemological idealism, the given must be presented in some determinate form before it is subjected to mental operations, and before we adjudicate its epistemic status—i.e. the given must be represented in, say, veridical perceptual judgements if it is to have the role of marking the extra-theoretic input necessary for empirical knowledge. If so, it must be possible that an immediate experience (feeling) have a plurality of contents.

[11] Frank Jackson, 'On the Adverbial Theory of Perception', *Metaphilosophy*, 6 (1975), 127–35. The other symposiast was Michael Tye, 'The Adverbial Theory: A Defence of Sellars against Jackson', *Metaphilosophy*, 6 (1975), 136–43. Although not one of the symposiasts, a response to Jackson by Sellars was also published: 'The Adverbial Theory of the Objects of Sensation', *Metaphilosophy*, 6 (1975), 144–60.

senses redly and triangularly' (or 'S senses in an of-a-red manner *and* S senses in an of-a-triangular manner'). But this translation cannot capture the difference, in the case of simultaneous after-images, between sensing a red triangle along with a green square *and* sensing a red square along with a green triangle, for the conjunctive analysis yields the same result in both cases. On the other hand, if the sensation of a red triangle is translated as 'S senses redly-triangularly'—a distinct mode of sensing—then, Jackson argues, 'redly' appears to modify 'triangularly' rather than 'senses', and so is not a mode of sensing at all. Here Jackson's main worry seems to be about handling stacked or embedded modifiers. In his example, 'He spoke impressively quickly', we need to get right the target of the first adverb, 'impressively': that it modifies 'quickly' rather than 'spoke', so the original sentence entails 'He spoke quickly' but not 'He spoke impressively'. Since this is the case, 'impressively' has distinct meanings in the two sentences 'He spoke impressively', where it indicates a manner of speaking, and 'He spoke impressively quickly', where it appears as a second-order mode or manner of 'speaking-in-a-quick-manner'. The problem, as I interpret Jackson, is not just the difficulty of saying how an adverbialist would decide which of these modes of sensing is the more fundamental—if such a decision is required, it might destroy the foundational claims of the immediate apprehension, by importing conceptual machinery or inferences into what is supposedly only a sensory apprehension or acquaintance—but also the counter-intuitive consequence that if sensing redly-triangularly is a distinct mode of sensing, it could not then bear the relation to sensing redly which we believe is captured by the quite natural belief that S's having a sensation of a red triangle entails that S is having a red sensation. Jackson's main contention is that these analyses—the conjunctive and the distinct mode—are the only two available to adverbial theorists; and since each leads to an unacceptable consequence, any adverbial theory will fail to provide an adequate account of sensory acquaintance.

My initial suspicion is that Bradley would respond to this dilemma by grasping the first horn.[12] This response depends on Bradley's use of 'unity' and cognate expressions in a systematically ambiguous way. He needs both that direct apprehensions

[12] Sellars and Tye attempt to avoid this dilemma by going through the horns.

provide elements, if they are to ground perceptual and other judgements about the empirical world, and that these elements be, at the very least, no more than 'conjoined' or presented together if immediate apprehensions are not to entail mental operations. Moreover, if immediate experience is to be not only 'self-transcendent'—where this means it can ground 'references away' to ideal objects[13]—but also the foundation of justified empirical beliefs, its elements must be determinate as well as determinable. So, in one sense of 'unity'—which I will, for convenience, call 'conjunctive unity'—a set of phenomenological items is a unity just in case they are presented together or, in other words, are the contents of one experience. They are what Bradley in one place calls a 'coexisting mass' (*AR*, 198; also cf. 'immediate inherence' at *ETR*, 33). It is in this sense that the multiple contents of an immediate experience form a unity or a totality. And this sort of unity would seem captured by a conjunctive adverbial analysis.

But if these apprehensions are to give rise to true judgements about the empirical world, we must, as Jackson has argued, have some understanding of how we get all these elements arranged into various fundamental and non-fundamental modes, and of how we get the right features connected up so that the red triangles and the green squares do not get all muddled up. That is, we need some idea of how to begin to establish the proper 'connections' among the features of immediacy. And in Bradley's case, this involves a second sense of 'unity'—which I will call 'connective unity'—explicated in terms of 'intelligible connections'. Establishing intelligible connections will probably require a theory of the causes of sensory apprehensions and coherence tests whereby logical and nomological relations are established between and among perceptual claims, physical and other laws, and the attributes of immediate experience with which we have direct acquaintance. (I will say more about connective unity later.)

This suggests an initial possibility: if we take Bradley's distinction between 'conjoined' and 'connected' seriously, as indicating two different types of unity,[14] we can see how Bradley might

[13] e.g. *AR*, 201; *ETR*, 155.

[14] It must be acknowledged that my treatment is, as it were, phenomenological or epistemic. As far as reality is concerned, whatever elements it has are presumably connected; for, were this not true, reality would not be the monistic system which Bradley requires. So the issue before us here is the various ways that the one systematic reality is, or can be, apprehended by us.

respond to the Many-Property Problem. Since the features of immediate experiences are merely conjoined, we have a number of adverbial modifications which could, at this level, be given only a conjunctive analysis. It becomes the task of conceptual thinking, using available theories and coherence criteria, to map out the *connections* which will ultimately provide a connective unity.[15]

In passing, it is worth noting that Bradley might well hold that Jackson's second interpretation of an adverbial account also displays part of the truth about immediacy. He *might* say that, if we focus on the presentational aspect of immediacy—on the fact that multiple contents are somehow given—we need the conjunctive analysis to indicate that the contents remain non-conceptualized presentations of the various features of the external world. On the other hand, if we focus on the finite centre of an immediate experience, it seems we will want something closer to the distinct mode account, since the multiple contents are non-relational manners of, as it were, jointly sensing. Then the problem for empirical knowledge is to arrange the multiple adverbial sensings so as to render them representations of physical objects, after-images, or whatever. And this allows for Bradley's claim that part of the task at the next level is separating out the features presented in immediacy.

Thus, there are two ways of viewing immediacy: the former, captured by the conjunctive analysis, is from the perspective of what will evolve from immediacy as the properties and qualities of physical objects; the latter, captured by the distinct mode interpretation, is from the perspective of what will evolve from immediacy as a self having intentional mental states the contents of which are propositions about these objects and qualities. If I am right that Bradley would be tempted to try to retain something of both of these adverbial analyses, we then face the question of

---

[15] In his debate with G. E. Moore, C. J. Ducasse offered a conjunctive adverbialization of a *sensum* with multiple contents, but hinted that he would take the sort of line I am suggesting Bradley would have taken. Ducasse is responding to Moore's worry that a sensation of blue is always of an extended blue area, such as a blue patch or a blue line. In expressing this worry, Moore came close to formulating the Many-Property Problem. For this debate see Moore's reply to his critics and the epistolary exchange between Moore and Ducasse in P. A. Schilpp (ed.), *The Philosophy of G. E. Moore* (La Salle, Ill.: Open Court, 1942), ii. 223–51, 653–60, 687 and n. I have discussed this in my 'Moore's Refutation of Idealism: The Debate about Sensations', *Idealistic Studies*, 24 (1994), 1–20.

whether he can do so consistently. I will ignore this complication, even though it poses a serious problem.

Unfortunately, this does not yet offer a clean exit from the problem, for it leaves some unanswered questions. For one, do not the features of the immediate unity (as a conjunctive unity), even if these are interpreted as multiple adverbial modifications of one presentation, entail relations of some sort? The features or elements—the multiple contents—must be distinct from one another, and this introduces relations at once.

I think Bradley has two possible answers to this charge. The first is to claim that while there are no relations within immediacy, the way we are forced to think of immediacy makes it appear—at least to the inattentive—as though there are. The second is to confess that there really are relations within immediate experience after all. While the first of these might garner general agreement, the second looks to be a wildly unorthodox interpretation. Nevertheless, there may be reason to believe that Bradley actually held both of these views.

The first possibility, that there only appear to be relations within immediacy, might be argued on abductive grounds. Full-blooded perceptual or observation claims (judgements) require immediate apprehensions as the point of empirical input. But the analysis of these immediate apprehensions may necessarily have to borrow distinctions from perceptual judgements which are couched in our normal physical-object language. That is, Bradley may have taken a proto-Sellarsian view that the features or attributes yielded by an adverbial analysis of direct perceptual acquaintance are analogous to conceptual properties indicated by words in the physical-object language, and he might further have held that their deployment is justified by the explanatory power they afford. We can begin to explore this possibility by asking what Bradley thinks is really being discussed when we talk about immediate sensory apprehensions. One thing which is not in the picture at all here, for Bradley, is the notion that a feeling or immediate sensory apprehension is a complex phenomenological state with phenomenological contents which could be the 'objects' of a first-person report. The contents of immediacy are not available in that sense, so cannot be the targets of first-person assertions. To treat them in that way would entail a 'self' which reports and a set of distinct 'objects' which are reported on; and this would render immediacy relational and cognitive at once.[16] Immediacy is not experienced in such a way that it allows for this sort of self-reflectiveness. Indeed, if such reports were even implicitly self-reflective, then the contents of immediacy would necessarily become propositional objects of reflection, thereby rendering a feeling (an immediate experience) a propositional attitude. And whatever else an immediate experience is, it clearly cannot be an intentional mental state. These considerations provide reasons for interpreting Bradleyan immediate experiences as 'adverbial' in some sense.

If we call a mental state which can have another mental state as its object a second-order mental state, then a first-order mental state will be one which cannot, for whatever reason, have a mental state, even itself, as its object. Bradleyan immediate experiences, to the extent that they are mental states at all, will be first-order states, since they lack any kind of object, propositional or otherwise. What causes some of the difficulty with understanding Bradley's account of immediacy is the problem of how we are to talk of these first-order states without giving the impression that they break apart into sensory objects and properties attended to by some experiencer. An adverbial account of immediacy is supposed to prevent this collapse. But we need a language for talking of the contents of first-order mental states. And here we will probably have to admit that since there is no special language available, we must employ the normal physical-object language that is ready to hand.

Thus, we cannot say, while *having* an immediate experience, what it is an experience of. But we can provide a second-level analysis of sensation which indicates what features these experiences have and must have if they are to be the direct, unmediated acquaintance-events upon which observation judgements are built. This analysis will proceed in the language of terms and relations—because it is operating at the level of judgements—and, within the sphere of empirical knowledge, will proceed in terms of physical-object predicates which are, in discussions of immediacy, employed analogically to the way they are used in their more normal place, in perceptual judgements and observation reports. Moreover, it seems that something like this is in Bradley's mind when he warns against confusing 'the feeling which we study with the feeling which we are' (*AR*, 205), or

---

[16] Cf. *AR*, 208 and 209.

when he says that the contents of immediacy, the 'various aspects' of a 'felt complex', 'can all be separated by distinction and analysis' (*AR*, 203–4),[17] by which he also means they can *only* be separated by higher-level operations involving conceptualization and analysis.

The second possibility, that there really are relations within immediacy, depends on whether the bonds holding the contents of a conjunctive unity together are also merely analogues of relations, or are themselves relations. Here there may be an ambivalence in Bradley's position.

Every unity involves some plurality of items held together in some way. The difference between the two basic types of unity lies in the nature of the bonds of the plurality involved. In a conjunctive unity the bond is mere conjunction. Here there are diverse items (or contents of an experience), but they display 'mere difference' reflected by the 'mere "and"' (*ETR*, 194). Together these items are a 'mere' or immediate totality (*ETR*, 179). This kind of unity apparently *does* display relations, but only 'mere' relations.

This means that we must be careful what we claim about the unity of feeling. An immediate experience or feeling is a conjunctive unity which is non-relational in the sense that there are not two distinct things—a subject and an object—related here. The adverbial analysis of immediacy saves this thesis. Further, immediate experience is non-relational in that it does not display relations which *connect*—that is, which really relate, in Bradley's weighty sense of 'relate'—the 'terms' or multiple contents of experience. This is because relations (in the weighty sense) must disclose the intelligible connections—the how and the why—of the unity involved, and immediacy does not do this. Indeed, it

---

[17] Perhaps Bradley has in mind something like a Sellarsian view. The key to Sellars's view is his translation of 'S senses a red triangle' as 'S senses (a red triangle)ly'. Retaining the indefinite article and 'triangle' instead of 'triangular' is important, for now it is possible to see the attributes of a visual sensation as 'the analogues of the sensible attributes of the objects . . . which are their standard causes'. Thus, the adverbial attribute-analogues are part of a theory of sensory acquaintance which would be justified just in case that theory displays adequate explanatory power and wins out over competitors via an elimination argument. Sellars takes 'a red triangle', as it occurs in the phrase 'a (of a red triangle) sensation', as not being a referring expression; although 'of a red triangle' is a predicate with syntactic and semantic structure. In 'S senses a red triangle', the adverbial predicate 'is playing a special role in which its conceptual properties as the specific adverb it is are conveyed by the fact that these same words in physical object discourse stand for an attribute having analogous conceptual properties' (Sellars, 'Adverbial Theory', 150).

cannot, since it is presentational and below the level of judgement. (And this is why Bradley at times says that immediacy is unintelligible (*ETR*, 314); because at this level we cannot establish the connections, the relations in the weighty sense, of immediacy's multiple contents. We cannot understand why the multiple contents of immediacy have presented themselves in this fashion, for the conditions of the uniting bonds remain unknown.)

Yet, the multiple contents of immediacy do present relations, albeit the relations of the 'mere "and"', which signal a conjunction of contents (an 'immediate inherence' (*ETR*, 33)). This is a 'relation' in what I will call Bradley's 'weak' sense, and probably corresponds in some contexts to an 'external' relation. Indeed, if an external relation is one which is somehow 'there' but *makes no difference to its terms*, then in the conjunction of adverbial sensings which composes immediacy we have external relations. It is the relation expressed by what Bradley calls the 'sensuous "is"' (*ETR*, 256). In this way the conjunctive analysis available to adverbial theorists in response to the Many-Property Problem maps on to a Bradleyan felt totality or conjunctive unity.

It is the process of analysis (which is actually the double process of analysis and synthesis) which moves us from mere conjunctive contents (a conjunctive unity) to connected wholes (a connective unity). It does this by exposing the *conditions* that explain the how and the why of the mere conjunction of elements. Immediate experience is required for this higher-level unity, because it supplies the *pieces* which analysis will connect. Thus, connection presupposes conjunction.[18] And for empirical knowledge, true perceptual judgements (which establish at least some of the connections between objects, their qualities, and the perceiver) depend on the presented external relations (conjunctions) of immediate sensory apprehensions. Given this, we can see why Bradley wants to say that immediacy remains throughout all other levels of experience, and is, in one sense, their foundation. (It also explains why Bradley claims that 'accidental conjunction' is the 'mark of genuine memory' (*ETR*, 371). This is because the 'merely conjunctive', or merely 'associational', aspect of memory signals that we have arrived at a recall of a felt unity (a conjunctive unity), and are thereby as close to the original felt experience as we are ever able to get.)

---

[18] Cf. *ETR*, 315.

At this point I must confess that it may be that, instead of saying, as I did a moment ago, that 'in the conjunction of adverbial sensings which composes immediacy we have external relations', it may only be possible to claim that here we have an *analogue* of an external relation. If only this weaker claim can be established, the second possibility collapses into the first. Of course, it is just at this point that Bradley is ambivalent. The more he presses the *presentational* aspect of immediate apprehensions, the more he wants to say that the contents of immediacy are there as distinct features *merely* conjoined. That is, they exhibit external relations. Yet, if relations are *established* via certain mental operations, we have reason to hold that what is present in immediate experience is describable only as an *analogue* of an external relation. (Or perhaps it might be possible to say that, once mental operations are engaged in the task of establishing connections, we have moved to a perspective from which the established relations are taken as internal relations.) Resolving this ambivalence, however, is a task for another occasion.[19]

To sum up, I have argued that we gain some illumination on Bradley's doctrine of immediate experience—at least as it functions within the sphere of empirical knowledge, as an account of sensory acquaintance—by interpreting it along the lines of an adverbial theory of sensory apprehension.[20] An adverbial interpretation is appealing, because it helps to explain how Bradley can hold that while an immediate experience or feeling is non-relational in one sense (because it is a 'manner' of sensing which thereby does not entail objects opposed to a subject of the experience), it is also relational in a 'weak', and perhaps analogical, sense (because it has multiple contents displaying the 'mere' relations of conjunctive unity).

[19] There is perhaps a further complication here: viz. whether Bradley thinks of relations as the products of intellectual acts, rather than as items simply occurring *in rerum natura*. At *PL*, 96, he seems to endorse the former view; yet in other contexts (e.g. *PL*, 10, 147, 290) he seems to accept the latter. Deciding what to say about this requires detailed examinations of the contexts of his remarks about relations, but for the theme of this essay the former would suggest that the diversities within immediacy—and within reality itself—could, at most, be taken as analogues of qualities or terms exhibiting relations.

[20] There is still more to be said about whether Jackson has posed a genuine dilemma for adverbial theories, which Tye and Sellars believe he has not, and about whether Bradley's view—which, I contend, grasps the first horn of that dilemma, as did Ducasse's—is ultimately satisfactory. I have said something on the latter in my 'Moore's Refutation of Idealism'.

9

Bradley's Doctrine of the Absolute

T. L. S. SPRIGGE

———◆———

INTRODUCTORY

There is a strong temptation, when attempting to interest philosophers of today in a historical thinker with currently unfashionable metaphysical commitments, to concentrate on aspects of his thought which seem independent of these. The result is often to relegate what was central from the thinker's own point of view to the sidelines. One could point to several treatments of historical philosophers of this character. With Bradley there is a temptation like this even for someone, such as myself, who actually goes along with much of his metaphysical outlook, but who likes to maintain a certain façade of respectability. Nor is this difficult with Bradley. He had interesting opinions on matters which can, up to a point, be disentangled from what many today see as his more outlandish beliefs. Still, *someone* at this conference should concern himself with these, and perhaps it is as well that it should be someone who partly shares them. So I shall present what I believe to be the core of Bradley's doctrine of the Absolute, and explain what I find so persuasive about it.[1]

My account will be in three stages. First, I shall present in my own way, rather than his, what I believe to be the core of the doctrine of the Absolute, and the case for its existence, stripped to its essentials, and freed from certain complications which I do not believe to be altogether helpful to it. Second, I shall say

[1] This essay includes some material from my *James and Bradley: American Truth and British Reality* (Chicago and La Salle, Ill.: Open Court, 1993). It is used with the kind permission of the publishers.

something about how my presentation departs from the letter of Bradley's own case. Third, I shall say something concerning what seems to have been its main personal significance for Bradley.

1. WHAT THE ABSOLUTE IS

First, we must consider what the Absolute is supposed to be. The answer is that it is the universe as it really is, as opposed to as it seems to be to ordinary human thought. However, in speaking of the universe as it truly is as the Absolute, Bradley is making certain definite claims about it which may be summarily presented as follows.[2]

(1) The Absolute, or totality of all things, is not a mere aggregate or assemblage of things; it is much more truly one than many. This means both that it is an organized system, and that it has, to a supreme degree, those features which make one regard something as a single thing rather than as a collection of things, and therefore has these features in a much higher degree than do what count as ordinary single things in daily life.

(2) The Absolute is a timeless experience or state of mind, inconceivably rich in the elements which go to make it up, but still having something like the kind of unity which belongs to a human person's experience as it occurs at any moment. It contains every experience which any conscious being has had or will have, and thereby contains everything, since for Bradley there is nothing except experience. Just as what a human hears, feels, sees, thinks, and so on at any one moment is multiple, yet makes up one single experience, so does every ingredient of the world go to make up this single vast cosmic experience, which is the Absolute, or, the universe as it really is.

(3) The Absolute is not a person. A person must feel itself in contrast to a world, which provides its environment, whereas the Absolute experiences everything as an element in its own being.

---

[2] 'The way of taking the world which I have found most tenable is to regard it as a single Experience, superior to relations and containing in the fullest sense everything which is' (*ETR*, 245–6). The doctrine of the Absolute is most fully stated in *AR*, chs. 13–15, 26–7.

(4) Although the Absolute is the *All*, there is a sense in which the *All* or *Whole* is present in each of its *parts* or *aspects*. As a first suggestion of what this means, one might say that it is present in all its parts somewhat as someone's personality may be present in all his acts, or in which the total character of a work of art permeates all its elements.

If the Absolute is all there really is, how come we can talk about anything else? Well, in a sense we cannot. However, Bradley distinguishes two other sorts of reality from the Absolute: namely, finite centres of experience and the constructed object world.

A finite centre of experience is, roughly speaking, the total psychical state which constitutes what it is like to be some sentient individual at a particular moment.[3] Or rather, it is anything of the same basic sort as what constitutes this. It is not very different from what other thinkers might call a total state of consciousness, though Bradley gives a more restricted meaning to 'consciousness'. In a somewhat different sense, a finite centre of experience is a continuant of which such a state is a momentary phase.

The constructed object world is the shared posit of a system of communicating finite centres achieved through synthetic judgements of sense which interpret any given perceptual fields as different fragments of a single spatio-temporal whole extending them in a manner homogeneous with them in character. Its existence consists simply in the pragmatic value of such positings. There may be many different object worlds constructed by different systems of communicating finite centres.

Both finite centres and the object world are simply appearances of the Absolute. However, it seems to me that they are so, for Bradley, in effect, in two somewhat different senses, which I shall distinguish as that of being part-like abstractions from it and that of being useful posits for the purposes of coping with it. Not that Bradley himself makes this distinction, but it seems needed to make sense of his position.

Finite centres of experience are appearances of the Absolute in the first sense. Suppose we start with the conception of them as simply parts of the Absolute, components in its being. Then we must modify this when we realize that the concept of 'part' implies

---

[3] The best statement of the doctrine of finite centres is 'What is the Real Julius Caesar?', in *ETR*, ch. 14. The most relevant parts of *AR* are chs. 19 and 21.

more independence of being from the whole and its other parts than these centres have from the Absolute and other finite centres. Perhaps we may think of them as standing to the Absolute somewhat as its various surfaces, or two-dimensional cross-sections, stand to a three-dimensional solid (taking a physical-realist view for the purpose of illustration). To single out one of these for attention is rather like singling out a part of the solid; yet they do not have that independent fullness of being possessed by the parts of a solid in a more proper sense—for example, the bricks of a house, which can be separated from the house and the other bricks, and this without any necessary effect on their individual character.[4]

In contrast, things in the object world are appearances of the Absolute rather in the sense that they exist simply as useful posits made by or within finite centres of experience as attempts to understand that total reality of which they feel themselves to be only fragments.

Bradley does not formally distinguish these two different senses of 'appearance', and indeed holds views which tend to assimilate them, but it is hard to understand him unless we make some such distinction. However, we must not overemphasize it. What unites them is that, to be an appearance of the Absolute, something must be such that, first, to think of such a thing as existing is to get some partial grasp of how things really are with it, and, second, that that partial grasp also somewhat distorts its real nature. Now things in our object world, and our object world as a whole, clearly answer to this description if Bradley's view of them is correct. The conception of them is helpful as a way in which finite centres can cope with their environment—that is, with, so to speak, their own situation within the Absolute—practically, but it also misleads as to the real character of the universe. In contrast, finite centres of experience seem more like genuine parts, or at least part-like features, of the Absolute, and as such rather

---

[4] I would not put too much emphasis on the fact that parts actually can be separated from the whole (or once were, as with the bricks of a house). For that concerns a change in time, which is not what is in question here. The question is rather whether an item just like a certain part of a certain whole as each is at a particular moment or eternally (eternally either in the sense in which an event is eternally located in its own one moment or in some more deeply metaphysical sense) could have existed without being such a part of it at such a moment or eternally.

more than mere useful posits. However, the conception of them too is, in the end, more a convenient way of getting hold of something important about the Absolute than an absolute truth about its articulation into parts or aspects. For the idea of it as thus articulated involves certain contradictions or incoherences which show that it cannot do adequate justice to how the Absolute really is a psychical many-in-one. Thus finite centres of experience also exist, in the end, only as useful posits.

But who or what posits them, one may well ask, if they themselves are only useful posits? One answer may be that the Absolute posits them itself, in order the better to understand itself, though it is a form of understanding, which, at some other level, it must transcend. Another answer is that we are here moving to a level which cannot properly be expressed in conceptual thought.

But though the concept of a finite centre is, in Bradley's opinion, ultimately unsatisfactory, I believe that it is one we must use in trying to give a conceptual statement of what Bradley believes to be as near to truth as we can come, and that talking thus we may say that they are part-like features of the Absolute, and even speak of them as 'parts' thereof when it is convenient to do so.

Putting matters thus, we may say that to claim that the Absolute exists is to claim that there is a single infinite centre of experience, the Absolute itself, of which all finite centres are fragments, and that everything else which in any sense exists is either a part of it, an aspect or feature of it, or something usefully posited by one of its parts, features, or aspects.

THE CORE ARGUMENT FOR THE ABSOLUTE

The Argument for the Absolute

So much by way of clarification of what it means to say that there is such a thing as the Absolute. Now we must consider what grounds there are for saying that there is such a thing.

I suggest that the basic argument is as follows:

(1) (premiss) Everything is related in some way to everything else (*principle of universal relatedness*).

(2) (premiss) Terms can only be related in virtue of being united with each other, usually together with other things, to

constitute a whole which is more of a genuine individual than are any of them singly (*holistic principle*).[5] (This principle may require the following qualification:[6] One term P can stand in a relation to another term W in virtue of uniting with other things to constitute it. In this case either W must be more of a genuine individual than P, or the terms which constitute W must do so in virtue of the fact that they combine with W to constitute a more comprehensive whole which is more of a genuine individual than it or they are. Relations which conform to this principle may be conveniently called 'holistic relations'. *Thus the holistic principle affirms that all relations are holistic.*)

(3) (lemma) Everything which *is* must be included in a whole which is more genuinely an individual than anything included in that whole (from 1 and 2).

(4) (premiss) Everything which genuinely *is* is experiential, that is, either (a) a whole (or centre) of experience or (b) an element in such or (c) an aggregate (or mereological sum) of items experiential in one of these first two senses (*principle of universal experientiality*).[7]

(5) (premiss) One or more experiences can only unite to form a whole if either that whole, or some larger whole in which they are included, is an individual unitary experience.

(6) (conclusion) There must be a single unitary experience which includes everything else and which is more of a genuine

---

[5] 'Relations are unmeaning except within and on the basis of a substantial whole, and related terms, if made absolute, are forthwith destroyed. Plurality and relatedness are but features and aspects of a unity' (*AR*, 125). See also *AR*, 512, and many other passages.

[6] The qualification basically deals with propositions to the effect that one thing is a part of another. To deal with multiple relational propositions affirming that *n* things (*n* > 1) are joint parts of an *n* + 1th thing would require an obvious further elaboration of this qualification. Bradley officially denied that relations could be more than two-term, but this seems to me inessential to his case.

[7] 'We perceive, on reflection, that to be real, or even barely to exist, must fall within sentience' (*AR*, 127). The idea of an aggregate of experiences which is not itself experienced would not be accepted by Bradley, but I have put it in as a provisional possibility, to be discounted in (7), as I can thereby bring out better the role of the holistic principle in establishing a Bradleyan view of the world.

individual than anything included in it. This is what is referred to as the Absolute.[8]

(7) (conclusion) Aggregates of what is experiential in senses (a) or (b) of premiss (4) must also be experiential in sense (a) or (b).

To these seven propositions I add three more, which could be divided into three further premisses and three further conclusions but which it will be simpler to present along with the case for them in a more informal way.

(8) The Absolute includes everything, past, present, and future, in an eternal standing now. For if there is a definite truth about the whole of the past, as there must be, the past must be included in the Absolute along with what we are now calling the present in an eternal *Nunc Stans*. This *Nunc Stans* must also include what we are now regarding as the future, for we are simply its past, and we have just seen that a reality's past exists alongside it in the Absolute.[9]

If this argument is present in Bradley at all, it is only so in a very hidden form, and there are even remarks which may seem to contradict it. But something of the sort is needed to establish Bradley's full doctrine.

(9) Every component of a unitary experience is affected in a unique way, within its own bounds (so to speak), by the character of the whole to which it belongs and the part it plays in giving it that character. Thus in a certain sense it reflects that character. This is a phenomenological claim which applies, as it seems to me, to every sensation which helps to constitute our state of consciousness at any particular moment. In this sense the relations between the components of an experience are not merely holistic, but *strongly* so. By this I mean that the inherent character of each term reflects the character of the Whole, in the sense indicated, in virtue of

---

[8] Thus the universe is not merely an aggregate of experiences without being an experience itself.

[9] I develop the kind of argument which I believe Bradley really needs here in my 'The Unreality of Time', *Proceedings of the Aristotelian Society*, 92/1 (1991–2), 1–18. Its relevance to Bradley is made clearer in my *James and Bradley*, ch. 4, para. 3.

helping to constitute which the terms are related.[10] It follows that, since the Absolute is a single cosmic experience containing everything else, then everything else in a certain sense reflects its character, thus justifying the fourth defining characteristic of the Absolute given above.

This is doubtless among the more contentious of the claims which I am making in my reconstruction of Bradley's case for the Absolute. I note therefore that even without it we could arrive at a somewhat weakened doctrine of the Absolute in which the fourth defining feature would be toned down. Our conclusion would still be sufficiently striking.

(10)   Since there is nothing beyond it towards which it could feel any sort of nisus, the Absolute must be in a state of overall satisfaction, and be describable as in some sense perfect.

Do the Conclusions Follow from the Premises?

Let us ask first whether these conclusions follow from the premises, in particular, whether (6) follows from what precedes it. It would take me too far afield to say much more about the cogency of (8), (9), and (10). Although they are required as part of a satisfactorily complete demonstration of the existence of the Absolute, as Bradley characterizes it, (1)–(6) are sufficient for the demonstration of the existence of a Bradleyan Absolute in some very challenging sense.

One objection may be this. Proposition (3) is supposed to follow from (1) and (2) along lines which could be indicated as follows. Suppose that we start with items a and b. They must be related, and must be so in virtue of constituting a whole together, or doing so with some further group of items, which we will lump together as X. Then we have a whole W, constituted by a, b, and X. Now presuming W is not the whole universe, there must be one or more further units related to it—call them Y—and this must be so because there is a whole, W2, which is constituted by W and Y. It seems that this series must go on until you get to a whole W which is not related to anything else (except to the parts

---

[10] For a more precise statement see my The *Vindication of Absolute Idealism* (Edinburgh: Edinburgh University Press, 1983), 218 ff.

that constitute it) and which will be more of a genuine individual unit than anything comprised within it.

Now someone might claim that, though premisses (1) and (2) certainly do imply that if we start with any terms which are related to each other, we must have a series of this sort, it does not follow that the series must have an end. There are several ways in which a Bradleyan might reply to this, doubtless all of them somewhat contentious. The simplest probably is this. Suppose we take some particular a, not itself the whole universe, and such that there is nothing, short perhaps of the whole universe, which is more genuinely an individual than it. Now let us regard the totality of what is entirely outside a as itself a vast object Z. Then a and Z must be related, but they can only be so because they constitute together a larger whole, the total universe, which is more of an individual than Z.

If something along these lines is acceptable, I think we should agree that the premisses establish the conclusion, (6).

So let us now examine the premisses from which (6) is derived in turn, to see what can be said for each of them.

Examination of the Premisses

(1) Is it reasonable to take it that everything is related to everything else?

Let me point out first that even if it were not true, it would be very reasonable for each of us (who are related to each other) to use the expression 'the universe' to mean the totality of everything to which we stand in any kind of relation. (*Being in some relation or other to* is clearly a transitive relation; so, since we are each of us in some relation to each other, it follows that it will be the same totality to which we each refer by 'universe' thus used.) Then such expressions as 'everything' may be taken to mean 'everything in the universe', and the argument as concerning the nature of the universe in this sense—our relative universe, if you like.

Bradley, I believe, would claim that (1) is true, without the need of any such explanation, on the grounds that even the most utter form of separateness is a kind of relation, and that everything must be related to everything else either by some form of unity or by some form of separateness. I find it hard to evaluate the claim that even the most utter separateness is a form of relationship. It seems like saying that not to be in a relation is itself a way of being related, and I think it safer not to use this rather specious-sounding claim without attempting more backing for it than can be given here. It is probably better to take it that, even if this is in some sense true, its truth is better taken as a conclusion from the establishment of the Bradleyan Absolute than as a premiss to be used in arguing for it.

Our discussion of the second premiss, however, will shortly provide us with reason for a certain revision of premiss (1).

(2) Is the holistic principle correct?

It will help in considering this to make a distinction which Bradley only ever makes in the most passing way: that between what are sometimes called ideal and, in contrast, real relations. Bradley did have reasons within his own system for not making much of this distinction, but in presenting a case for his Absolute which does not presuppose its own conclusions, we should regard the distinction as having prima facie some force, even if, once the Absolute is attained, we would have some reason for taking it as without ultimate validity.

In distinguishing between real relations and ideal relations, I shall confine my attention to relations between concrete particulars. (Tacitly I have been ignoring the status of what today are commonly, and very misleadingly, called 'abstract objects'—in particular, universals. Bradley's position is, I think, roughly, that a universal like red is both identical and different from itself as it occurs in its different instances. As different from itself, it is a particular; as identical, it is a universal. To take this into account would unduly complicate my account, and so I have taken expressions like 'everything' as referring primarily to concrete realities, with the assumption that universals can be fitted into the scheme by reference to the doctrine of identity and difference.)

An ideal relation is a relation of contrast or affinity in character, or of degree of some quality, where this has a meaning which is non-derivative from any possibility of practical alignment with a measuring apparatus (e.g. of a brighter colour hue than, twice as beautiful as). And it does not seem to me at all obvious that ideal relations answer to the holistic principle, though there are also considerations which might imply that they do.[11]

---

[11] Ibid. 180–94, 250–3.

Now consider real—that is, non-ideal—relations. It seems to me that these are all either relations of juxtaposition of one sort or another, or part–whole or whole–part relations, or presuppose a relation of one of these sorts between their terms. (This is all rather rough-and-ready, but more precision is impossible here.) It also seems to me that, while the holistic principle raises problems (to which I cannot now attend) if it is taken as covering ideal relations as well as real relations, it is difficult to resist if qualified so that it concerns only real relations—in short, is understood as the claim that all real relations are holistic.

To take account of this revision of the second premiss, some revision is required also of the first premiss if we are to avoid claims about ideal relations which are not really necessary to the case for the Absolute. The first premiss, then, should now be taken as laying down a requirement for things to be in some real relationship to each other, and must be taken as saying that everything is related to everything else in some real way—that is, in some way which goes beyond a mere affinity or contrast, or difference of degree in some quality. (The character of this and other required revisions of the premisses should be clear enough without a full formal restatement of them.)

Thus modified, it may seem less certain, though in fact I think it is something that most of us find it hard not to believe. However, we can continue to protect it absolutely by defining the Universe as consisting of the totality of everything to which we are in any kind of real relation. This does not make claims about it merely trivial, for questions about the nature of the Universe are surely normally about it understood in this sense.

I have described the holistic principle, thus revised, as difficult to resist. However, I would have some sympathy with someone who was persuaded only of a less bold version of it. In this less bold version, the claim that terms in a real relation are so in virtue of constituting a whole together which is more of a genuine individual than either of them is singly would be replaced by the claim that they are so in virtue of constituting a whole which is *as* genuine an individual as either of them taken singly. (Applied to the qualification to cover the whole–part or part–whole relation, the revised version requires that the whole either itself be more genuinely an individual than the part, or that its unity depends on its being a part of something which is more genuinely an individual than it.)

To me, at least, this less bold version of the holistic principle seems absolutely compelling, and it will in fact suffice for purposes of my reconstruction of Bradley's argument for the Absolute. So let me try to bring out why I am so convinced of the holistic principle, at the very least in this form, by considering a few examples which I think point to a general truth.

What is it to learn the spatial relations between things, but to learn how they combine together to make up a certain sort of spatial whole (or do so together with other things)? What is a temporal relation but that of combining together to make up a certain sort of unitary temporal event (or doing so together with other things)? What perhaps of causal relations? Well, the most usual view is that the holding of a causal relation between terms consists in the fact that the holding of some other relation between them is an instance of some law. But in that case a causal relation can only hold between things which are in some other relation (that determined by the law). And it seems to me that this cannot be a mere ideal relation, but must be a real relation answering to the holistic principle. What of the relation between a thought and its object? Well, that is too immense an issue to take on here, but I would claim that you cannot think about a particular to which you are not in some real relation, and that this requires that there be some appropriate whole to which you and it belong, which is not less of a genuine individual than either you or it (e.g. a human community and its physical infrastructure).

I have argued these points at some length elsewhere, and shall not elaborate them further now.[12] Suffice it to say that to me it seems that all real relations are holistic in the sense indicated, or at the least presuppose holistic relations. The person who thinks otherwise must try to think of two or more items as in some real relationship to each other—that is, one which is not merely ideal—and claim that this is not, in the end, a matter of thinking of them as forming, or helping to form along with other things, a totality with the same or greater degree of individuality as each of them possesses considered alone. I find myself quite unable to do this, and believe that this is a sign of insight, not of defect. Something of the same sort was recognized by Husserl

---

[12] Ibid. 211–13 and 239–41 on causation, and 241–7 on the relation between thought and its object.

as holding whenever distinct objects are recognized as in so-called external relations. (I think 'external' relations in his sense covers all non-ideal relations holding between separate individuals.)

The matter is plainly similar in the case of external relations, from which predications such as 'A is to the right of B', 'A is larger, brighter, louder than B etc.', take their rise. Wherever sensible objects—directly and independently perceptible—are brought together, despite their mutual exclusion, into more or less intimate unities, into what fundamentally are more comprehensive objects, then a possibility of such external relations arises. They all fall under the general type of the relation of part to parts within a whole.[13]

That the bolder version of the holistic principle is also true I believe, but it is less obvious. However, if we substitute the less bold requirement in the argument, then we will still reach the following conclusion: that there must be a single unitary experience which includes everything else and which is as genuine an individual as is anything included in it. Thus there must be such an all-encompassing unitary experience which is as genuine an individual as my present state of consciousness. That seems to me quite enough to prove Bradley's Absolute. For once granted that the universe as a whole is a single unitary experience, then surely there are all sorts of reasons for thinking that it must be more genuinely unitary than is any human state of consciousness. Proposition (3) is not a premiss, but a lemma, derived from propositions (1) and (2), so let us move on to the final premisses for the conclusion (6).

(4) and (5). Are premisses (4) (the principle of universal experientiality) and (5) (that one or more experiences can only unite to form a whole if either that whole, or some larger whole in which they are included, is an individual unitary experience) acceptable?

Take (4) first. Personally I accept this, but it would be too big a thing to argue for extensively here. It is obviously crucial for Bradley's metaphysics. My own main argument is that one cannot genuinely imagine anything not itself either quite evidently itself an experience or free of any characteristics which it could have only as a component in an experience (with the possible

[13] Edmund Husserl, *Logical Investigations*, trans. J. N. Findlay (London: Routledge and Kegau Paul, 1970), ii. 794–5.

prima facie exception, to be discounted on the basis of further reflections, of aggregates of experiences).[14] This argument is often rejected through confusing it with the claim that one cannot imagine anything without imagining it as an experience or a component in an experience. But to imagine it without imagining it as included in an experience, or as it could only be as included in such, is not the same as imagining it as, so to speak, positively not in experience, and it is the latter that is required if one is to imagine things lying outside mental life.

Other objections are that what one can or cannot imagine has no bearing on what one can conceive, and that neither of these has any bearing on what might be. But I suggest that one does not have the kind of deep grasp of what a thing is which metaphysics seeks unless one can acquire a genuine sense of something of its essence in a manner which comes under 'imagining' taken in a broad sense, and as regards possibility, one cannot believe in the existence of things with a feature F unless one can conceive feature F, and the argument is that if F means *totally unexperienced*, one cannot conceive it. It would be wrong to conclude that I cannot believe in the existence of things inconceivable by me, for I can conceive the predicate 'inconceivable by me' on the basis of reflections about how the congenitally blind may stand to colours as qualities presented within experience. What I cannot conceive is *something totally non-experiential*, there being no kindred basis for the construction of such a concept.

And what of (5)? Well, it does seem to me very difficult to see how experiences can form any kind of whole which is not either a unitary experience or an element of a unitary experience.

It is worth pointing out that even without (4), and with a slightly different version of (5), one could reach Bradley's Absolute.

(4a)   There are such things as unitary experiences of the type which constitute the state of consciousness of a human being at some time.

(5a)   No sort of whole is conceivable which would include more than one of these unitary experiences which was not itself some kind of unitary experience (or part thereof).

---

[14] See *Vindication*, esp. 110–40.

Although I could not expect a modern physicalist to accept (5a) and would expect him to accept (4a) only in what I would consider a debased form, I still believe that anyone who really recognizes the kind of being which pertains to a unitary experience should agree with these propositions. And it should be fairly obvious that they would do the trick, even without the strong pan-experientialist claim of (4).

All in all, while I cannot adequately argue every point every inch of the way in the present short compass, I do believe that an argument along these lines makes an extremely strong case for the existence of the Absolute. Indeed, I find it hard to resist myself.

COMPARISON OF OUR ARGUMENT FOR THE ABSOLUTE WITH BRADLEY'S OWN PRECISE POSITION

Although I believe that the argument which I have presented is thoroughly Bradleyan in spirit, it may seem to diverge somewhat from Bradley's own precise position.

I will admit, first, that it concentrates on certain aspects of Bradley's case for the Absolute to the exclusion of others. For example, it downplays the role in Bradley's reasoning of the claim that finite things contain internal contradictions which can only be resolved by seeing them as components in larger wholes, ultimately of the Absolute. The reason for my selective approach is that I want to concentrate on a line of argument in Bradley which I personally wish to recommend as peculiarly convincing.

But do the argument and conclusion which I have presented actually diverge from Bradley? I shall consider this under three main headings:

(i)   What Bradley actually held about relations.
(ii)   Did he think that nothing exists except experience?
(iii) Did he think that the Absolute was actually composed of finite centres of experience?

Bradley's real view on relations

About the only thing which many philosophers know about Bradley is that he thought relations unreal. Perhaps they wonder what he can have meant by this.

They probably know that he did not mean—what one might at first expect—that the basic existents (one can hardly say the basic existents of the world, for there would hardly be a world in this case) are out of any kind of togetherness with each other. What they believe, usually, I suppose, is that Bradley thought that there was only one thing.

This is not exactly false, but it is rather misleading. A better way of putting it is to say that, for Bradley, the universe is, indeed, more of a genuinely individual thing than are any of its components, and that the usual conception of it as constituted of innumerable distinct things, each with a quite separate character of its own, but somehow bonded together by something called 'the relations' between them, is false because demonstrably impossible.

I shall avoid entanglement in the details of his arguments about relations. Worthwhile as it may be sometimes to evaluate these as they stand, I think that too much attention to their rather dubious details has detracted attention from what is really the main point he is trying to get across. And I believe that this really comes to much the same as saying that the genuine relations which link things are strongly holistic. (Though, as I have indicated above, a sufficiently striking case for something very like Bradley's Absolute could be made with only the insistence that all *real* relations are strongly holistic.)

Bradley would say that this was not an adequate way of conceiving things, because the relations still either have to stand outside their terms, and then require something else to bind them to the terms, in an endless regress, or they lie within the terms taken together in a manner which presupposes that the terms are, so to speak, already together without their aid. But, as I understand it, to talk of strongly holistic relations just is a way of talking about the togetherness which Bradley is concerned to emphasize.

Does Bradley believe that nothing exists except experience?

It may be suggested that (despite the famous passage at the beginning of ch. 14 of *AR*) it is rather misleading to say that for Bradley the Absolute consists only of experience. For an experience commonly includes judgements which posit the existence of things other than itself. Let us call these its deliverances. (The expression 'intentional object' is too closely associated with

approaches other than Bradley's to be used here.) Now the deliverance of an experience, as opposed to the judgement which posits
it, is not exactly a part of it in the way in which what is strictly
perceived of an object is a part of the experience to which the
perception belongs.[15] Nor, so it might seem, need it be part of
any other experience. Yet surely the deliverances of experience,
including such things as number systems, belong to the Absolute
as truly as do the experiences in which they are posited. In fact,
Bradley would seem to hold that the Absolute achieves its awareness of total systems of this sort by putting together the mere
fragments of them which are all that are grasped in any single
finite centre. So it seems that the Absolute thinks of there being
things which are neither part of its own psychical stuff nor necessarily even thought of by any finite individual. And because the
Absolute thinks of there being such things, in an important sense
there *are* such things. For, as Bradley sees it, that which is postulated in a satisfying and harmonious thought can properly be
described as having *being*. Such being pertains not only to our
physical environment, but to such other things as the abstract
entities of mathematics, philosophical systems, hierarchies of value,
and other such deliverances rather than components of experiences
of various kinds. And surely these deliverances do pertain to the
Absolute, which, therefore, seems not to be solely experiential in
character.

One approach might be to distinguish between the actual constituents of the Absolute and what pertains to it without being
in the same way part of what makes it up. On this view 'to be'
is 'to be thought or to be experienced' but it is only that which
is experienced, and not merely thought, which is an actual constituent of the Absolute, though the latter pertains to it.

But that cannot be quite correct. For Bradley's pan-experi-
entialism implies that, at the level of the Absolute, all judgements
which posit something not experienced must be corrected by
judgements which ascribe an experiential character to these posits.

---

[15] Not everyone would accept that what is strictly perceived is part of the perception of it. But for Bradley, I believe, the presented things which are the basis
for the synthetic judgements of sense, through which we conceive them as components of a larger object world, are so, and I would follow him in this. Certainly
they are part of our sentient experience as needing to be described in any description of 'what it is currently like to be us'.

And, what is more, he holds that the very distinction which holds for us between actually experiencing something and merely thinking about it is somehow transcended in the Absolute.

To understand this, we must recall his account of judgement as the alienation of some feature of one's own experience from its home therein to become a concept which is projected on to reality beyond. Thereby (as Bradley sees it) it becomes a mere 'wandering adjective'. For it has been deprived of its original home in the experience of the thinker, without having been given a proper home in the beyond on to which he projects it.

This is somewhat puzzling. On the one hand, it has not really lost its home in the mind of the thinker, and on the other, if the thought which predicates it is literally true, it does have a home in the beyond. Perhaps Bradley means that for us it has been deprived of its status as an element of the concrete fact of our own experience, but that, since we have no direct access to its home in the beyond, it is not presented to us as the genuinely concrete reality it is there, but only as something characterized in a rather abstract way. In the Absolute, however, the contrast between a universal as a predicate of what is thought about and a character present in the judging thought itself somehow disappears.

This is fairly straightforward where thoughts about the character of another's experiences are in question, but it is difficult to see how it is to be interpreted in relation to thought and perception of the physical. Bradley's doctrine here has been well expressed by Dawes Hicks (commenting on Bradley's remark that 'Nature may extend beyond the region actually perceived by the finite, but certainly not beyond the limits of finite thought'[16]):

> Somehow, what we merely think must, in the Absolute, be perceived; and the nature which we know conceptually will in the Absolute, where all content is reblended with existence, gain once more the form of being immediately felt or sensed, i.e. an intuitional (anschauliche) form.[17]

Thus suppose I am in a car and have various beliefs about what is contained below the bonnet. Then the universals which specify the character and location of these are, indeed, exemplified in my experience, or at least would be so if what I am believing

---

[16] *AR*, 277.
[17] G. Dawes Hicks, 'Mr Bradley's Treatment of Nature', *Mind*, 34 (1925), 61. Cf. *AR*, 146.

were fully realized in my imagination, but they are attributed to a reality beyond my experience. Thus they seem to have two distinct loci: first, as characteristics of imagery which I do actually experience, but which I must transcend in order to think, and second, as characteristics (so far as my beliefs are correct) of what I am thinking about, but do not directly experience. However, the Absolute experiences the identity amidst difference of the universals in these two loci, and thus heals the division between their felt occurrence as a character of concrete experience and their merely postulated occurrence as features of a reality beyond.

I do not see how else we can understand the coming together of the conceived and the immediately experienced in the Absolute. Yet it has apparent implications to which Bradley denies he is committed. For it suggests that there is something within the Absolute, with a certain distinctness from my own experience, which is what the engine of the car and so forth really is. What could this be? For pan-psychism it might be the group of feelings which constitute the 'in itself' of its ultimate physical units. (Though as the noumenon behind the ordinary physical reality it would have only the more purely structural of the universals which figure in my thought.) Another possibility is that it would be an element in a certain margin of experience, X, not filtered through any finite centre, which Bradley acknowledges might be the 'in itself' of nature.[18] But Bradley insists that he is not committed either to pan-psychism or to the existence of such a margin. Yet without one of these, it is hard to see how the engine can be anything more substantial than a shared posit that is the common deliverance of judgements united in the Absolute. And that leaves it unclear how the Absolute can heal the breach between thought and felt being, apart from the case in which what I am thinking of figures as an actual component of someone else's experience, with which it can be united in the Absolute.

It is true that Bradley plays with the idea that everything physical is perceived by some finite mind,[19] but he is no more committed to this than to the other possibilities just canvassed, and this means that, in so far as I think of what no one perceives, even the Absolute cannot heal the breach between perception and thought. It seems that it could only do so if it were given a much

---

[18] See *AR*, 241–2, 466–8; *ETR*, 350–1 n. 1. (Note that the references in the *ETR* note are to the 1st edn. of *AR*.) [19] See *AR*, 244.

more Berkeleyan role than Bradley seems willing to give it, as a
universal perceiver of physical nature.[20] (My way out, it will be
seen, is pan-psychism.)

Does Bradley Think that the Absolute is Actually Composed of Finite Centres of Experience?

But granted that the Absolute consists of nothing but experience,
does it include any experiences not either themselves total experiences, of the kind which Bradley calls 'finite centres of experience',
or included in one?

Well, we have just seen that Bradley is not a 100 per cent certain that there are no experiences which are not filtered through
any finite centre ('elements experienced in the total, and yet not
experienced within any subordinate focus'[21]). Still, on the whole,
he is inclined to reject their postulation. (It does not follow that the
same experience cannot occur within two or more such centres.
For Bradley, it certainly can, though the sameness will be an
identity-in-difference, a concept which I cannot explore here.)

So if we drop the notion of such dissociated experience, it does
not seem too far from the truth to say that, for Bradley, the
Absolute consists of finite centres and their contents synthesized[22]
in a single cosmic experience, with the important qualification
that the absolute experience has its own overall character ('some
content beyond that which falls in the experiences as several'[23]),
and that this character suffuses, more or less vividly, all its components, so that they could not possibly have existed in their own
inherent character except as just such ingredients in just such an
absolute experience (so that one can say equally that it owes its
character to them as they owe theirs to it). This seems to me to

---

[20] Bradley speaks rather scathingly of Berkeley's conception of the role of God.
See *AR*, 250 n. But since it was the conception of the divine and human minds
as external to one another to which he objected, one might have expected a more
pantheistic form of Berkeleyism to have some appeal for him.   [21] *AR*, 467.

[22] The past tense here does not imply that the synthesis is either temporally or
logically subsequent to what it synthesizes.

[23] *ETR*, 350 n. 1. There is, perhaps, some difficulty in distinguishing this
admitted extra content of the whole as the whole from some experiential matter
not 'filtered' through finite centres. Bradley would surely hold that there is an
inevitable straining of our conceptual resources on such matters. My own solution is to distinguish between more part-like and less part-like features of the
Absolute.

justify speaking of the Absolute as composed of finite centres of experience, provided it is stressed that it is no mere *aggregate*, whatever exactly that means, still less the set of all such centres, and that it has its own experience of itself as the Whole, an experience with, for example, an emotional quality and value which do not pertain to any of its finite components.[24]

ITS HUMAN SIGNIFICANCE FOR BRADLEY

In Part XII at the end of Hume's *Dialogues Concerning Natural Religion*, Philo, expressing what is usually thought to be Hume's opinion, says, reflecting on various arguments for theism:

If this really be the case, what can the most inquisitive, contemplative and religious man do more than give a plain, philosophical assent to the proposition, as often as it occurs, and believe that the arguments on which it is established, exceed the objections which lie against it?

We might ask what more the doctrine of the Absolute can be for Bradley? Is it merely a move in a recondite conceptual game, or is it the basis of something like a living religion or philosophy of life, it may be asked.

Well, surely part of its appeal was as providing answers to a variety of important intellectual questions about such things as the nature of thought, reasoning and truth, the logic of relations, and the ultimate significance of morality. Finding what he thought to be the truth on these matters was more than a game for him, and is so, surely, for anyone who professes to be a philosopher.

But what did it mean for him in more human terms, in terms of philosophy of life or lived religion? Well, it is worth remarking that Bradley seems to have been highly ambivalent in his attitude to Christianity. In *Ethical Studies* the tone suggests that he felt basically at one with the Protestant Christian tradition. In some of the essays of his middle years the tone is distinctly hostile. But, whatever his changing thoughts about Christianity, he certainly thought it important for human life that we should not lose our

---

[24] See *AR*, ch. 26 *passim*. It must be admitted that at *AR*, 469, Bradley objects to saying that the Absolute consists either of souls or of finite centres; but, granted no verbal formula is satisfactory for what is (doubtless rightly) supposed to be beyond conceptualization, I think a conceptualization along the lines above is helpful rather than otherwise.

sense that there is an underlying spiritual significance to the world, and that we can relate to something appropriately called 'the divine'.

His view seems to have been that there are many different ways of doing this, such as are provided by various different religions. The mythology of these is, so far at least as historical religions go, never metaphysically true, but they serve in different ways to promote effective engagement with Reality, and therefore are pragmatically true, to varying degrees, just as are different scientific theories, which are also always based on necessary mythology. The value of a metaphysics like Bradley's is that it shows that Reality in truth is such that these religious mythologies provide suitable forms of adjustment to it, even if they do not provide much ultimate truth about it. It also serves to show that morality has an objective basis in the fundamental identity underlying all phenomena, including ourselves: 'Unless there is a real identity in men, the "Inasmuch as ye did it to the least of these" becomes an absurdity.'[25]

Bradley says at one point that the world has need of a new religion.[26] I take it that he thought it possible that this one might be somewhat nearer to the metaphysical truth than are any of the traditional ones. It is strange that he never considers whether something like Advaita Vedanta Hinduism, once purged of superstition, might not become such a religion.

There is an aspect of Bradley's thought which is seldom or never noted today, but which, if it had received fuller emphasis, might have made him a more fashionable thinker in the present climate—that is, a strain of pantheism which might have been invoked in aid of a so-called deep ecological philosophy.

I shall simply illustrate this by a few quotations.

A God who has made this strange and glorious Nature outside of which he remains, is an idea at best one-sided. Confined to this idea we lose large realms of what is beautiful and sublime, and even for religion our conception of goodness suffers. Unless the Maker and Sustainer becomes also the indwelling Life and Mind and the inspiring Love, how much of the universe is impoverished! And it is only by an illusion which is really stupid that we can feel ourselves into, and feel ourselves one with, that

---

[25] Bradley, *Ethical Studies*, 2nd edn. (Oxford: Clarendon Press, 1927), 334–5. (The note there is one of the original ones of the 1st edn.)   [26] *ETR*, 446–7.

which, if not lifeless, is at least external. But how this necessary 'pan-theism' is to be made consistent with an individual Creator I myself do not perceive. (*ETR*, 436)

Positively the right and duty of self-assertion on the part of the Whole and lesser Wholes and against the individual follow. And of course the use of force where required follows, (force as compulsion of others).

This self-realization is to have no limits—no higher region of any kind which is separate and has more than a relative value.

Hence no denial of right to exist to any class or part of the finite world. Early Xtianity [affirmed?] this principle though only of all *human* beings—mainly on a mistaken ground. But we cannot stop there. We cannot exclude what we call the lower animals. We cannot even exclude what we call the inanimate world. There is no downward limit. To treat these things as matters of indifference is not moral.

Nothing is excluded but on the other side all is a matter of degree. There are no equal rights in the human world or outside it. You must sacrifice the welfare of part to whole within that world—and also out-side it. It is monstrous to say that for us man has no more right than lower animals or inanimate nature. It is also monstrous to say that these have no right as against him. The covering of a hideous world with the greatest possible number of inferior beings so long as they are human is not the end—even for us.[27]

CONCLUDING REMARK

Personally I agree with Bradley that the doctrine of the Absolute really does provide the solution to certain purely intellectual puzzles. But just as it stands in Bradley, I think that it still does not take the existence of physical reality seriously enough, too much suggesting that it exists only as a shared construction for finite centres of experience. I escape this myself by combining the doctrine of the Absolute with a pan-psychist view of nature towards which Bradley sometimes seems sympathetic, but which he never finally endorses or sees as necessary to his metaphysics.

In my opinion there is a compelling case for the pan-psychist view that the inner essence of what we call physical reality is

---

[27] From a 'A Note on Christian Morality', in IIB9 (chest II, pile B9) in the Bradley collection held at Merton College, Oxford. I have used the fair copy made by his sister. It has been published in *Religious Studies*, 19 (1983), 175–83, ed. G. Kendall.

psychical in character. The physical world of daily life, our 'life-world', is how a more fundamental reality appears to us, rather than something with an independent existence in the character it presents to our senses and imagination. A natural view to take is that this more fundamental reality is the physical world as basic science seeks to describe it and whose features would only finally be limned in a perfected physics. I accept this, but I believe that, in the end, natural science can describe only the abstract structure of the world. When it tries to show more concretely what it is which actualizes this structure, it falls back on imaginative aids which are simply extensions of that ordinary life-world which can exist only for human perception or for an imagination which extends it. But if nature exists as something more than a sensory appearance and as more than mere structure (as it surely must, for there must be something producing the experience and something concrete possessing the abstract structure), then it must have some hidden inner character and forms of togetherness and mutual influence between its parts. To me it seems that the best hypothesis as to what these can be is that they are somehow psychical, and that our own consciousness is an aspect of the psychical 'in itself' of what presents itself to common sense and science as our brains. Such a view helps to explain the relation between the mental and the physical (the former being the inner essence of the latter), and derives its view of reality as it is in itself from the only reality of which we know the concrete inherent character, mental experience akin to our own (though of course the mental inner essence of things other than processes in brains will not be—for the most part, at any rate—discursively cognitive in anything like the same way).

Thus I believe that the world ultimately consists of innumerable flows of experience, some of them of the high level which constitute our own streams of consciousness, others streams of mere dumb feeling with a certain volitional charge. As all these intermingle, they constitute a system with a certain overall structure which is what science seeks to capture in its description of the physical world, and of which our own life-world gives a less precise indication.

But how do these streams form any kind of unitary world within which they can exchange mutual influence? To think of them as in space and time, as we picture these in our imagination, is to reduce them to mere appearances, while to describe them in determinedly scientific terms is to specify only their structure. The only solution, I believe, is to suppose them united in an absolute experience, and to interpret space and time as either the sensory presentation of, or the abstract structure of, one main way in which they belong together there.

On this account, there is an Absolute Consciousness or Experience answering to a great extent to Bradley's account of the Absolute. But this Absolute Consciousness contains centres of experience which sense or chart their position alongside each other within it as something spatial and temporal. And, indeed, space and time represent, rather than misrepresent, this; only they leave its inner psychical character hidden. It will be seen that a conclusion like this develops Bradleyism in a somewhat Spinozistic direction.

For me, this makes it more satisfactory; for in spite of Bradley's being much less anthropocentric in his picture of the universe than were most absolute idealists, the main mood of his thought hardly does justice to the non-human immensities of the reality in the midst of which we find ourselves, and risks implying that the world is mainly a scene for human activity, or at least the activity of finite beings of much the same sort. Developing Bradleyism in this Spinozistic direction thus saves it from any suggestion of that cosmic impiety regarding our vast natural environment for which Santayana so criticized idealism in general.

This does not necessarily rule out the possibility, dear to Bradley, that the existence of the Absolute ensures that there is some point to the world, of a kind which materialism cannot find. Perhaps this emerges particularly in moral and mystical experience. At any rate, the doctrine of the Absolute, or of a cosmic consciousness of the universe at large, vindicates the sense we have at times of the ultimate unity of all things, and also, surely, the moral principle that the welfare of all should be the concern of each, seeing that the same common essence of consciousness burns in us all.

BIBLIOGRAPHY

ALLARD, JAMES, 'Bradley's Intentional Judgments', *History of Philosophy Quarterly*, 2 (1985).
—— 'Bradley on the Validity of Inference', *Journal of the History of Philosophy*, 27 (1989).
—— and STOCK, GUY (eds.), *F. H. Bradley: Writings on Logic and Metaphysics* (Oxford: Clarendon Press, 1994).
ARMSTRONG, DAVID, *A Materialist Theory of Mind* (London: Routledge, 1968).
AYER, A. J., *Language, Truth and Logic* (New York: Dover Publications, 1952; 1st edn. 1936).
—— *Philosophical Essays* (London: Macmillan, 1954).
—— (ed.), *Logical Positivism* (Glencoe, Ill.: Free Press, 1959).
BALDWIN, THOMAS, *G. E. Moore* (London: Routledge, 1990).
—— 'Moore's Rejection of Idealism', in R. Rorty *et al.* (eds.), *Philosophy in History* (Cambridge: Cambridge University Press, 1984).
—— 'The Identity Theory of Truth', *Mind*, 100 (1991).
—— 'The Projective Theory of Sensory Content', in T. Crane (ed.), *The Contents of Experience* (Cambridge: Cambridge University Press, 1992).
—— (ed.) *G. E. Moore: Selected Writings* (London: Routledge, 1993).
BARWISE, JON, and PERRY, JOHN, 'Semantic Innocence and Uncompromising Situations', in P. A. French *et al.* (eds.), *Midwest Studies in Philosophy* (Minneapolis: University of Minnesota, 1982).
BELL, DAVID, 'How "Russellian" was Frege?', *Mind*, 99 (1990).
BLANSHARD, BRAND, *The Nature of Thought* (London: Allen & Unwin, 1939).
—— 'Bradley on Relations', in A. Manser and G. Stock (eds.), *The Philosophy of F. H. Bradley* (Oxford: Clarendon Press, 1984).
BOGHOSSIAN, PAUL, A., 'The Status of Content', *Philosophical Review*, 99 (1990).
BRADLEY, JAMES, 'F. H. Bradley's Metaphysics of Feeling', in A. Manser and G. Stock (eds.), *The Philosophy of F. H. Bradley* (Oxford: Clarendon Press, 1984).
—— 'The Transcendental Turn in Bradley's Metaphysics', in W. J. Mander (ed.), *Perspectives on the Logic and Metaphysics of F. H. Bradley* (Bristol: Thoemmes, 1996).
—— (ed.), *Philosophy after F. H. Bradley* (Bristol: Thoemmes, 1996).
CAMPBELL, C. A., *Scepticism and Construction: Bradley's Sceptical Principle as the Basis of Constructive Philosophy* (London: Allen & Unwin, 1931).

CAMPBELL, KEITH, *Abstract Particulars* (Oxford: Blackwell, 1990).

CANDLISH, STEWART, 'Bradley on My Station and its Duties', *Australasian Journal of Philosophy*, 56 (1978).

—— 'Scepticism, Ideal Experiment, and Priorities in Bradley's Metaphysics', in A. Manser and G. Stock (eds.), *The Philosophy of F. H. Bradley* (Oxford: Clarendon Press, 1984).

—— 'The Truth about F. H. Bradley', *Mind*, 98 (1989).

—— 'Das Wollen ist auch nur eine Erfahrung', in R. Arrington and H-J. Glock (eds.), *Wittgenstein's Philosophical Investigations: Text and Context* (London: Routledge, 1991).

—— 'The Unity of the Proposition and Russell's Theories of Judgement', in R. Monk and A. Palmer (eds.), *Bertrand Russell and the Origins of Analytical Philosophy* (Bristol: Thoemmes, 1996), 103–35.

—— 'Resurrecting the Identity Theory of Truth', *Bradley Studies*, 1/2 (1995).

CARNAP, RUDOLPH, *The Logical Structure of the World,* trans. R. George (Berkeley: University of California Press, 1967).

CARTWRIGHT, RICHARD, *Philosophical Essays* (Cambridge, Mass.: MIT Press, 1987).

COLLINGWOOD, R. G., *The Principles of Art* (Oxford: Clarendon Press, 1938).

—— 'The Metaphysics of F. H. Bradley: An Essay on *Appearance and Reality*', unpublished, in the Collingwood Papers, Bodleian Library, Oxford.

CROSSLEY, DAVID, 'Justification and the Foundations of Empirical Knowledge', in J. Bradley (ed.), *Philosophy after F. H. Bradley* (Bristol: Thoemmes, 1996).

—— 'Moore's Refutation of Idealism', *Idealistic Studies* 24 (1994).

DAVIDSON, DONALD, *Inquiries into Truth and Interpretation* (Oxford: Clarendon Press, 1984).

—— 'A Coherence Theory of Truth and Knowledge', in E. LePore (ed.), *Truth and Interpretation* (Oxford: Blackwell, 1986), repr. in A. Malachowski (ed.), *Reading Rorty* (Oxford: Blackwell, 1990).

—— 'Afterthoughts, 1987', in A. Malachowski (ed.), *Reading Rorty* (Oxford: Blackwell, 1990).

—— 'The Structure and Content of Truth', *Journal of Philosophy*, 87 (1990).

DAWES HICKS, G., 'Mr Bradley's Treatment of Nature', *Mind*, 34 (1925).

DENYER, NICHOLAS, *Language, Thought and Falsehood in Ancient Greek Philosophy* (London: Routledge, 1991).

DERRIDA, JACQUES, *Margins of Philosophy*, trans. A. Bass (Brighton: Harvester Press, 1982).

—— *Limited Inc.* (Evanston, Ill.: Northwestern University Press, 1988).

DIAMOND, CORA, *The Realistic Spirit* (Cambridge, Mass.: MIT Press, 1991).

DUCASSE, C. J., 'Moore's "The Refutation of Idealism"', in P. A. Schilpp (ed.), *The Philosophy of G. E. Moore* (La Salle, Ill.: Open Court, 1942), 1.

ELIOT, T. S., *Knowledge and Experience in the Philosophy of F. H. Bradley* (London: Faber & Faber, 1964).

—— 'Leibniz's Monads and Bradley's Finite Centres', *Monist*, 26 (1916), repr. in *Knowledge and Experience*.

EVANS, GARETH, *Varieties of Reference* (Oxford: Clarendon Press, 1982).

FERREIRA, PHILLIP, 'Perceptual Ideality and the Ground of Inference', *Bradley Studies*, 1/2 (1995).

FREGE, GOTTLOB, *Logical Investigations*, trans. P. T. Geach and R. H. Stoothoff (Oxford: Blackwell, 1977).

—— *Posthumous Writings*, ed. H. Hermes, F. Kambartel, and F. Kaulbach, trans. P. Long and R. White (Oxford: Blackwell, 1979).

—— *Collected Papers*, ed. B. McGuinness (Oxford: Blackwell, 1984).

—— 'Thoughts', in *Collected Papers*, also in P. F. Strawson (ed.), *Philosophical Logic* (Oxford: Oxford University Press, 1967), and Frege, *Logical Investigations*.

GOLLWITZER, HEINZ, *Europe in the Age of Imperialism* (London: Thames and Hudson, 1969).

GREEN, THOMAS, H., *Prolegomenon to Ethics*, 2nd edn. (Oxford: Oxford University Press, 1884).

GRIFFIN, NICHOLAS, *Russell's Idealist Apprenticeship* (Oxford: Clarendon Press, 1991).

—— 'What's Wrong with Bradley's Theory of Judgment?', *Idealistic Studies*, 13 (1983).

—— (ed.), *The Selected Letters of Bertrand Russell*, i: *The Private Years (1884–1914)* (London: Allen Lane, 1992).

—— and LEWIS, ALBERT C. (eds.), *The Collected Papers of Bertrand Russell*, ii: *Philosophical Papers 1896–1899* (London: Hyman Unwin, 1990).

GROSSMANN, REINHARDT, *Meinong* (London: Routledge, 1974).

HEAL, JANE, *Fact and Meaning* (Oxford: Blackwell, 1989).

HOLDCROFT, DAVID, 'Holism and Truth', in A. Manser and G. Stock (eds.), *The Philosophy of F. H. Bradley* (Oxford: Clarendon Press, 1984).

—— 'Parts and Wholes: The Limits of Analysis', *Bradley Studies*, 1/1 (1995).

HUSSERL, EDMUND, *Logical Investigations*, trans. J. N. Findlay (2 vols., London: Routledge and Kegan Paul, 1970).

HYLTON, PETER, *Russell, Idealism and the Emergence of Analytic Philosophy* (Oxford: Clarendon Press, 1990).

HYLTON, PETER, 'Russell's Substitutional Theory', *Synthese*, 45 (1980).

INGARDIA, RICHARD, *Bradley: A Research Bibliography* (Bowling Green, Oh.: The Philosophy Documentation Center, 1991).

ISHIGURO, HIDÉ, 'Inscrutability of Reference, Monism, and Individuals', in J. Hopkins and A. Savile (eds.), *Psychoanalysis, Mind and Art* (Oxford: Blackwell, 1992).

JACKSON, FRANK, 'On the Adverbial Theory of Perception', *Metaphilosophy*, 6 (1975).

JAMES, WILLIAM, *The Principles of Psychology* (2 vols., New York: Henry Holt, 1890).

—— *Some Problems of Philosophy* (New York: Longmans, Green, 1911).

—— *Collected Essay and Reviews* (New York: Russell and Russell, 1920).

JOACHIM, H. H., *The Nature of Truth* (Oxford: Clarendon Press, 1906).

KAPLAN, DAVID, 'Dthat', repr. in P. Yourgrau (ed.), *Demonstratives* (Oxford: Oxford University Press, 1990).

—— 'Thoughts on Demonstratives', in P. Yourgrau (ed.), *Demonstratives* (Oxford: Oxford University Press, 1990).

—— 'Opacity', in L. E. Hahn and P. A. Schilpp (eds.), *The Philosophy of W. V. Quine* (La Salle, Ill.: Open Court, 1986).

—— 'Demonstratives', in J. Almog *et al.* (eds.), *Themes from Kaplan* (Oxford: Oxford University Press, 1989).

—— 'Afterthoughts' [to 'Demonstratives'], in J. Almog *et al.* (eds.), *Themes from Kaplan* (Oxford: Oxford University Press, 1989).

KENDALL, GORDON (ed.), 'A Note on Christian Morality', by F. H. Bradley, *Religious Studies*, 19 (1983).

KRIPKE, SAUL, *Wittgenstein on Rules and Private Language* (Oxford: Blackwell, 1982).

LACKEY, D. (ed.), *Russell: Essays in Analysis* (London: Allen & Unwin, 1973).

LEIBNIZ, G. W., 'The Monadology' (1714), in *G. W. Leibniz: Philosophical Papers and Letters*, ed. L. Loemker (Dordrecht: Reidel, 1976).

LEPORE, ERNEST (ed.), *Truth and Interpretation* (Oxford: Blackwell, 1986).

LEVINE, JAMES, 'Putnam, Davidson and the 17th Century Picture of Mind and World', *International Journal of Philosophical Studies*, 1 (1993).

LEWIS, C. I., *Mind and the World-Order* (New York: Dover Publications, 1929).

LINSKY, LEONARD, 'The Unity of the Proposition', *Journal of the History of Philosophy*, 30 (1992).

MCDOWELL, JOHN, *Mind and World* (Cambridge, Mass.: Harvard University Press, 1994).

—— 'Singular Thought and the Extent of Inner Space', in P. Pettit and J. McDowell (eds.), *Subject, Thought and Context* (Oxford: Clarendon Press, 1986).

MacNiven, Don, *Bradley's Moral Psychology* (Lewiston, NY: Edwin Mellen Press, 1987).

Malachowski, A. (ed.), *Reading Rorty* (Oxford: Blackwell, 1990).

Mander, W. J., *An Introduction to Bradley's Metaphysics* (Oxford: Clarendon Press, 1994).

—— (ed.), *Perspectives on the Logic and Metaphysics of F. H. Bradley* (Bristol: Thoemmes, 1996).

Manser, Anthony, *Bradley's Logic* (Oxford: Blackwell, 1983).

—— 'Bradley and Internal Relations', in G. Vesey (ed.), *Idealism: Past and Present* (Cambridge: Cambridge University Press, 1982).

—— and Stock, Guy (eds.), *The Philosophy of F. H. Bradley* (Oxford: Clarendon Press, 1984).

Marcus, Ruth Barcan, 'Rationality and Believing the Impossible', *Journal of Philosophy*, 80 (1983).

—— 'A Backward Look at Quine's Animadversions on Modalities', in R. Barrett and R. Gibson (eds.), *Perspectives on Quine* (Oxford: Blackwell, 1990).

Monk, Ray, and Palmer, A. (eds.), *Bertrand Russell and the Foundations of Analytic Philosophy* (Bristol: Thoemmes, 1996).

—— 'The Nature of Judgement', *Mind*, 8 (1899), repr. in T. Regan (ed.), *Moore's Early Essays* (Philadelphia: Temple University Press, 1986).

Moore, G. E., *Principia Ethica* (Cambridge: Cambridge University Press, 1903).

—— *Philosophical Studies* (London: Routledge, 1922).

—— *Philosophical Papers* (London: Allen & Unwin, 1959).

—— *Lectures on Philosophy*, ed. C. Lewy (London: Allen & Unwin, 1966).

—— 'The Refutation of Idealism', *Mind*, n.s. 12 (1903), repr. in *Philosophical Studies*.

—— 'External and Internal Relations', *Proceedings of the Aristotelian Society*, 20 (1919–20), repr. in *Philosophical Studies*.

—— 'A Defence of Common Sense', in *Philosophical Papers*, repr. from J. H. Muirhead (ed.), *Contemporary British Philosophy*, 2nd ser. (London: Allen & Unwin, 1925).

—— 'The Subjectivity of Sense-Data', in P. A. Schilpp (ed.), *The Philosophy of G. E. Moore* (La Salle, Ill.: Open Court, 1942), ii. 653–60 (reply to Ducasse).

Moser, Paul, *Empirical Justification* (Dordrecht: Reidel, 1985).

Neurath, Otto, *Philosophical Papers 1913–1946* (Dordrecht: Reidel, 1983).

—— 'Soziologie im Physikalismus', *Erkenntnis*, 2 (1931), repr. in Neurath, *Philosophical Papers*, as 'Sociology in the Framework of Physicalism', and in A. J. Ayer (ed.), *Logical Positivism*, as 'Sociology and Physicalism'.

NEURATH, OTTO, 'Protokolsätze', *Erkenntnis*, 3 (1932–3), repr. in Neurath, *Philosophical Papers* and in A. J. Ayer (ed.), *Logical Positivism*.

PARRET, HERMAN, 'Perspectival Understanding', in H. Parret and J. Bouveresse (eds.), *Meaning and Understanding* (Berlin: de Gruyter, 1981).

PASSMORE, J., 'Russell and Bradley', in R. Brown and C. D. Rollins (eds.), *Contemporary Philosophy in Australia* (London, Allen & Unwin, 1969).

PEARS, DAVID, 'The Relation between Wittgenstein's Picture Theory of Propositions and Russell's Theories of Judgment', *Philosophical Review*, 86 (1977).

PUTNAM, HILARY, *Mind, Language and Reality* (Cambridge: Cambridge University Press, 1975).

QUINE, W. V. O., *Word and Object* (Cambridge, Mass.: MIT Press, 1960).

QUINTON, ANTHONY, 'Spaces and Times', *Philosophy*, 37 (1962).

—— 'Absolute Idealism', Dawes Hicks Lecture on Philosophy, British Academy, 1971 (Oxford: Oxford University Press, 1972).

ROBERTS, G. W. (ed.), *The Bertrand Russell Memorial Volume* (London: Allen & Unwin, 1979).

ROYCE, JOSIAH, *The World and the Individual*, 1st ser. (New York: Dover Publications, 1959).

RUSSELL, BERTRAND, *A Critical Exposition of the Philosophy of Leibniz* (Cambridge: Cambridge University Press, 1900; subsequently, London: Allen & Unwin).

—— *The Principles of Mathematics* (Cambridge: Cambridge University Press, 1903; subsequently, London: Allen & Unwin).

—— *Philosophical Essays* (London: Longmans, 1910; subsequently, London: Allen & Unwin).

—— *Our Knowledge of the External World* (Chicago: Open Court, 1915; first pub. 1914).

—— *Mysticism and Logic* (London: Longmans, Green and Co., 1919).

—— *Introduction to Mathematical Philosophy* (London: Allen & Unwin, 1919).

—— *Logic and Knowledge*, ed. R. C. Marsh (London: Allen & Unwin, 1956).

—— *The Problems of Philosophy* (Oxford: Oxford University Press Paperback, 1959; 1st edn. 1912).

—— *My Philosophical Development* (London: Allen & Unwin, 1959).

—— *An Outline of Philosophy* (London: Allen & Unwin, 1961; first pub. 1927).

—— *The Collected Papers of Bertrand Russell*, ii: *Philosophical Papers 1896–1899*, ed. N. Griffin and A. C. Lewis (London: Hyman Unwin, 1990).

—— *The Collected Papers of Bertrand Russell*, vi: *Logical and Philosophical Papers 1909–1913*, ed. J. Slater (London: Routledge, 1982).

—— *The Collected Papers of Bertrand Russell*, vii: *Theory of Knowledge: The 1913 Manuscript*, ed. E. R. Eames (London: Allen & Unwin, 1984).

—— *The Collected Papers of Bertrand Russell*, viii: *The Philosophy of Logical Atomism and Other Essays 1914–1919*, ed. J. Slater (London: Allen & Unwin, 1986).

—— *The Collected Papers of Bertrand Russell*, ix: *Essays on Language, Mind and Matter 1919–1926* (London: Routledge, 1994).

—— 'An Analysis of Mathematical Reasoning' (1898), in *Collected Papers*, ii.

—— 'Meinong's Theory of Complexes and Assumptions', *Mind*, 13 (1904), repr. in D. Lackey (ed.), *Russell: Essays in Analysis* (London: Allen & Unwin, 1973).

—— 'On the Nature of Truth', *Proceedings of the Aristotelian Society*, n.s. 7 (1906–7); part repr. as 'The Monistic Theory of Truth', in *Philosophical Essays*.

—— 'Knowledge by Acquaintance and Knowledge by Description', *Proceedings of the Aristotelian Society*, 11 (1910–11), repr. in *Mysticism and Logic*.

—— 'On the Nature of Acquaintance', *Monist*, 24 (1914), repr. in *Logic and Knowledge*.

—— 'The Relation of Sense-Data to Physics', *Scientia*, 4 (1914), repr. in *Mysticism and Logic*.

—— 'The Philosophy of Logical Atomism', *Monist*, 28 (1918), repr. in *Logic and Knowledge and Collected Papers*, viii.

—— 'Logical Atomism', in J. H. Muirhead (ed.), *Contemporary British Philosophy* 2nd ser. (London: Allen & Unwin, 1925), repr. in *Logic and Knowledge* and *Collected Papers*, ix.

—— and WHITEHEAD, ALFRED NORTH, *Principia Mathematica* (3 vols., Cambridge: Cambridge University Press, 1925–7; 1st edn. 1910–13).

SALMON, NATHAN, 'A Millian Heir Rejects the Wages of *Sinn*', in C. A. Anderson and J. Owens (eds.), *Propositional Attitudes* (Stanford, Calif.: Center for Study of Language and Information, 1990).

SCHILPP, P. A. (ed.), *The Philosophy of G. E. Moore* (2 vols., La Salle, Ill.: Open Court, 1942).

SCHLICK, MORITZ, *The Problems of Philosophy and their Interconnection*, ed. H. Mulder *et al.*, trans. P. Heath (Dordrecht: Reidel, 1987).

—— 'On the Foundations of Knowledge', trans. P. Heath, in Schlick, *Philosophical Papers*, ii, ed. H. Mulder and B. F. B. van de Velde-Schlick (Dordrecht: Reidel, 1979; first pub. 1934).

SELLARS, W., 'The Adverbial Theory of the Objects of Sensations', *Metaphilosophy*, 6 (1975).

SIEVERS, K. H., 'F. H. Bradley and the Correspondence Theory of Truth', *Bradley Studies*, 2/2 (1996).

SMART, J. J. C., 'Sensations and Brain Processes', *Philosophical Review*, 68 (1959).

SPADONI, CARL, ' "Great God in Boots!—The Ontological Argument is Sound" ', *Journal of the Bertrand Russell Archive*, 23–4 (1976).

SPRIGGE, TIMOTHY, *The Vindication of Absolute Idealism* (Edinburgh: Edinburgh University Press, 1983).

—— *James and Bradley: American Truth and British Reality* (Chicago and La Salle, Ill.: Open Court, 1993).

—— 'Russell and Bradley on Relations', in G. W. Roberts (ed.), *The Bertrand Russell Memorial Volume* (London: Allen & Unwin, 1979).

—— 'The Self and its World in Bradley and Husserl', in A. Manser and G. Stock (eds.), *The Philosophy of F. H. Bradley* (Oxford: Clarendon Press, 1984).

STICH, STEPHEN, *From Folk Psychology to Cognitive Science* (Cambridge, Mass.: MIT Press, 1983).

STOCK, GUY, 'Bradley's Theory of Judgement', in A. Manser and G. Stock (eds.), *The Philosophy of F. H. Bradley* (Oxford: Clarendon Press, 1984).

—— 'Negation: Bradley and Wittgenstein', *Philosophy*, 60 (1985).

STOVE, DAVID, *The Plato Cult* (Oxford: Blackwell, 1991).

STRAWSON, P. F., *Individuals: An Essay in Descriptive Metaphysics* (London: Methuen, 1964).

—— (ed.), *Philosophical Logic* (Oxford: Oxford University Press, 1967).

TARSKI, ALFRED, *Logic, Semantics, Metamathematics* (Oxford: Oxford University Press, 1956).

TAYLOR, A. E., 'Francis Herbert Bradley, 1846–1924', *Proceedings of the British Academy*, 11/2.

TYE, MICHAEL, 'The Adverbial Theory: A Defence of Sellars against Jackson', *Metaphilosophy*, 6 (1975).

VESEY, G. N. A. (ed.), *Idealism: Past and Present*, Royal Institute of Philosophy Lecture Series 13 (Cambridge: Cambridge University Press, 1982).

WALKER, RALPH, *The Coherence Theory of Truth* (London: Routledge, 1989).

WATLING, JOHN, *Bertrand Russell* (Edinburgh: Oliver and Boyd, 1970).

WILLIAMS, BERNARD, *Descartes: The Project of Pure Enquiry* (Harmondsworth: Penguin, 1978).

—— *Ethics and the Limits of Philosophy* (London: Fontana, 1985).

WILSON, FRED, 'Bradley's Impact on Empiricism', in J. Bradley (ed.), *Philosophy after F. H. Bradley* (Bristol: Thoemmes, 1996).

WITTGENSTEIN, LUDWIG, *Tractatus Logico-Philosophicus*, trans. C. K. Ogden (London: Routledge and Kegan Paul, 1922).

—— *Tractatus Logico-Philosophicus*, trans. D. F. Pears and B. F. McGuinness (London: Routledge and Kegan Paul, 1961).

—— *Philosophical Investigations*, trans. G. E. M. Anscombe (Oxford: Blackwell, 1958).

—— *Notebooks 1914–1916*, ed. G. H. von Wright and G. E. M. Anscombe, trans. G. E. M. Anscombe (Oxford: Blackwell, 1961; Chicago: University of Chicago Press, 1979).

—— *On Certainty* (Oxford: Blackwell, 1969).

—— *Letters to C. K. Ogden*, ed. G. H. von Wright (Oxford: Blackwell, 1973).

WOLLHEIM, RICHARD, *F. H. Bradley*, 2nd edn. (Harmondsworth: Penguin, 1969).

YOURGRAU, PALLE (ed.), *Demonstratives* (Oxford: Oxford University Press, 1990).

INDEX